The Sound of Summer

JIM MAXWELL
The Sound of Summer

A MEMOIR

ALLEN&UNWIN
SYDNEY · MELBOURNE · AUCKLAND · LONDON

First published in 2016

Allen & Unwin
83 Alexander Street
Crows Nest NSW 2065
Australia
Phone: (61 2) 8425 0100
Email: info@allenandunwin.com
Web: www.allenandunwin.com

Cataloguing-in-Publication details are available
from the National Library of Australia
www.trove.nla.gov.au

ISBN 978 1 74237 082 8

Set in 12/18 pt Sabon by Midland Typesetters, Australia
Printed and bound in Australia by Griffin Press

10 9 8 7 6 5 4 3 2 1

MIX
Paper from
responsible sources
FSC
www.fsc.org   FSC® C009448

The paper in this book is FSC® certified.
FSC® promotes environmentally responsible,
socially beneficial and economically viable
management of the world's forests.

For Tim Cohen,
cricket lover and friend forever

Contents

Foreword

It's hard to imagine summer in Australia without Jim Maxwell . . . his voice is the one you hear each year that confirms the footy is over. He seems to have been there forever. When Jim began broadcasting on ABC Radio all those decades ago the Rolling Stones were young and Rock Hudson was straight.

For thirteen seasons I shared a microphone with him—it was to be a journey of discovery for both of us!

You see, Jim came out of the Alan McGilvray stable . . . I was from the Seinfeld barn. Not much in common. And yet, it must be said, after a period of adjustment, our deep love of the game bound us year after glorious Test cricket year! It was one of the most enjoyable periods of my life.

Summer, of course, is a different headspace to winter: people chill out, the world passes us by, you wear thongs—and spend more time in the car. The automobile is ABC cricket's greatest vehicle . . . people everywhere over the years have reminisced with me about something they heard on the ABC while driving. And the voice of Jim Maxwell is a constant, rebounding off the upholstery. His style is a relaxant. He makes you feel comfortable. Old-school dentists could use *ABC Grandstand Cricket* instead of gas. The most obvious trait of the Maxwell delivery is that it contains no fluster. If calmness behind the microphone was an Olympic event, Jim would share the podium medals with Richie Benaud and Peter Alliss. Economy of word is their signature. There is rarely overstatement . . . control is paramount . . . and precision.

I particularly admire Jim's use of the pause. So many times an ABC studio host would build up the first morning cross to Jim at the ground with an enthusiasm that would make Boris Johnson sound like Bernie Fraser, only to be greeted by the Maxwell pause—not awkward dead air, just a moment of balance, two-and-a-half seconds of nothing—before Jim would pick up the commentary. It was a sense of timing to behold. These pauses were so pregnant you could imagine waters breaking. Vintage Maxwell!

Not enough can be made of the author's knowledge of the game, forged from four decades of going to work, watching, listening and forming opinion. And ultimately delivering it forthrightly in that unmistakeable tone.

Jim is more than a broadcaster—he is a journalist. He respects the game, the players and its values, but he does not tow the party line. He will ask the tough, but well considered, question. I found his interviewing technique fascinating. Some days he could be *Conversations with Richard Fidler* . . . or, if he had a vulnerable administrator in his sights, he could be Leigh Sales off her long run. You sense half volleys came with the job, but he loved nothing more than the odd bouncer.

Then there are his phrases. Whereas the late Tony Greig introduced 'he's hit it like a tracer bullet', I believe Jim invented the term 'nurdle', which is to brush the ball away for a single behind the wicket. He was the first commentator I heard use it and it is now in Wikipedia. Another Maxwellism is his oft used 'Take me out to the "ball game"', when a batsman has struck one out of the yard. He may well love proper cricket, but Jim is not averse to delighting in a crude swipe that sends the ball into the stands.

As the doyen of *ABC Grandstand Cricket*, the responsibility of ensuring the broadcast had the right feel more often fell to Jim. He, above anyone else in my time, created an atmosphere where the overseas commentator—so integral to our coverage—felt at ease.

Jonathan Agnew, Neil Manthorp, Bryan Waddle and Fazeer Mohammed were four who added much to our product. With Jim steering the ship, everyone was a happy sailor. The international callers were there to add to the coverage . . . to bring different voices . . . to give insights into Australia's opponents . . . and all seemed to enjoy cricket the ABC way. Jim Maxwell had much to do with that.

And there are both his loyalty and his toughness . . . no greater example was his support of the late Peter Roebuck through his difficult times and the inner strength Jim showed when Peter eventually took his own life.

I saw his eyes moisten on air only twice . . . once at the MCG when a glowing tribute was broadcast to celebrate his 200th Test match and the other when I signed off for the final time in 2014. Of the latter, maybe it could have been more relief than anything else. Hah! Hah! Still, I am richer for spending so much time working with Jim and I know that this book of memoirs will reflect his outstanding contribution to cricket in this country.

Kerry O'Keeffe

Preface

In August 2016, I was part of the ABC team covering the Rio Olympic Games from an outside broadcast van located in an industrial park in Redfern, Sydney, thousands and thousands of miles from the events we were calling.

Unfortunately, this is where sports broadcasting and reporting is heading thanks to vastly reduced budgets. For all our technological advances we are not that far away from the days when we called the Tests from England via telex and coconut.

At least it meant sleeping in my own bed at night and, as it turned out, that was an enormous blessing. If I'd been in Rio . . .

I was getting up at 3.30 a.m. most mornings, but on the morning of 16 August I was up at 2 a.m. to prepare for the day's sailing. It was the ninth day in a row I was up before the sparrows. The night before I had been at a Sydney Cricket Association meeting and hadn't got to bed until around 11 p.m. so I wasn't feeling that good, to be honest.

My heart had been racing for a couple of weeks and my blood pressure was up, but what do you do? The games won't call themselves. You have a cup of coffee or three. The show has to go on.

This was a special morning, as I had lined up my friend Peter Shipway, veteran of 31 Sydney to Hobart races and the current Admiral's Cup skipper, to help us out.

Peter is an 'old salt' and I thought he would spice up the coverage of Tom Burton's big race. As it was, we'd wasted our time, as the event was cancelled that day. We didn't know that until we arrived at the broadcast van. So we sat there through the night doing the odd update. At 6.25 a.m., Karen Tighe threw to us from the Ultimo studio and I attempted a small introduction for Peter, but just as we were about to do the cross I came over all strange.

My whole right side became numb. I felt confused. Disoriented. The timing was terrible, so I pressed on as best I could, attempting to say a few words, but my thoughts were jumbled. I slurred and mumbled and stumbled but got something out. By this time, I knew something was really wrong and so did everyone around me.

Peter picked up his cue like a pro and did his bit, but as soon as he was finished everybody rushed to me and lay me down on the floor. Somebody called an ambulance.

Tim Gavel was in the truck and picked it straight away: 'Jim's just had a stroke,' he said.

I didn't know what to think. I was poleaxed. I just lay there, my mind racing, waiting for the ambulance to come. By the time they stabilised me and carried me out of the van there was a large group watching.

'This has turned into a spectator sport,' I said in an attempt at humour.

I remember our man from Brisbane, Corbin Middlemas, walking up as they were about to put me in the ambulance. He shook my hand and wished me luck. I don't need to tell you how surreal it all felt. Surreal and frightening.

When I got to the hospital I signed a form about some procedures or other and since then my right arm and my right leg have basically refused to respond to commands.

I was in reasonable form at the hospital. I remember that a few people from work arrived even before my family did and I announced that after 43 years I would finally be taking some sick leave. I had rarely had more than a day or two off for illness in my life. I found out during my enforced absence that I had accrued 672 days of sick leave!

I did have a stroke on air that morning. I was 66 and pushing it too hard. I should have been more careful because there had been a lot of warnings in the twelve months leading up to it.

There's not a lot of us in the cricket media, but I was the fourth to go down in the space of a year. We were men of all ages and dispositions. Wayne Smith, the *Australian*'s sports writer, had a very mild stroke the year before. Then, in the space of a few days at the end of the 2015–16 season, two more of us suffered the same fate.

Channel 9 cameraman Frankie Ilankovan has been on the scene for years and is one of the great characters of the job, loved by everyone. The sports reporters come and go, but Frankie is always there, training them up, rolling his eyes at their demands . . . The great man suffered a major stroke on the way to an assignment one day and was lucky that his workmates had the nous to drive out looking for him. They found him by the side of the road.

Frankie, like me, is paralysed down one side and was last heard of seeking ayurvedic treatment in his native India.

Preface

Frank was 57 and Wayne was 60, but *Age* cricket writer Jesse Hogan was just 33 when he suffered a major stroke a few days later. One of the nicest guys in the trade, it was touch and go for a while there. Jesse was in a coma for over a week and was lucky to survive. Today he is out of hospital and, like Frank and me, he is going through intensive rehabilitation as he learns to walk and talk again.

So, that makes three of us trying to get paralysed limbs to do what we want them to. It's a long, hard road, but things could be much worse.

I know how lucky I am to come out with only that to contend with. Early on I had some problems with confusion and slurring of words, but that passed quickly and now I just have to learn to be mobile again.

I have learnt that one in six people suffer strokes. That many of them suffer them and don't even know it has happened.

I have learnt that it is something we all need to be more aware of and that we need to fund more research into stroke prevention and treatment.

I have also learnt how important it is to be loved. My wife, Jen, only signed up a few years back and probably didn't think that I would be invoking the first part of the 'in sickness and in health' clause so quickly. She has been magnificent. It would be awful to be alone when you go through something like this and I am so grateful to have her and my sons, Hamish and Oliver, to help me out.

It might be some time before I am back on air, as commentary boxes are rarely conveniently located. In Hobart the media has to climb flight after flight after flight of stairs to gain access to the box as the only lift in that area is reserved for the VIPs. In Perth the lifts stop before the broadcast level and you have to climb stairs to complete the journey. Even when reached, the commentary box is a restricted space with little room to move about, and it takes a certain degree of physical mobility to slip in and out of the chair when coming and going from a shift.

Perhaps these are things we need to think about, but for now I have a more personal battle to contend with.

Life takes some strange turns.

Room 22, Rehab Ward, Sacred Heart,
St Vincent's Hospital, Sydney, September 2016

1

Early years

Good morning and welcome to our lounge room. Somewhere in Sydney. Sometime midway through the last century.

Before moving pictures, before my father reluctantly allowed a television into our house, before the internet, iPhones and all that jazz, before podcasts and video on demand, there was the radio.

Like most Australian families in the 1950s the crackling box in the corner was our home entertainment unit and our connection to the world outside. Of all the songs and sounds that came from it, it was the cricket that captivated me as a boy. The voices of the commentators, the distant sound of bat on ball, the swell of the crowd, the romance of foreign players and foreign grounds were a world I knew I wanted to be part of.

There was something about the game, something about listening to John Arlott and Alan McGilvray calling it from a corner of this country or England, that took root inside me early. Batsmen and bowlers know that once a certain level of skill is attained that cricket is a game played mostly within the confines of the head, which might explain why the game is so suited to the spoken word. It's no coincidence, I think, that many of the great writers and poets were attracted to cricket. It's a game that speaks to them and to anyone who listens. It's a long-form drama.

Of course I am no poet. I call the game, describe its dramas and relay its shifts, then wander about its boundaries when things get a little quiet in the middle.

My father was a probate lawyer in a second-generation family practice, my mother an academic with a love of language and other cultures, but by the time I was old enough to have any serious notion of what I wanted to do I had only one dream: to sit behind the microphone at cricket grounds and relate what was unfolding out there, the drama, the tension, the failings, the crowd and the occasional majesty of a great innings or bowling spell.

Maybe the truth was, like many of us, I just wanted to be close to the game. Getting paid to go to the cricket is a rare privilege and one I have neither taken for granted nor grown tired of.

I was born in Sydney, Australia, on 28 July 1950, the first and only son of Ian James Maxwell and Margaret Brome Maxwell (née Weigall). Mum and Dad were cultured people with a love of the arts, but that didn't exclude Dad from having a passion for the great game.

Radio was a big deal when I was young. It was the world wide web in a box. Radio and newspapers told us what was going on. Newspapers arrived twice a day and while the radio was constant it also had its cycles.

Mum and Dad had a state-of-the-art yellow Hotpoint set in the lounge. Of a Sunday evening there would be thoughtful lectures and discussions on weighty topics on 2FC that my parents would force me to endure because they thought it was good for my education, but it bored me silly. I wanted to listen to the cricket and if I wasn't listening to that I wanted to hear the popular music that played on an ancient Bakelite Radiola in my bedroom every night after 6 p.m. (I'd inherited that one when the main radio was upgraded.)

The Australian Broadcasting Corporation was part of every Australian's life, even if you were a kid. Back then you used to have *Kindergarten of the Air*, which was all songs and games, something like *Play School*. At school there were other educational programs that we'd listen to. At night there were the serials like *Hagan's Circus*, *Superman*, *Life with Dexter*. Radio was magic and sometimes the Maxwells would even go down to the Macquarie Auditorium to see them doing the serials live, which tells you just how big a deal the whole thing was.

When I was older the radio in my bedroom was tuned to 2UE every morning to the legendary Gary O'Callaghan (famous for reporting the Petrov Affair live from Mascot Airport) and Bob Rogers. These guys were huge celebrities at the time.

To this day I am not sure any other medium conveys the drama that radio does. I remember in December 1963 sitting in the lounge with Dad listening to Australia play South Africa when Col Egar no-balled Ian Meckiff out of cricket for throwing. That was something. A huge controversy at the time. Maybe I saw television highlights later, but what remains with me is *hearing* that happen. More than 30 years later I was on radio when Sri Lanka's Murali was likewise called for throwing on that fateful day at the MCG on Boxing Day 1995. I don't know why, but there is something about hearing a broadcast of these events that seems so much richer than watching them on television.

•

My first memories of listening to cricket are from the 1961 tour of England. We would sit in the lounge and tune in after dinner and then later I'd lie in bed listening to the game unfold on the other side of the world. Richie Benaud, the Shane Warne of his time, coming around the wicket at Old Trafford, bowling Peter May around his legs for a duck. That was radical! No leggie came around the wicket, but Richie was always a pathfinder in the game. Australian wicketkeeper Wally Grout had to tell the English captain what had happened. 'You're out, mate, he bowled you.' It was the Gatting ball of its time. The coverage would drop in and out, sometimes revert to short wave and hiss like a snake, adding to the whole romance and other-worldly feel to cricket being played so far away.

A whole generation of cricket fans was introduced to Ashes tours by the medium of radio. England was the birthplace of the game and had such an important connection with so many Australians. Lord's and The Oval, Trent Bridge, Edgbaston, Old Trafford and Headingley. Green fields and county games . . . it was all very romantic to Australians who hadn't let go of our love of the Old Country.

The broadcast of the 1964 Ashes tour was a lot stronger, and so is my memory of it. Bobby Simpson had taken over from Benaud as captain. The Aussies won 1–0 in a series that featured four draws. There was no thriller at Manchester this time. It was quite the opposite. Simpson got his first century and went on to make 311 in that fourth game at Old Trafford. The Australians batted into the third day to ensure England couldn't win the series. Despite those dull tactics, this was when I really started to listen to the game and the people who called it—those educated and erudite men who were our eyes and ears, men who wove narratives in and out of the unfolding drama.

That was when I realised how good one in particular was: an Australian by the name of Alan McGilvray. I knew his voice from home summers, but when I heard him among the English commentators he stood out. The great British broadcasters had their own style. John Arlott was the poet of the airwaves, master of the flowery approach, but McGilvray was the only bloke who told you what was going on; he gave you information about the battle rather than waxing lyrical. He cut to the chase—Australians tend to get to the point a little more quickly.

McGilvray, who I would work with later, told me he had a hard time of it when he first started working as the ABC man in the BBC box back in England in 1948. They didn't like the colonial approach much and let him know, but he stuck to his guns. He wrote many years later in *The Game Is Not the Same . . .* that 'The English practice was to be terribly lyrical. They would talk about the birds, and the clouds and all manner of things. Their commentaries were rich with colour and atmosphere, but it didn't seem to matter if they missed a ball or two while they were discussing dress trends for the gentry in the Long Room. My style was more direct. I would describe the ball, analyse every ball, give the score at least three times an over and often more . . . The BBC team saw that as dull.'

I met Arlott in 1977 at the Centenary Test in Melbourne. I wasn't working, but went down to enjoy the spectacle. McGilvray introduced us. It was the Englishman's first trip out since the 1954–55 series. I don't think he liked it too much Down Under. He was a homebody who covered every English Ashes between 1946 and his retirement in 1980, but who only ever toured with the team twice. By 1977 he was doing only one session a day behind the microphone. He was a melancholy man who wore a thin black tie as a mark of respect and regret over the death of his eldest son in a car accident.

When Arlott died in December 1991 he was buried in St Anne's churchyard on the island of Alderney, a line from one of his poems carved into the headstone: 'So clear you see these timeless things that, like a bird, the vision sings.' He was an extraordinary man who had great influence in the game. Ian Botham became a close friend, the two having bonded when Arlott taught him about wine when the younger man was just sixteen. Botham bought a holiday home on Alderney, and whenever he returns there he drinks a bottle of red by Arlott's grave, leaving the cork behind.

McGilvray used to say that the BBC actually came around and started using the more direct Australian approach, which is ironic given the way commentary has changed over the last decade or so in Australia. Maybe we have found a place where we got the best of both worlds, but we still never miss a ball. And we give the score regularly. That was the discipline imposed, indeed demanded, by Sir Charles Moses, who was head of the ABC, then by McGilvray and faithfully continued by me and my generation. That is a point of honour.

I am not sure what is on McGilvray's headstone, but I can tell you that there is a plaque in the corner of my local pub, the Lord Dudley, marking out his space at the bar. It is a curious coincidence that we shared a local watering hole.

The first time I ever went to the ABC studios I was taken by a friend of my parents, Mungo MacCallum snr, who was a famous broadcaster and journalist—as his son would be too—and a big deal around town. Mungo produced the first night of television on the ABC in 1956. He and his wife Diana Wentworth were good friends of ours and Mungo asked my dad if I would like to come in and watch him record as a panellist on a current affairs show. It was around 1958 and the whole process was all very formal.

I sat in the production booth and watched from my privileged position. Many years later when I was starting my own career I walked back into that same room and thought that not much had changed. Life was like that back then; things changed slowly. Well, they did at the ABC anyway.

•

I was an only child, born and raised in the enclave of Bellevue Hill, which is a part of Sydney reclaimed from the Bondi sand dunes. It sits on the ridge that separates the sea from the city. In 1804 convicts fought soldiers there, and it became known as Vinegar Hill, after an uprising in Ireland just a few years earlier. Governor Lachlan Macquarie wasn't too keen on this and ordered it be called Bellevue Hill and that was that. I am a little ashamed to say I don't know what the Aboriginal people called it. It is, quite conveniently, less than five kilometres from the Sydney Cricket Ground. The suburb was my home for more than twenty years before I moved out—I now live next door in Woollahra.

Bellevue Hill is famous for having some of the most expensive homes in Sydney, and that's saying something, because Sydney has some of the craziest real estate prices on the planet. In those days it was not like it is now. The rich people lived in the big houses on Victoria Road, but the Maxwells had a modest place on the corner of Bradley Avenue and Riddell Street. It was a good old Aussie bungalow that my parents bought in the early 1950s: three bedrooms, a lounge, a dining room, a little area out the back and an unusual open veranda that was used as a sleep-out on hot summer nights. It was probably built in the 1920s.

Our street was shelled by the Japanese in World War II. The two houses next to us were hit and we all knew the story because the old timers loved to tell it.

The Japanese were set on destroying Allied ships moored in the harbour and having twice done surveillance via a seaplane that came from a large submarine outside the harbour, they despatched three Ko-hyoteki-class midget submarines to do so. The midget subs slipped past the anti-submarine net into the harbour and things got hectic. Two were detected and attacked, but one fired a torpedo at the USS *Chicago*. It missed and sunk the converted ferry HMAS *Kuttabul,* killing 21 sailors. Eight days later one of the mother submarines—the I-24—launched an attack from outside the heads, firing ten shells towards the Sydney Harbour Bridge. Most landed in the nearby suburbs of Rose Bay, Woollahra and our street in Bellevue Hill.

There could have been a lot of damage done, but only one of the shells actually exploded.

In 2006 the midget sub that had done the damage was found on the ocean floor off the Northern Beaches. It had escaped but obviously had not met up with the I-24.

Our neighbour, old Mr Russell, used to have a few forks and spoons that he said were bent by the bombs, and he would show them off from time to time. He was on a pension from World War I and his wife was a seamstress. I can't recall many professional people in our street. Another neighbour, Sid Beverley, owned a garage. Frank Hann was a butcher and a motor racing driver at Bathurst and always had his head in the engine of a Jaguar. They were pretty ordinary middle-class Australian people who lived frugal lives without great expectations. Two wars in quick succession sobers people up.

I was a baby boomer, born in a time of relative peace. The most important thing for me in our neighbourhood was the rockery wall opposite our house. It's still there to this day, but if you drive by now there will be a row of cars parked there, which would have been a disaster when I was a boy. Every only child knows that a wall is your best mate when you haven't got anybody to play cricket or tennis with. I spent hours bouncing balls off that wall and another in our garden. You simply threw the ball at the wall, quickly took guard and played your best shot off the rebound. If you were Bradman you used a stump and a golf ball; if you were Maxwell you used a bat and a cricket ball and did your best.

When there were mates around we would walk down to Cooper Park for more expansive games. It was a simple life, simple pleasures. We dressed up and played cowboys and Indians, built cubbyhouses, raced billycarts and roamed the neighbourhood. When the passionfruits were in season I'd set up a milkshake stall. Nobody ever bought them, but we went through a fair bit of milk. I was my best customer.

None of the kids on my street went to my school. They mainly went to Bellevue Hill Public and then Sydney High or Waverley College. One went to Scots College. The social demographic was nothing like it is today. People didn't have a lot of money. Australia was a bit of a backwater then, we didn't know a lot about the world we lived in. It must have been a rude shock when the Japanese popped up in the harbour. It's unimaginable even today what it must have been like to be shelled in your own home.

Australians didn't travel overseas much. We lived in our own backyard and were happy there, satisfied with small mercies and modest thrills. An ice-cream was exciting. You got around on foot, a bus or even a tram. A car trip was a big deal—'an excursion' was what they called it, from memory. There used to be a tram that wandered out our way and as we got older we'd jump on and off it, riding the running board all the way to Bondi or Coogee or the city. If you timed it right you didn't have to pay the fare. I got to know other parts of the city, but the west remained a mystery. When you lived so close to the ocean and the cricket ground, there wasn't much call to go inland. I was no explorer!

My mother, Margaret, was an intelligent and engaging woman with an academic background. She was a secretary at the Institute of International Affairs until she was married—in those days when a woman got married she had to stop working. Mum didn't like that and it would become a hot topic at the dinner table when certain relatives visited. She was in signals in the Women's Auxiliary Australian Air Force during the war. She had a sharp brain, and spoke Russian, French and Italian, which were of limited use in her social circle. Mr Falcomata was the greengrocer and she could speak Italian to him, but that was about it. Australia was a bit of a monoculture back in those days. Particularly where we lived.

Mum decided there might have been a bit more to the Spanish culture, so she learnt the language and that led her to join the Good Neighbour Council in the 1960s. She became particularly involved with the people from Chile and Argentina at a time when there was a lot of South American migration. When you came here in those days you weren't put on Manus Island; you went instead to the Endeavour Migrant Hostel at South Coogee. Mum would go out there and chat with the newly arrived, help them out as they integrated. She also did some interpretive work with SBS on the Spanish language in the formative years for the multicultural broadcaster. She already had an Arts degree from Sydney University in the 1930s and once she got me through school she went back to study. For a while she and I would drive to the University of New South Wales every day. Let's just say Mum was keener on university than I was.

Mum was small, a bit feisty and would hold her own in any argument. She was no retiring housewife.

Dad was an intelligent man, a classicist, dux of Cranbrook School, and had his Arts/Law degree very early, maybe when only 22. He was a thespian too, he just loved acting, and was involved in the Sydney University Dramatic Society. I think if he had his time over again and not been caught up in the family law practice he would have been an actor, but people had a sense of duty in those days, so he took up his role at his father's law firm when his father died.

He was a heavy smoker, addicted to the bloody things that eventually killed him, but he was a fighter, and although he had emphysema for much of his later life he refused to give in to it.

Dad did go on the Orient liner *Orontes* with the Australian cricket team to England in 1938 (the same ship had brought the English here previously for the Bodyline series). It was a grand adventure for him, but his father died while he was away. He had to cut short his trip and return to put his law degree to use with his father's firm, Maxwell and Boyd.

That must have been some trip and while he may have regretted having to leave early it was what he found, or didn't find, when he got home that bothered him for decades to come. Dad used to live in the old family home on Ocean Street, Woollahra, and while he was overseas one of his sisters took it upon herself to do some spring-cleaning and threw out his collection of *Wisden Cricketers' Almanacks*. That annoyed him for decades to come and annoys me now, because I have spent a small fortune compiling my own collection when I could have inherited his.

After the war he was involved with the Sydney branch of the British Drama League, which was a semi-voluntary group that coordinated the production of plays. He'd done some acting himself, but I think that it was considered a bit frivolous when he was a young man. He and Mum kept up an interest in theatre and the arts all their lives. They seemed to have season tickets for everything. I think I got my dramatic delivery from Dad; he could really work himself up when telling a story.

Actually, when I was young they were concerned that I didn't speak properly and sent me off to elocution classes to help me get my mouth around words.

Dad wasn't fussed that I didn't follow him into the law and maybe that was because he could appreciate that the freedoms gifted people my age were the ones that he would have loved. I was lucky to be part of the post-war generation. Mum would often be on at me about what I was going to do with my life, but my father never put pressure on me to do anything, which is quite remarkable, particularly given the emphasis on schooling.

My paternal grandfather was on the founding council of Cranbrook School and was its first treasurer. My father and his three brothers went there and there was never any question that I would too. Both my sons went as well. It was and remains a strong part of my life.

Surrounded by playing fields and set on Sydney Harbour, Cranbrook was just two kilometres down the hill from our home. I was there from my first day at school until my last, including two years doing the HSC. Not because I didn't pass, but because I was a year younger all the way through and my mother thought I was too young to take off the school uniform and enter the world. It didn't bother me, as by that time the Cranbrook cricket team, of which I was captain, was the centre of my life and I was happy to keep playing.

School was so close I could walk there and back and usually did, but then the decision was made, despite its proximity to home, that it was a good idea for me to board there.

I think the reason was my parents thought it would socialise me a little better, as I was an only child. Of course it might also have freed them up a little too. I started boarding school in Year Five when I was about nine years old and it was a bit of a shock to the system.

As you would expect, there was a real emphasis on discipline, routine and sport at school. We'd get up at 7 a.m. and under the supervision of a house master brace ourselves for a character-forming cold shower. For one term I had to get up at 6.30 a.m. and wait shivering in the old portico for the papers to arrive and then distribute them. After showers you'd line up in the courtyard for shoe parade; if they weren't clean you had to see to them before breakfast. It was an institution in the old British tradition and we even had those heavy grey clothes that we wore in summer, and hats too. They caned us if we were bad, and while I wasn't always the best-behaved I managed to avoid that most of the time. The food was shocking, something you never forgot. A man called Oz was the cook and he had two big women, Rosemary and Catherine, who were his helpers. Institutional eating is, like cold showers and corporal punishment, not for the faint-hearted. Lambs fry and bacon, tomato slop, soggy toast . . . that was character-forming too.

I went home on the weekend, but not every weekend. We had sport on Saturday at school and you were free after that, but you had to have an exeat card and sign out before they would let you go. We were allowed out only a certain number of times a term. You could take one of your mates home, which was a bit of a treat for the kids whose parents lived too far away. You had to be back on Sunday night for chapel. Lights were out at 9 p.m. and next thing you knew you were in the queue for the first cold shower of the week.

Being a year younger than everyone in my class caused its own problems. I used to get picked on and whacked around a bit. I don't think I was scarred by it, but I wasn't always happy with it. That's what happened in those days and it was nothing too awful. It was bullying to a minor degree, but that just seemed to be the way things were. After four years, when I was about to start my third year at senior school, I'd had enough of boarding. I wasn't enjoying it and I was a bit more established and I just wanted to spread my wings. I needed a change. I protested to my parents, I said 'I don't want to do this anymore.' There wasn't any argument about it and that was that. I wasn't a boarder anymore.

2

The game

When did the seed of cricket take hold, or was it always there? I like to think it all began the day I caught the 333 bus with my mates Ken and Stephen Hann to the SCG to watch the West Indies play in January 1961. That was a revelation to me and to so many in this country.

The tour kicked off with that historic tied Test in Brisbane, which set the tone. We'd heard it on the radio and couldn't believe the finish. The Australians won the second Test in Melbourne and then the show came to the SCG. I paid a shilling at the gates, sat on the Hill and watched these magnificent Caribbean athletes do things that were unimaginable. Gary Sobers went berserk with the bat, scoring 168 off 234 balls. Benaud's mob took the new ball after tea and Sobers scored 70 in 70 minutes.

It was exhilarating cricket. Despite all the runs being scored Alan Davidson finished with 5–80 in that innings.

I couldn't take my eyes off these men from the Caribbean. As I wrote earlier, Australia was a monoculture then, and I had never seen men like this playing cricket like this before.

That was probably the only time I sat on the Hill, which was an experience in itself. The crowd was as much a part of the show as the cricketers. It was nothing like the exclusive vantage point I grew accustomed to on the other side of the ground in the Members, where collars were mandatory and polite behaviour expected. It was the perfect setting for a game like this. There was a cultural divide at the ground: the better-off in the traditional stands, the working class on the grass opposite.

Like many visiting teams, the West Indies came and practised at Cranbrook, where I got to see them up close. It was almost a life-changing moment. They were superb athletes, lithe and elegant, and they moved joyously, cackling as they went. This was another form of cricket, far removed from the reserved style of play the English had taught the world.

We were a pretty ignorant society in those days and I was living a secluded life, with little idea of what was going on in the world. I had seen the occasional Aboriginal person before, but there were none in my world. The sad truth was that I had grown up in a country that didn't admit blacks, that embraced the White Australia Policy and was ignorant of its own indigenous population. Either that or in denial of them. At school we studied all about Captain Cook and the Eureka Stockade in history, but nothing about the people who had been here for at least 40,000 years. A decade later boxer Lionel Rose and the magnificent tennis champion Evonne Goolagong made names for themselves as champion black athletes, but back in the summer of 1960–61 the visiting Calypso cricketers captured the hearts of a nation of cricket lovers.

They certainly captured mine and showed me a side of the game I had no idea existed.

Dad played for I Zingari—Italian for 'the Gypsies'—a famous cricket club that had its origins in England and has been going in Australia since 1888. Its colours are red, black and gold, which symbolise 'out of darkness through fire into light'. Former Test cricketers like Ian Craig, Jimmy Burke, Martin Donnelly and Ted White played with them and they had a lot of good first-class players. Many fine grade cricketers played, including Graham Reed, who later became a first-class umpire, and match referee.

Dad got involved before the war, but he was strictly a lower-order batsman who would occasionally get a bowl. It didn't matter to him; he just loved the game.

His older brother Ham played first grade at Paddington. Ham Maxwell is the first name on the honour board at Cranbrook for cricketers who made a century against Combined Associated Schools teams, and my boy Oliver Maxwell is there from more recent times. I am not there for my batting or bowling feats, but I at least gain a mention for captaining the school side, so there are three generations of Maxwells on the school honour boards.

The cricket influences weren't all on the Maxwell side and maybe Mum's genes had just as much say in the way my life went. Her grandfather, Albert Bythesea Weigall, an Englishman who arrived in 1863, was headmaster at Sydney Grammar, and had a profound influence on the school and the town of Sydney. The 'Big Chief', as he was known, was headmaster for 45 years until his death in 1912. The Weigall Ground was named after him (the setting for one of my greatest sporting triumphs—but more of that later).

Another relative, Gerry Weigall, was a famously eccentric English cricket figure forever remembered for his coaching and his aphorisms, some of which entered the lexicon of English cricket. Old Gerry had opened the batting at Kent and went on to coach the side and a number of Test players. A stickler for orthodox batting technique, he is said to have coined the phrases 'never run on a misfield', 'never cut in May' and 'never hook until you have made 84'. He was quite a character apparently. The great English writer E.W. Swanton said 'he may well sound a rather preposterous fellow . . . I can only say that every cricketer was his friend, and that he never spoke an unkind word about anyone.' He is also famous for running out three teammates while batting for Cambridge in a match against Oxford in 1892, which prompted C.B. Fry to observe that 'Weigall did more to win the match for Oxford than anyone on our side.' Gerry appears in the book *Great Characters from Cricket's Golden Age* by Jeremy Malies, which I have and love. He certainly sounds like one of the more interesting men to have played the game. Malies wrote to my mother when researching that book, as she was one of the few living people who knew Gerry, having visited Lord's with him in the 1930s.

My humbler experiences with cricket, of course, started in the backyard and moved out to the streets and parks. One of my best mates at school was a boy by the name of Tim Cohen and we'd worked out early that playing with cricket balls caused broken windows and was more trouble than it was worth. We eventually picked up the art of soaking and shaving tennis balls so that they bounced about the same height as a cricket ball. We would set imaginary fields, with the batsman taking guard in front of stumps scratched into the rockery wall.

Tim and I played cricket together for decades, both of us playing for the Old Cranbrookians after we finished school and touring with them too. He died in 2015 and I miss him terribly.

Our Tests were played out with proper teams and interrupted by disputes about how such and such a fielder could have made up so much ground to dismiss a Harvey or an O'Neill. Imaginary fielders were quite athletic in our minds and never spilled a catch.

Cricket was part of the Saturday ritual in the Maxwell house in the late 1950s and early 1960s. Dad would drag me into his law offices in the city in the morning, where I would sit bored out of my mind until he knocked off at lunchtime and we headed to Concord Oval for an I Zingari match. At least at the cricket I was free and I spent a lot of time exploring the canal that ran by the ground and into Canada Bay. That was when I first met Bill Douglass, who has been an IZ stalwart for 70 years, as a player, secretary, president and chronicler of the club's history. It's worth a visit to Camden Park to see the museum he has created.

I became a junior member of the Sydney Cricket Ground in 1962. Before that I got in on a ladies ticket, but as a full-blown member I had entrée to some of the great cricket matches and to a place that would become my occasional office for more than 50 years.

24

In the early days I think I spent more time ferreting around for empty bottles than watching the game. Tooth's brewery had the rights at the ground and if you could swoop on a discarded Blue Bow bottle you'd return it and get threepence. A lad could do alright with that sort of money. They eventually caught on to this and changed the rules, so you'd get a refund only if you bought another bottle. That might have been part of the reason I was drawn back to events happening out in the middle.

Cricket was different then. A lot of people have become accustomed to annual international tours, to the Boxing Day Test at the MCG and New Year's Test in Sydney, but international visitors didn't come as often when I was growing up.

Fortunately, state cricket more than filled the void. In fact the biggest date of the year was the Boxing Day Sheffield Shield match between NSW and Victoria. As a young Blue Bagger I loved the NSW cricketers. Neil Harvey, Norm O'Neill, Alan Davidson, Richie Benaud and Johnny Martin were my favourites and I was at the ground as often as I could be to see them and their jousts with Les Favell, Sam Trimble and Bill Lawry.

I remember 1962–63 when the Poms were here. Bob Simpson's catching at first slip was worth the price of admission. Davidson was swinging them, occasionally getting one to hold its line; the English batsmen were nicking them fine and 'Simmo' was pocketing catches that by rights should have been wicketkeeper Wally Grout's. I reckon Simmo was the greatest slips fielder ever. Just phenomenal. 'Davo' got five for not much and won us the game with the help of Garth McKenzie. Simmo made 91 before he was bowled by Fred Titmus; the innings still lives in my mind.

Australia won by eight wickets on the fourth day, and as they were running off the SCG the rain started and didn't stop.

The South Africans came in 1963–64 and the stand-out of that series was Graeme Pollock's batting in the NSW tour game and the third Test match. He made centuries with spectacular driving through the off side in each match. Peter Pollock bowling fast and Joe Partridge bowling big inswingers from the Paddington end had Australia on the edge, but Benaud and McKenzie saved us with the bat, McKenzie memorably lashing David Pithey for a six into the top deck of the Members Pavilion in a stand of 160. It was Benaud's last series, cueing Bob Simpson's captaincy and tough losing tours to the West Indies and South Africa.

Pakistan was here for their first tour in 1964–65 and that was a dud season, although one memory lingers. They played NSW and a tail-ender called Farooq Hamid hit the biggest six I have ever seen at the SCG. It landed up near the dome of the Ladies Pavilion. Johnny Martin was the unfortunate bowler.

The Australian board would only give Pakistan one Test, which was in Melbourne and held over four days. A half-century later there is a push for four-day Tests, but at the time it was disrespectful. The legendary Hanif Mohammad scored 104 and 93 in a drawn match.

In the next summer, 1965–66, Bob Barber scored 185 in a 234-run partnership with Geoffrey Boycott—who later became my friend when we worked together on the BBC's *Test Match Special*—and the Poms won easily thanks to off-spin skill from Titmus and David Allen.

Simmo didn't play at the SCG Test but another NSW batsman, Grahame 'Tonker' Thomas, did. He opened the innings in place of Simmo and got a half-century. I remember he scored a double century against Victoria that summer too. He was part American Indian, made his debut against the West Indies in 1965 and played all five Tests of that series. He toured South Africa in 1966–67 but never got a game and retired from international cricket at the age of 28.

By the mid-1960s the sports bug had bitten me hard. I was playing cricket, writing my own sports magazine—*Cricket Chronicle*—for distribution among classmates and in my last years at school acting as a bookie for all the other kids. I would take anyone's business on almost anything. Most kids would have a 5-cent bet with me to pick the card on the whole rugby league round with points start. It was pretty good business because nobody ever won. In 1967 I got cleaned out by a boy who convinced me to take 20 cents on Wiedersehen in the Metropolitan at 25/1. Of course every bookie has to learn a lesson. Then I got knocked off again by a young kid from first year who had 20 cents on the card at 33/1. That hurt me for a while and it was some time before I could pay him out, which chewed out my pocket money, required a loan from my parents and brought about some reshuffling in the school pecking order.

I'd started playing cricket in the Under 13 C-grade side and gradually worked my way up the rungs. I was handy with bat and ball in the early years. Well, I could hit it and I had this almost wrong-footed inswinger that confounded young batsmen. By the Under 15s I was opening bowler and on one famous day I took 9–63 against Trinity. I bowled a lot of rubbish to be honest, but when I got it right they couldn't keep it out.

Unfortunately that was my peak and as I got older I got slower, or at least I didn't get any faster, and by the time I was playing open-age cricket I had resorted to a bluffing version of off spin. My straight breaks served me well enough for three years in the First XI thanks to the munificence of the old umpires who officiated our matches in a rather haphazard manner.

It was captaining that I really enjoyed and I had that role in the 15s and then in my last year of school with the Firsts.

In those days we played among the Combined Associated Schools, which was a grouping of six independent private schools. There was also an annual match against the Naval College at Jervis Bay and another two against a Combined Northern Districts High Schools, which is where I came up against future Australian Test star Gary Gilmour. I remember him smashing us for 70-odd one day at Cranbrook but we never got to face his bowling because the match was rained out, which was probably a good thing. Gary, or Gus as he was known, was one of the best all-rounders of Australian cricket and one of the great natural talents, but he was dogged by injuries, which eventually forced him out of the game.

Today school teams go on overseas tours to the UK, Sri Lanka, South Africa and India. In the 1960s trips to Newcastle and Jervis Bay were much anticipated and created associations that still connect half a century later.

The biggest game of the year, aside from the rivalries with the other schools, was against the Old Boys. Scheduled to coincide with the end-of-year speech day, it was a two-day match that began the day before and was interrupted for the speeches, which were held in a marquee on the practice wicket that adjoined the ground. When the speeches were done we would return to the field and finish the game.

I was well established as captain by this stage and in my last year we got walloped in the first innings by the Old Boys. On the Saturday I said to the boys that we had nothing to lose and we may as well just go for it, which was my approach to captaining. I was always one to take risks or set a funky field. Anyway, we managed to get 120 ahead and I declared our innings over. Everyone thought I was mad and that we should have dug in for a draw, but I figured it was better to risk losing if it gave us a chance to win. Fortunately I had at my disposal the talents of Jerry Thiedeman, who played in the NSW schoolboy side with the fearsome fast bowler Jeff Thomson. A left-arm spinner and right-handed bat, Thiedeman was an exceptional cricketer. When he bowled he turned the ball so far that some-times I would have every fielder on the off side just daring the batsman to hit across his line.

Anyway, with Jerry at one end and me at the other we managed to convince the old umpires to keep the game going even though it was getting ridiculously dark, and we somehow managed to roll the Old Boys and pull off a famous victory. We got a few decisions to go our way that may not have survived the DRS today, but we won and were very happy.

Those games don't happen at Cranbrook anymore and it's a shame. Now speech day is held off campus and the boys are away adventuring at Outward Bound or the like and study is a higher priority than it once was.

The games against other schools were proper cricket matches, with no over limits, so you had to judge when and if to make a declaration. I loved the whole tactical part of captaining the Firsts side: placing creative fields, making bold declarations, trying to outsmart the other team. It was that analytic approach that attracted me to McGilvray's commentary and made the game so intriguing.

Some of the great memories I have of schoolboy cricket are of the umpires who would stand in the games. They were World War I veterans. Old men, hard of hearing, poor of eyesight and erratic of judgement, they were great characters and we cultivated their favour. There was Ernie Bockman, who made appalling decisions and would then justify them for overs to come. He'd give you an LBW, upsetting the batsman, and say 'that was out, that one was out . . . that hit him right in front' and I would say 'you are right, Ernie'. He loved dancing and he'd had his left testicle shot out at Ypres, or so he told us. Another was Fred Paris, known as the

One-Armed Bandit because he'd lost his arm at Passchendaele. Signalling a six was a bit awkward for him, as you can imagine—it was a bit like a bloke doing an exaggerated bye signal. They were all lovely fellows but poor judges. You'd get fired on a lot of shocking decisions, but that was the way it was and you just had to cop it, because you knew it went both ways.

There was an old bloke by the name of George who used to keep his blood sugar up by munching on biscuits out in the middle. When he got to square leg he would often take the chance to sit down. One day I was bowling and knocked the bail off in my delivery stride, but managed to bowl the batsman. George gave him not out.

'Why?' I asked.

'Because you can't knock the bails off when you bowl, so it's a no-ball,' he said.

'You probably can't but it isn't a no-ball,' I said.

'I am the umpire—you get on with the game,' he said.

Fifty years on Steven Finn did the same thing playing for England and they changed the laws. That was after a match against South Africa where the batsmen complained it was distracting them—he did it three times in the first over—and when he did it and the batsman snicked to slip it was ruled a dead ball. As a result the International Cricket Council changed the rules, and it would now be a no-ball.

The cricket facilities at Cranbrook were outstanding and because I was a member at the SCG I could also go down and use the nets at the old No. 2 ground, where there were two turf wickets available on certain days of the week. That was a favourite thing to do because you would often be in the nets alongside members of the state team.

I was something of a bold hitter and I remember one day we were down at the Sportsground end and I top-edged one into the Sydney Sports Ground. Someone must have seen it because the next thing you know Warren Saunders, Peter Philpott and a few other state players had made their way over to see this kid who could hit the ball so far. After I played a few more shots they walked away—my moment of glory was over. If it had been 40 years later I might have got a BBL contract.

In one match against Sydney Grammar in the 14As on the Weigall Ground named after my relative I managed to get onto one that went over the road and into the old Advanx Tyre factory opposite the ground. It was a fair distance and everybody was pretty impressed. The kids could probably do it easily these days, but back then we weren't using those ridiculous bats that have made the game so loaded against bowlers.

Bats were such a precious thing when we played. Dad would take me to the Alan Kippax sports shop in Martin

Place and his good friend Mr Crawford, who was the brother of the famous tennis player 'Gentleman Jack' Crawford, would look after us. Getting a new bat, oiling it up and knocking it in was one of the great anticipatory pleasures. I loved the smell of linseed oil. It's incense to an old cricketer.

Eventually I had to leave school and take the first tentative and confused steps into the outside world, although I had no idea where I was going.

I think by this stage we had a television at home. Dad had held out for some time, begrudgingly hiring a set in the summer, but he was never keen on the idea. When television started broadcasting games I think he saw the need for the Maxwells to get with the times. Radio, however, remained at the centre of my life. In 1967, when I was doing the HSC for the first time, I had seen a job advertised to work as a specialist trainee in the sports department at the ABC. It was my dream career, sport and radio combined.

Years later, after my mother's death, I found the clipping in a pile of strange things she had kept. Applicants needed the 'Leaving Certificate or its equivalent and have a good general knowledge of sport and a keen and active interest in sporting activities. An acceptable speaking voice and potential for training in the writing of sporting scripts and the broadcasts of commentaries is necessary. The work is interesting and offers good prospects in the sporting field in both radio and television.'

The wage was $2891–$3531 per annum, but lower rates applied to persons under 21. So I would have been paid even less than that.

Unfortunately they weren't interested in me. In fact, they gave the job to Peter Meares, who was a few years ahead of me at Cranbrook, a very good sportsman, and enjoying a fine career centred on his love of sport.

In 1969 I strode reluctantly into the world of academia and enrolled in an Arts degree at the University of NSW, where I was supposed to study subjects like the history and philosophy of science, but I found myself a little distracted by the Randwick racecourse, conveniently located across the road. There were a few pubs in the vicinity too. Mum was at university by this stage and she used to drive me out there every day. It was her world; she had a car park on campus and was Australian President of the International Federation of University Women, a role she was quite passionate about. It was her window to a world of many impressive women, who became friends and encouraged Mum to travel.

I went to lectures and all that business, but it wasn't for me. I was restless. I wanted to get a job. I wasn't one for sitting around and contemplating (apart from cricket). I reckon the only interesting thing that happened that year was when they stopped all the lectures and we gathered in one of the theatres to watch Neil Armstrong and his mates land on the moon.

Of course 1969 was a pretty intense time in Australia and the rest of the world, with the Vietnam War heating up and the protest movements gaining momentum. I wasn't political; in fact I was very much a product of my conservative environment.

One of my friends at school, who went on to become a history teacher, used to try to tell me how stupid our involvement in the Vietnam War was and I would argue that the bloody commos would come Down Under if we didn't stop them. I swallowed the line from Robert Menzies that the invasion of the south was a direct threat to Australia.

I was up for the draft that year and I remember that of all people Lindsay Hassett pulled the marbles out that decided who was going. He must have taken pity on me. I was born on 28 July but got lucky, as Lindsay pulled out 27 and 29.

Conservatism may have run in the family. Mum's brother-in-law, Leslie Bury, was a minister in the Menzies, Holt, Gorton and McMahon governments. He was a contender to be prime minister after Harold Holt disappeared in the surf at Portsea in 1967. That influence was around me and I just didn't rebel against it.

I remember Mum haranguing Uncle Leslie every Christmas about the position of women in society and how badly they were treated, particularly in the public service, where if they got pregnant they had to leave. She was very strong on women being involved in public life, but strangely hated the feminist movement that was starting to find a voice. Maybe it was just too strident for her. She always said there could be no tokenism and that women had to get there on merit.

Uncle Leslie was the Minister for Labour and National Service in Harold Holt's first ministry and had introduced conscription in Gorton's government. Phil Lynch was the Minister for the Army and protestors used to have a slogan 'Lynch Bury and Bury Lynch'. Quite clever.

I remember being at the centre of another raging political controversy eighteen months later when the Springboks toured Australia. It was too heated for the usual under-age kids to be ball boys, so they wanted a few older blokes to have a go and hence I got the job at the SCG. Boy that was a crazy tour.

The anti-apartheid activists did everything they could to stop the games. Up in Queensland, Premier Joh Bjelke-Petersen was so keen to stop them he declared a state of emergency and built a fence around the ground. In New Zealand a bloke in a plane buzzed the ground and dropped flour bombs on the players. In Sydney they had barbed wire up to stop people invading the field.

Before the game somebody tried to saw down the goal posts and during it the players were pelted with oranges and assorted missiles. There were even billiard balls. They had police wagons on the side of the field and were throwing people in there as they went.

It was after the rugby tour and discussions with activist and later Labor MP Meredith Burgmann that Bradman saw the light on apartheid and cancelled the next tour by South Africa.

Anyway, I didn't really engage with university life. I was still hanging around with my mates from school and by now I was playing with the Old Cranbrookians Cricket Club. We'd have games on the weekend and were very well organised at the time. I think within a year I was secretary and then on the committee and editor of the OC magazine.

At the end of the year I was sure of what my uni results would say and that it would be ugly, but my mother announced that we would be touring the world with her South American friend, Val Franco. That was some trip. Mum made use of her political and family ties to make sure we were well looked after. We were hosted by every Australian ambassador everywhere we went. We were picked up at the airport in Bangkok by an official car. We went to dinner with the Australian ambassador to Greece, Hugh Gilchrist, a remarkable man who wrote a seminal three-volume work, *Australians and Greeks*. He had been at Cranbrook with my father, so the connection was historic. In Rome I got a lecture from the ambassador, Walter Crocker, who sat me down after dinner at his house and grilled me about what I was going to do with my life. It stuck in my mind, so much so that years later, when he was Lieutenant Governor of South Australia, I sought him out on one of my Adelaide trips. At the time I was nineteen years old and wandering around the world with my mother and her friend, with no idea of where I was going. He gave us the official car and driver to go and look at the ruins in Ostia.

Spain really opened my eyes; it was an amazing experience. We were there just before Franco's regime fell. It was around Christmas time and we went down to the Valle de los Caídos, or Valley of the Fallen, where all the dead from the civil war were buried. The power of Catholicism was overwhelming. It was everywhere and in your face and quite extraordinary. I had really had little to do with Catholics until then; most of the ones I knew were tough buggers from Waverley College, the Christian Brothers, who I only ever met on the sports field.

We were in Greece when I slipped out and slipped up. Thinking I could navigate my way around, I got bailed up in some dodgy bar that I think must have been a brothel. The bloke demanded I avail myself of the local delights and when I declined stood over me and made me fork out 25 quid for the drinks. It was pretty intimidating and I would have paid anything to get myself out of there. Things like this didn't happen in the Eastern Suburbs! I never told Mum. I was too embarrassed. It goes to show how young and naive I was.

After that we went on to London and stayed at the English Speaking Union near St James Park. It was a pokey little place, damp in the middle of winter. Quite charmless, but there were so many relatives to visit and dues to be paid. We then came home through the United States and enjoyed more generous hospitality in Washington, where my uncle, the aforementioned Leslie Bury, had worked at the World Bank until Robert Menzies lined him up to become the member for Wentworth in Sydney.

I'd applied for a job at the ABC again in 1969 but nothing had come of it and when we arrived back in Bellevue Hill at the start of 1970 my future was not looking too bright. My results from university had arrived at home and it's fair to say they weren't flash . . . I'd failed every subject.

Mum was not amused but my father was more laid back. It was obvious to him that I was no academic. On reflection it was a pretty enlightened attitude from a man who had to some degree curtailed his dreams to do his duty by the family's law firm. He placed no such expectations on me. Mum was a bit different. She had a line she used to trot out around this time: 'you don't want to be a lotus-eater'. It was Mum's highbrow way of telling me not to be indolent, a bum or a drop-out. She told me I had to get a job and I said the only job I wanted was the one at the ABC, which was never going to come around again.

On the good offices of my cousin Peter Bury, I got a job as a clerk in the superannuation department at National Mutual Life, which was about as much fun as it sounds. At least I was earning money and my first investment was a Mini Cooper S when I turned 21. I had wheels at last, but I was still living at home and I didn't wander too far. Cricket was still a constant and when they moved me into the trust deeds area I found myself spending plenty of time with Tom Spencer, who was a wrist-spinner with Manly and a good cricketer. Restless still, I moved on to work for a Dutch insurance company AMEV, but the change didn't cure my restlessness.

I applied again to the ABC in early 1971 and was rejected once more.

I stayed in touch with Tom Spencer and in 1972, after what might have been the longest year of my life (office work was not my thing), he suggested I join him on the Australian Old Collegians Cricket Association tour to the UK and various exotic destinations. Naturally there was talk of lotus-eaters at home, but Dad could see the attraction. These tours were magnificent events. They were basically for people who loved the game and who had enough money to pay for an overseas trip, and there were some good players. Michael Hill, a Shield cricketer with NSW and a Newcastle lawyer, was our vice-captain and there were plenty of good first-grade cricketers, such as Mal Elliott and Ian Howell from Manly, Peter James from Sydney University and a strong group of Newcastle players, all managed enthusiastically by Bruce O'Sullivan.

We left Sydney on 13 May and weren't due to return until 21 August. In between we played 90 games, starting in Honolulu and then progressing through the United States, Canada and Bermuda before heading to England.

I hadn't changed much as a cricketer. I think I had the most ducks, but I hit a lot of sixes, which in a way were more memorable. I hit Don Shepherd for two sixes at Swansea—the ground where Sobers hit six sixes. Don was a classic English county bowler and took more than 2000 wickets, was voted one of *Wisden*'s cricketers of the year in 1970, but never got to play for England. He later became a broadcaster for the BBC in Wales.

I opened the batting on the odd occasion on tour, but cricket wasn't ready for the David Warner approach back then, and even if it was I didn't have our David's talent or concentration.

In England we picked up a few more players, mainly from I Zingari Australia, so we formed two teams and had double fixtures. We stayed at the old White House Hotel next to Regent's Park. When the organised tour finished I stayed on and went back to London and played with Hampstead. A couple of boys from Queensland, John Loxton and John Maclean, had been playing with them and had to return, so I took a spot in their house for a short time before I realised my money was running out.

I got on a British Caledonian plane back to Australia. It stopped in Singapore where we all had to catch a bus to the hotel. A bloke got up and sang. His voice, which was pretty good, rattled the windows of the bus. Turned out he was Johnny Farnham. Later John Farnham.

I got off the plane in Perth because there was someone there who had taken my interest, but pretty soon I had to face up to reality and get home. Only problem was I didn't have a cent and had to ask Dad to send me the money. I think it was about $129. I spent days staring from the train window at the desert and the spinifex tumbling aimlessly along the Nullarbor. That just about summed up my situation in life. No job. No qualifications. Drifting. No interests outside cricket and on my way back to Mum and Dad's.

Funny, however, how life can turn.

Anyway, I eventually got home, walked in the front door and Mum said 'it's good to see you and by the way I cut this out of the paper the other day'. It was an ad for a traineeship in the ABC sports department.

3

Cricket chronicles

Irealised early on I was never going to make a career out of playing cricket and it was obvious to my parents that the world of academia was not for me, but perhaps through the media there was a chance to be involved with the game and earn some money.

There were early signs. Among the things I found in my mother's possessions after she died are early incarnations of my self-published cricket magazines.

They started life in 1963 as *The Cricketer's Newspaper* and were sold to my classmates for threepence. An early surviving copy, neatly handwritten in red pen (Mum would type them up for me later), contains a match report from the Shield match between Victoria and South Australia and a scorecard from the first Test between England and the West Indies.

Showing a degree of creative flair, I clipped a head shot of Ted Dexter from a newspaper and glued it to the lined page in the section 'This Week's Pin Up'. This was cut and paste in its truest sense.

Published on Thursdays, there was a bit of editorialising, but the magazine was mainly score-driven.

By 1965 the publication was known as *Cricket Chronicle* and had reached a level of professionalism that my maturing readership demanded. Now selling for sixpence, the front cover boasted a table of contents: Editor's Notes, Crossword, Quiz.

The first to complete the cricket-based crossword and the quiz stood to win the princely sum of two shillings (20 cents, post-February 1966). A budding rival for the Murdochs, I was also pulling in revenue by running guessing competitions, usually asking readers to name future squads, which had entrants parting with a bit more cash in the hope of winning the big prize.

A September 1965 edition featured an obituary for Bill Woodfull and short biographies of every member of the MCC side that was to tour Australia that summer.

The owner-publisher was soon making the most of his editorial control. I had opinions on all manner of cricket topics and expressed them with confidence.

The December 1967 edition starts with an exhaustive assessment of the touring Indian squad, concentrating on its lack of both pace and experience against pace, but it was on the topic of broadcasting that I really came into my own and thumped the pulpit.

'One can only view the New South Wales Cricket Association's decision in not televising any matches this summer with disgust, remorse and perhaps sympathy. In refusing to grant the Australian Broadcasting Commission rights to make such telecasts, even of the last session of play, the NSWCA is no doubt hoping that the crowds will come back to the game, but as far as I can see they have only worsened an already unhealthy situation, and Sheffield Shield cricket and its like will lose a lot of the popularity it has had. These telecasts serve to keep the game alive in many respects, for there are many people in country areas who will now be unable to see any cricket at all. Even in England, where attendances are worse than they are here, the game is televised, even Sunday games . . .' and on I went.

I also championed the cause of New Zealand cricket by slamming administrators for not playing Tests against our neighbours after they had a victory against an unofficial side led by Les Favell. 'But no, they passed the New Zealanders off with pathetic excuses of "our program's too full", "we've already got the Indians coming" . . .'

Dear reader, your young editor was quite the progressive, even launching into a call-to-arms on the issue of Sunday cricket.

'Despite the "great objections of churchmen", despite the "Sunday cricket would not draw the spectators" opinion of "leading" administrators, and despite the fact the NSWCA is unable to afford the "high cost" of "hired labour" on the Sabbath, Sunday cricket has managed to prosper in the more "backward" cricketing states of Western Australia and Queensland ... In Sydney we know that the SCG Trust is against any sport on Sundays. In the football season they told the New South Wales Rugby League that excessive use of the ground would ruin the surface for cricket. And when the cricket season arrives, we discover that this policy is still being carried out. What's the trouble? Is cricket on four successive days going to ruin the surface for football, or is the SCG Trust anti Sunday cricket because of tradition. Maybe they can't afford to pay the ground staff. For the moment, at any rate, we must continue to play cricket for six out of seven days of the week to the detriment of the game as a public drawcard. May our Sunday prayers be well directed, to terminate this narrow minded and incomprehensible attitude.'

I must have had the cricket authorities shaking in their boots.

Two decades later I took over as editor of the *ABC Cricket Book*, a publication beloved by many a tragic who sits at games filling in the scorecard and flicking through the articles. The editorials were a little less forthright and my crossword/quiz competitions had fallen away.

My mother also kept my scorebook from those days. I would catch the bus with my best friend Tim Cohen and we would sit in the upper deck of the M.A. Noble Stand, by the ABC box and behind the wicket, studiously filling in our books, which came with the MCC Laws of the Game printed inside. It was a way of engaging with the game and something we did with great pride. Occasionally we would go out the back for a quick game with a tennis ball in the break, but by the time we were thirteen or so we were keen on watching the cricket. That was how we spent our school holidays.

We also went to White City for the NSW Tennis Championships. They were five-set matches with no tie breakers, so there were some long afternoons watching Roy Emerson, Clark Graebner, Cliff and Nancy Richey and Margaret Smith (later Margaret Court).

I was quite busy in the summer of 1964, keeping the scorecard for a first-class game between Pakistan and NSW in early December. I note that Tim and I swelled a crowd of just over 4000 on the first day and a little over 13,000 across the three days. I was back again for Queensland and NSW at the SCG in January. Trimble's undefeated 252 dominated the scorecard. In the next game Sobers hit 138 for South Australia. There's even a score sheet for the third Test between Australia and South Africa the following season.

I saw some great players that summer. Ian Chappell, Doug Walters, Bill Lawry, Wally Grout, Graeme and Peter Pollock, Bob Simpson, Les Favell, Barry Jarman, Rex Sellers, Asif Iqbal . . .

•

The *ABC Cricket Book* has a long history and was first published in the 1930s basically as a guide for cricket fans to find out when the broadcasts were on. I have a couple of early copies and they sell for an absolute fortune.

The foreword to the first edition in 1934 says 'the Australian Broadcasting Commission will throughout the tour broadcast authentic and detailed descriptions of the play. The observations of experts expertly recounted and this booklet is offered to listeners in the hope that it will assist them to understand those descriptions fully and to follow the tour with yet greater interest.'

A 1938 edition boasts that 'The Australian Broadcasting Commission has been fortunate enough to secure the services of a particularly competent body of former leading players and authorities on matters concerning cricket to present to the public an authentic and detailed picture of the forthcoming Test Cricket Matches in England.'

There are pen-pic bios of all the commentators. Former MCC captain Arthur Gilligan is acclaimed for his 'most unbiased outlook'. Former Australian captain Bill Woodfull, Bertie Oldfield ('an interesting and competent talker on cricket topics'), Monty Noble, Victor Richardson and Alan McGilvray were also on the panel.

E.K. Sholl from the ABC's head office was in charge of 'organising the cable service from which the synthetic ball-to-ball descriptions will be constructed'. He had experience from the 1935–36 tour of South Africa in a similar capacity.

The composition of the team was diverse. NSW opening bowler Hal Hooker, Victorian broadcaster Mel Morris and former children's radio personality John Chance were all on board. There was even Dudley Leggett, the Federal Officer for Outside Broadcasts, formerly in charge of school broadcasting in Queensland, who was 'in charge of the organisation of the present Cricket Broadcasts, and will be glad to receive any suggestion for their improvement'.

Can you imagine the reaction if we offered this invitation today? Might be suggesting a few changes in the personnel.

The first editions contained a glossary of terms, some of which have fallen out of use over the years or been fine-tuned. The original program told us that 'in the describing of any game it is unfortunately necessary to make use of a number of technical terms . . . such terms are especially valuable in that they convey briefly and clearly a lucid description'.

A *full tosser* was not the bloke who delivered one but the delivery itself. *In-swerve* was not an inswinger, but refers to the drift a leg-spinner got, *out-swerve* the opposite. A *cross-bat cover-hit* was basically a front-foot cut shot.

I took over as editor of the *ABC Cricket Book* in 1988. It was still a pretty basic publication in those days and I set out to improve the quality of the writing and make it a little bit more than a simple preview of the season's cricket accompanied by the odd article.

As an example of lifting the quality, I asked Scobie Malone author Jon Cleary to write a piece about his cricket life in London as an Australia House player in the 1950s; comedians Roy Slaven and H.G. Nelson wrote an irreverent article or two; ABC journalist Marius Benson did a piece on the politics of South African cricket; and Bill O'Reilly wrote a wonderful story when the Pat Hills Stand was renamed in Bill's honour at the SCG.

My editorials carried over the tradition established in the *Cricket Chronicle*. In 1992–93 I was already fretting about the future of Tests. 'Were it not for the one-day game, cricket would be struggling for survival and as time passes one wonders how much longer Test matches can survive as the one-dayers are paying its bills.' Strange how things change. Maybe I had got a bit ahead of myself. I hadn't heard of T20 but it sounds like I should have. 'As our working lives reshape so does the opportunity for more part-time employment and more leisure time, for cricket it is twilight time, the cool shades of evening for boys and girls to play alongside the oldies and not just within their age group.'

I was complaining about the cost of admission even then. In 2015–16 Geoff Lemon wrote a piece for our website on exactly the same issue. It caused quite a stir, and led to a reappraisal and reduction in admission prices by as much as $20 a ticket for 2016–17. The boy who thundered in those 1960s self-published editorials finally got his way, ensuring more people get to see the cricket.

4

I join the ABC

So, I typed up another letter to the ABC and hoped for the best.

This time, my third attempt, I got my foot in the door, but it was a protracted process and dragged on over months.

My luck must have been in. Not long after being accepted into the second round of interviews I won second place in a Melbourne Cup sweep and stuffed almost $400 into my empty pockets—where it didn't stay for very long.

There was only one thing to do with it and that was to spend it on an Old Cranbrookians tour of New Zealand (full cost: airfares, accommodation and hire cars, $305). It was a turn of fortune that proved to be invaluable for my job application. Peter Meares, who had beaten me for the position the first time around a few years before, was on the trip and I pumped him for all the information I could get.

Peter was very generous. He sat with me in the stands during the games and helped me as I practised my commentary, knowing that the ABC wanted me to do an audition in January at either White City or the SCG. If I had been smarter, I could probably have claimed the trip on tax as a study tour.

When I got back to Sydney I was sent to the back of the Noble Stand with a Swedish Nagra tape recorder, and told to do some commentary while Johnny Watkins and Bob Massie snicked their way to an 83-run partnership in the Test against Pakistan. That ninth-wicket stand got Australia enough runs to give the bowlers something to aim at in what turned out to be an extraordinary Test. Dennis Lillee bowled with a busted back and Max Walker took six wickets. It was Johnny Watkins' only Test, but things turned out better for me.

The head of ABC sport, Bernie Kerr, told me later it was the audition that got me the job, so I have Peter Meares to thank for his tuition—and the horses for allowing me to afford the fees on our 'study tour'.

I started at the ABC on 6 April 1973. Bright-eyed and nervous.

The organisation I joined was still a place where men smoked pipes and wore hats while women answered the phones and 'manned' the typing pool, but also an organisation changing to reflect a country doing the same. It was an institution with all the attendant rituals and eccentricities.

The days when newsreaders wore a tuxedo at the microphone had passed, but the plummy English accent had not died off completely. A lot of the 'voices of the ABC' sounded English—indeed some were—and if you weren't from the Old Country it seemed you had to do your best to sound like you were.

When I arrived Martin Royal, the newsreader, was still a big name and he was a Pom; John Chance, probably the most famous voice in Sydney, had just wound up. He was the man who told you 'the number you have dialled is not correct. Please check the number and dial again' when you made an error dialling on the landline. Maybe Australians liked being corrected by a well-spoken, English voice.

That English accent—faux or not—had, however, started to irritate people. It had been contentious for a while and the ABC was moving more to what you might call a cultured Australian voice.

The sports department in the 1970s was a hard-drinking and hard-working environment. My first six months were spent learning the ropes. There was a retired announcer called Gordon Scott who came in to help me with my elocution. He'd have me reading from a book with emphasis on certain words in an attempt to teach me and other apprentices how to put a bit of life and timing into our outpourings.

Most of the trainees wanted to get out and call the footy (rugby league), but when we went to games we were there to observe. I sat behind Alan McGilvray and soaked up the way he described cricket matches, got a feeling for his approach. He always said you can copy technique, but not style.

There's a basic science to calling any sport, especially cricket, and I don't think giving away the tricks ruins the magic of it. The essential thing when calling the action is—much like when you are facing a bowler—to get into position early.

As the bowler approaches you say 'Lillee comes in to bowl' but you cut away before he lets the ball go and get up the other end as fast as you can and 'it's short, Boycott NICKS IT . . . HE'S CAUGHT AT FIRST SLIP!' Once you have the hang of it you are catching the wave of noise that rises with the occasion, but to do that you have to be just ahead of the crowd. When it works it is seamless and apparently effortless.

My first summer in the job, New Zealand was the visiting team. I went out early for a couple of Shield games, taking up my spot behind McGilvray and letting it all sink in.

I join the ABC

In December 1973 they threw me in to call a four-day match between NSW and the Kiwis at the SCG. God I was nervous. I reckon if the tapes survived you would hear me sweating over the crackles and fumbles. There was a guy called Mike Shrimpton in the game who batted about as well as I called, but somehow he got his way to an undefeated 100. It was an ugly innings and he got dropped a few times by the locals. Perhaps it was a metaphor for my early career.

Young Gary Gilmour, who I'd encountered in that school match a few years before, opened the bowling for the Blues and finished the game with seven wickets. Kerry O'Keeffe, who would become a big part of my life many decades later, was also in the home team and bowled well in NZ's second innings. Both the Hadlees played for the visitors, who lost the match by seven wickets.

It was the 1970s and young people seemed to be licensed to be cocky and ready for everything, but I have to admit I was intimidated. I was on the air with real cricketers like Jim Burke, the Australian batsman who had scored 100 on debut against England in 1951 and an infamous undefeated 28 in a four-hour knock in Brisbane seven years later.

Poor Jim, he was a friendly, happy guy who got into financial trouble a few years later and tragically committed suicide. At the time Keith Miller said that Jim didn't have a soulmate, despite his wide circle of sporting and business associates. He was a stockbroker long on gold, and I think the investments he thought had gone bad actually turned around. Jim was a popular commentator on radio and television. He shot himself a few days before he was due to cover the sixth Ashes Test in February 1979.

McGilvray had been a good state cricketer himself and was the grand old man of the game. He was the voice of Australian cricket, the man who was there every time you flicked on the radio, the man who had in many ways inspired me to become a cricket commentator.

And then there was me, a young bloke who may have hit some sixes occasionally, but had no real experience of playing big cricket, no experience of calling the game, but was now a cricket commentator, sitting in the box surrounded by giants.

Back in those days we did the Shield games in half-hour bursts on radio and at 3.50 p.m. ABC television would pick up the coverage until stumps at 5.30 p.m. Norman May was the main man on those broadcasts, and it was all very rudimentary. There were a couple of cameras that were almost static and a very straight commentary. We didn't do any to-camera pieces or analysis in breaks, and there were no replays.

On radio it was a no-frills approach, introduced from the studio in Forbes Street, Darlinghurst, with, 'for descriptions of play in the Sheffield Shield match between New South Wales and Queensland we take you to Alan McGilvray at the Sydney Cricket Ground'. It was very formal. We were instructed to describe the play, give the score regularly and introduce the summariser, say Jim Burke or later Dave Renneberg, at the end of the over.

After a few years I did a little bit of television myself on a Saturday program called *Sports View*, which covered the rugby union and rugby league. I was the frontman for that regional coverage, but television lacked the appeal of radio. Radio was personal, more intimate and lent the opportunity to create pictures for people's imagination. Television was comparatively superficial.

Even when Channel Nine started doing the coverage of cricket with all its bells and whistles, it didn't make us old-timers in the radio box think we'd missed out or been left behind. To be honest we told ourselves that most people would be looking at television pictures but with the sound down and the radio turned up, because we didn't have ads and we had continuity and authoritative analysis. I've met a lot of people who said that this was how they watched the game. A lot still do, despite what Tony Greig may have said on the matter. Tony reckoned it was a myth created by radio commentators.

On television you are a slave to pictures—unless you are Richie Benaud. He made an art form of television commentary, establishing the idea that silence was golden. He was the king of the pregnant pause. I believe the game can carry itself. I have to say, though, that our friends at Sky TV in the UK do a great job calling what they see without xenophobia or cheerleading, offering humour and knowledge without bias or in-jokes.

●

The old ABC studios were where the Horizon apartments now stand in Forbes Street. Our offices were at 164 William Street and you had to run up the hill and across the road with your script to deliver the sports news at 6.30 p.m. In those days all the interviews had to be pre-recorded—it was rare to have anyone in the studio live.

Sporting Highlights was on before the famous *Blue Hills* serial for fifteen minutes. When they axed that show in 1976 we went to half an hour and for a while there we were doing a full half-hour of sport, but then we got punted for the *PM* program, which was also on Radio National.

The whole nature of covering cricket on radio and television has changed so much since the mid-1970s. It was very formatted and straight-laced back then. You very rarely had anything approaching a conversation, diversions were banned, the whole thing was a lot stiffer and certainly very different to the last thirteen years with Kerry O'Keeffe (but it had changed even before he came along).

In the old days you provided your own statistics too, which meant you had to lug around the *ABC Cricket Book* and a heap of *Wisden*s. And you had to do your homework. You didn't have that almost instant access to data you have today; you couldn't google or look it up on one of the dedicated stats sites. There were scorers, but scorers just kept the score, which is still pretty much the case with a lot of them in this country. The best scorers anticipate the milestones and give the information to commentators as it happens. Currently Ric Finlay, Graham Pellen, Gerard Cameron and the ever-green Laurel Kirton stand out in our summer coverage. Overseas Andrew Samson has eclipsed the field with his instant ability to find a fact or answer a question faster than parliamentarians in question time.

The game has changed with access to the audience via texts, tweets and the rest. We are getting information from all sorts of sources and on all manner of topics. I always enjoyed it when we would hear from farmers who were harvesting crops, truckies on the road, families heading off on holidays, who would be tuned in to the coverage. In recent years, thanks to social media, we can have immediate interaction with the crowd, with a worldwide audience.

The changes in technology have been significant, but from where I sit not so enormous. The microphone is always there and the game is your canvas.

The broadcast is a relatively simple exercise today. Plug in a few leads, dial up and you're away. And if something goes wrong—as it always did on my early visits to the subcontinent—we can phone in live coverage.

Of course it was a lot different when McGilvray was broadcasting the so-called synthetic Tests, which have become part of broadcast folklore. When Bradman's side toured England in 1938 the technology wasn't up to it—short wave transmissions would have dropped in and out—so they did it with cables, smoke and mirrors. Working in the Market Street studio in Sydney the commentators—Vic Richardson, Monty Noble, Hal Hooker and Alan McGilvray—would receive one-line updates from England via cable and with the aid of some stored local knowledge and background crowd noises they 'created' a live call. The commentator made the sound of the bat hitting ball by striking a pencil on a piece of wood or coconut.

They got away with it most of the time, although McGilvray told of an occasion when the cable—they were in a code which probably resembles the way people talk now on SMS or Twitter—informed them that MC was out in the first Test of the 1938 series at Trent Bridge. This was rather unhelpful as Stan McCabe and Ernie McCormick were batting at the time.

Figuring that McCabe had passed his 100 and was most likely to be the one, McGilvray took a gamble and announced him out, summed up his innings and got on with calling the game. As more cables arrived it became obvious that McCabe was still batting and McCormick was in the dressing room. Honesty was the best policy, so Alan apologised and corrected the error. The philosophy behind the broadcasts was to create a live 'feel' but not to con people.

McCabe went on to make 232 in an innings Bradman called one of the finest he had seen.

They used the synthetic method for the 1934 series and a combination of it and short wave in 1938, but then decided to rely on the short wave after that. I still remember it dropping in and out when I was a boy. Those strange waves of sound that would come from the other side of the globe had a sci-fi feel.

When I started, the routines were different too. We would cover the Shield cricket in those half-hour bursts. Most games started on a Friday. We did that until somebody decided that state cricket no longer held enough interest against the regular local radio output.

The Shield games were hard to cover as there was no crowd and no atmosphere. You were like an actor on the stage with ten people in the audience. It was a struggle but that was my apprenticeship. I was way down the pecking order when it came to doing Test matches. At that time we had long-serving commentators in their forties who still hadn't been allowed into the box for a five-day game. I had to earn my stripes and get in the queue.

I was very lucky as it turned out. In January 1977 I did my first Test match, Pakistan versus Australia, when I was 26. I remember working on that game with Iftikhar Ahmed, a pioneering Pakistani commentator. He was an excitable caller, never more so than when the ball took an aerial route. 'It's up in the AAAAIIIRRR,' he would yell even if the ball was scooting along at ankle height. McGilvray led the batting for us, along with Lindsay Hassett. I was very much the junior partner.

We started our coverage at five minutes before the first ball was bowled. There were no interviews beforehand at the toss and none after the day's play. We didn't have that access, for a start. The captain might speak to the press at the end of the match, but if the writers from the fourth estate wanted a story or an interview they had to find their man at the bar. Of course you wouldn't get that access today because they wouldn't be in the bar—they would be drinking water and playing PlayStation in their rooms!

Nobody really expected Pakistan to be competitive in that series. The Australians, with Lillee and Thomson, looked unstoppable. They'd beaten Intikhab Alam's Pakistan in 1972–73 (3–0), Mike Denness's England in 1974–75 (4–1) and Clive Lloyd's West Indies in 1975–76 (5–1). Pakistan was in a right muddle before the series, fighting with their board about better pay, with a cabinet minister intervening to make sure the tour went ahead.

Australia's fortunes took a tumble when 'Thommo' did his shoulder in the first match of the series. Lillee bowled brilliantly, Max Walker did a good job as a replacement in the last two games, but the side seemed unsettled by the recent retirements of Ian Chappell, Ian Redpath, Ross Edwards, Ashley Mallett and Terry Jenner. Imran Khan gave our batsmen a few headaches. He did things with the Kookaburra I had never seen done before. Zaheer Abbas matched Greg Chappell run for run, both batsmen finishing with 343 runs at an average of 57 for the series.

The Australians were supposed to win the deciding game in Sydney easily and there were a few raised eyebrows when Greg Chappell won the toss and chose to bat in humid conditions on a wicket that had a bit of life in it. It was a gift for the Pakistanis and they made the most of it. Imran destroyed the Australians, picking up twelve wickets for the match, and Asif Iqbal made a stylish century to ensure the advantage wasn't lost.

Pakistan had tied the series 1–1 and I had made my Test commentary debut.

The ABC had extensive television rights in those days: rugby league, the Commonwealth and Olympic games . . . we did everything on radio and television, so you got to cover a variety of sports in both media.

Of course we learnt how to splice audio tape, but the specialist trainees also went to the ABC training school in Kings Cross, where we were shown how to write for film and to create and edit radio stories. By the early 1980s I was covering the rugby league every weekend . . .

ABC television covered the trots from Harold Park every Friday night. They would broadcast the first leg of the daily double, play an episode of *The Two Ronnies*, then come back for the second leg live before showing replays of what people had missed while they were away.

Everything moved more slowly then—a video tape took ten seconds to roll before it got to air, it wasn't instant as it is today—so you had to learn to adlib. You didn't have autocue; there was no such thing.

Occasionally I used to present the trots in Norman May's absence. Norman was renowned for his on-camera brilliance, unscripted, adlibbed, wearing an ABC mono-grammed khaki jacket, shirt, tie, underscored with shorts and thongs out of vision. And sometimes a cask of refreshment nearby.

The ABC sports staff used to lunch at The Strand hotel in William Street. There was a lot more drinking in those days. More drinking than lunch. McGilvray led the charge, but the old hands like Norman May, Allan Marks, Bill McGowan, Ron Davies and Geoff Mahoney all knew how to pull their weight. The apprentices would try and hang in with them while keeping our own counsel as much as we could. McGilvray would say 'Son, you will never learn anything if you don't listen.' He was a bit intimidating and as he got older he got more pontifical.

In 1983 Bernie Kerr had moved on as head of sport and Derek White took over. He came from television and had been looking after *This Day Tonight*. We were a bit wary of him because until then everyone who had been involved in sport had a sporting background, but he didn't. He started to make some changes, which turned out to be beneficial for the younger blokes like me.

One of the most controversial moves he made was to take Lindsay Hassett off the air without consulting McGilvray. That didn't go down well at all, but then he decided that I should do the 1983 World Cup in England, and things got really interesting.

McGilvray was still the main man and this decision caused a lot of angst. There was a time there when Mac wouldn't talk to me. That might have been because I may have got cocky and been a bit of an upstart, but we did have a falling-out that endured until he retired in 1985.

•

Pardon me if I get a bit misty eyed as I look back to the days of the ABC before it was pecked at by reduced funding, the emerging digital platforms and the politically pernickety/correct, but I walked into an institution that was a quintessential part of Australian life. The commercial media was localised and limited, but Aunty was Australian and ubiquitous. The people in the country relied on us and the people in the city were pretty fond of what we did too.

Working in the media has changed so much and most of the change has happened recently, especially for my friends in the newspapers, who appear to be pigeons flapping around a recently arrived cat. Disruption is a word you hear a bit these days and the old ways of delivering information have been well and truly disrupted.

It's fascinating how radio is one medium that has hung tough—possibly even gained some strength.

You don't need a great big valve job Radiola to tune in now—you can listen on your laptop, phone, tablet, on a device as big as a pack of chewing gum, even a portable transistor radio . . . and if you can't listen live, you can hear it later on a podcast.

Radio was always something of a portable medium. Transistors saw to that. While the television stayed in the corner of the lounge and occasionally made it outdoors, the radio was with you in the kitchen, the shed and the car, by your side as you fished, and discreetly attached to your ear at an inconveniently timed wedding. And it was doing all these things long before the internet.

The wireless was, as the name suggested, wireless well before 4G. With the digital age, radio has become even more accessible. Thanks to the proliferation of digital channels there's the chance to broadcast on multiple topics at the same time and the ABC has embraced this.

Unfortunately, just as we have the chance to do so much more we are restricted by budgets and bellyaches from our political leaders. There are more opportunities but fewer resources to exploit them, yet the cricket endures. Our coverage of the 2015–16 summer was as good as I remember, but then there was no will to send somebody to New Zealand for the tour in February, which was quite disappointing. I know all the newspapers are attempting to do more with less, but they will not miss a Test tour.

Cricket has taken something of a back seat. In 2013 the decision not to send anybody on the tour of India provoked an outcry from Senator John Faulkner, who made a speech to the Australian parliament about the situation:

> Australians love cricket—playing it, watching it and talking about it. We also love the sound of cricket on ABC radio. For generations Australians have grown up listening to Test match cricket on ABC local radio . . . Unfortunately, in recent times the ABC has made a decision—perhaps driven by budget or financial considerations—not to broadcast Test match cricket played overseas. Last year in April, when Australia played a three-Test series in the West Indies for the Frank Worrell Trophy, the ABC was not there . . . This year many Australian cricket fans have been disappointed by the ABC because it decided not to send a commentary team to India to broadcast the current series there . . . The national broadcaster has been broadcasting Test match cricket since December 1924 . . . It had provided continuous coverage of all Australian Tests in the West Indies since 1965 before last year's disappointing decision . . . In 1947, when India played their

first ever Test series as an independent nation, here in Australia against Bradman's team, the ABC was there to cover the five-Test series.

In 1998, in the series known as the Tendulkar versus Warne series, the ABC was there. When Australia won their world record sixteenth consecutive Test win in Mumbai in 2001, the ABC was there. In 2004, when Michael Clarke made a century on debut and Australia won their first Test series in India since Bill Lawry's team in 1969, the ABC was there.

But in 2013 nothing—nothing at all. In 2013 ABC listeners were not allowed to hear the joy of another Michael Clarke century, as they heard in 2004 . . . Later this week ABC listeners will not be able to hear the Australian cricketers again give it their all and try for a consolation win as they did in 1998 . . . Apparently the ABC bean counters decided that sending a team to commentate in India would cost too much money. Apparently ABC programming officers decided that 120-odd hours of Test cricket in April was too much. I do note for the record that some believe there can never be too much cricket on the radio . . .

Senator Faulkner is, as you can tell, a big cricket fan and a keen amateur cricketer himself, but even with friends in high places little changed.

5

Taking it on the road

As a new boy from Down Under I was warmly welcomed to the BBC host commentary team by the *Test Match Special* producer Peter Baxter, with no inkling of the shock that was about to hit the tournament in Australia's first match in the 1983 World Cup.

In the box for Australia's opening match against Zimbabwe at Trent Bridge in Nottingham was cheerful visiting commentator Bob Nixon, a retired Zimbabwean dentist who had just been elected to parliament in a by-election in Bulawayo. He looked edgy as his countrymen managed to make a competitive total thanks to an all-rounder who'd played in the Lancashire League, Duncan Fletcher, whose 69 not out anchored the 6–239 score. Australia looked sloppy in the field, dropping five catches, and I started to get an uneasy feeling.

In the chase Zimbabwe caught brilliantly, a catch from Andy Pycroft in the deep one of several stunners that restricted Australia to 7–226, Fletcher taking 4–42, and producing an upset thirteen-run win. I had the pleasure of working with Brian Johnston, Peter Parfitt and Nixon in that memorable game.

Australia's cricket was mediocre at best, a shambles of grouchy players, and in Kim Hughes they had a leader who wasn't respected by the old hands. In the preceding Australian summer Australia regained the Ashes under Greg Chappell's leadership and won the triangular one-day series, beating New Zealand in the final. On paper Australia's World Cup squad looked strong, with Graham Yallop, Allan Border, David Hookes, Dennis Lillee, Jeff Thomson, Geoff Lawson and Rod Marsh. Greg Chappell was not willing to travel, so Kim Hughes regained the captaincy.

Going into the last round-robin match they still had a chance of qualifying for the semi-finals if they could defeat India at Chelmsford. Hughes cried off with an injury and David Hookes led the team, ignominiously. Another slipshod performance in the field, including 24 extras from wides and no-balls, allowed India to get 247. Roger Michael Humphrey Binny ran through Australia's woeful batting alongside Madan Lal, despatching them for 129.

Memorably I worked alongside Trevor Bailey for the first time during that game. 'The Boil' had a superior tone that infuriated some Australian listeners, maybe especially those who remembered his stonewalling batting in Ashes series, when he had a different nickname—The Barnacle. He'd had a remarkable sporting career, scoring more than 20,000 runs and taking over 100 wickets in 61 Test matches. He'd also been a very good footballer, playing with a Walthamstow Avenue side that won the FA Amateur Cup in 1951–52 before a Wembley crowd of 100,000. The following season, he played in the side that reached the fourth round of the FA Cup.

Those were the days when you could play football in winter and cricket in summer. It would never happen now, although Australia's Ellyse Perry has managed to forge a career for herself at the top level in both.

I found The Boil engaging, knowledgeable and sometimes prone to schadenfreude when it came to the failings of the Australian side. At Chelmsford I asked what he thought of the Australian left-arm spinner Tom Hogan. 'Australia has been sending left-arm spin bowlers here for years and frankly none of them can bowl.'

In that match against India, Brian Johnston, the perennial joker, set me up with his ice-cream trick. Having kindly bought me a vanilla two-scooper in a cone, 'Johnners' suggested that I get ready for the resumption, and as I sat next to him he immediately took the cue and said, 'Well, Jim Maxwell has been kind enough to join me ... so Jim, can Australia score these runs?' I desperately tried to swallow my mouthful of ice-cream, which gave me an instant headache. Johnners guffawed in delight at catching me out.

Johnners' easygoing style rubbed off on a brash Aussie and I think from that point I realised that cricket was a game to be enjoyed. It was a reminder of advice I received from Max Rowley when I went to his DJ school in my adolescence: Bring a smile to everything you say. Translated to cricket commentary: Don't be too serious.

India knocked out England in the semi-final and in a famous victory at Lord's upset the hubristic favourites, the West Indies, by 43 runs. Kapil Dev's fine running catch to remove the master blaster Viv Richards was a turning point in a low-scoring match.

I will never forget the smile on Farokh Engineer's face in the BBC box at Lord's. He couldn't contain himself as the game unfolded. Of course he was happy that his side had done well against the odds, but it was other odds that were really bringing him joy. 'Jim, I got 66/1 about India winning the World Cup.' I never asked how much he'd bet, but I hope it was substantial.

My parents in the 1970s, outside our house. (Author's collection)

As a child, looking happy, cradling the cat, Sandy, which looks less pleased. (Author's collection)

Tug of war was part of the physical education regimen at Cranbrook Junior School, which I attended as both a day student and a boarder—even though I lived a short walk away. (Courtesy of Cranbrook)

The family home, a 'good old Aussie bungalow' at the corner of Bradley Avenue and Riddell Street, Bellevue Hill, which narrowly escaped being shelled by Japanese submarines in World War II. The two neighbouring houses weren't so lucky. (Author's collection)

CRANBROOK SCHOOL
VICTORIA Rd
BELLEVUE HILL
9TH Oct.
7.5 – 7.15 pm

Dear Mum, Dad and Sandy,
I hope you are all well. I just took a Biggles in Australia book out of the library. I am just about to start it. We played cricket to-day. I hit a four and caught someone out. May I please have some more ACTA-VITE. Are you coming down during the week? All is well at school

Adios
Amicas.

Love

A letter home, in which I recount my cricket exploits—and put in a bid for some more Acta-Vite. (Courtesy of Cranbrook)

7.00	GET UP. HAVE COLD SHOWER. GET DRESSED
7.15.	DOWNSTAIRS
7.30.	BREAKFAST.
8.00.	MAKE BEDS
8.15.	INSPECTION
8.20.	GO TO PLAY
8.45.	LINE UP.
8.50.	GO TO CLASS
11.00.	PLAY.
11.25.	CLASS
12.45.	LUNCH
1.15.	PLAY
1.30.	SPORT or CLASS.
3.10.	CLEAN SHOES and CHANGE. PLAY
5.00.	SHOE INSPECTION
5.5.-5.30	SHOWERS.
5.30-6.0	PREP.
6.0	DINNER.
6.30	PREP ⟩ FRIDAY FILM
7.30	BED. SATURDAY. T.V.
8.15..	LIGHTS OUT.

TATUM	WALL	SILVER	KENDAL PAGER.
WILLIS	PAGE.M.	RESTER. H.	WINDSOR
STIRLING	PERRIER	" S.	PFEIFFER.K.
DUPREE	BETTINGTON	BURGESS	FERGUSON.
PFEIFER	GRIEG	CARR	WINTERFLOOD
HILLDENT	JOSEPH	STOREY	WILSON
GKILL	MONKTON	LAEHY	MILSON
MACFARLAN	MAYNE	MARSHALL	OLOFINSKY.
FEARON			

From a cold shower at 7 a.m. to lights out at 8.15 p.m., every
minute of the school day was accounted for. (Courtesy of Cranbrook)

I caught the 333 bus to the Sydney Cricket Ground in January 1961 with my mates Ken and Stephen Hann to see Australia play the West Indies. Watching the West Indians play was a revelation. (Fairfax)

When I became an SCG member, I attended every game I could. I remember the third Test in the Ashes series in January 1963. Australia got the two runs they needed to win as rain set in on the fourth day, and the crowd invaded the ground. (Fairfax)

The phrase 'customer satisfaction' had not been coined in 1963, but sitting on the grass on the SCG Hill, having brought copious amounts of their own beer, these fans look well pleased. It was a different era. (Fairfax)

Bob Simpson (left) succeeded Richie Benaud (right) as Australian captain during the 1963–64 series against South Africa. I admired them both, and they would feature in different ways during my professional career. (Newspix)

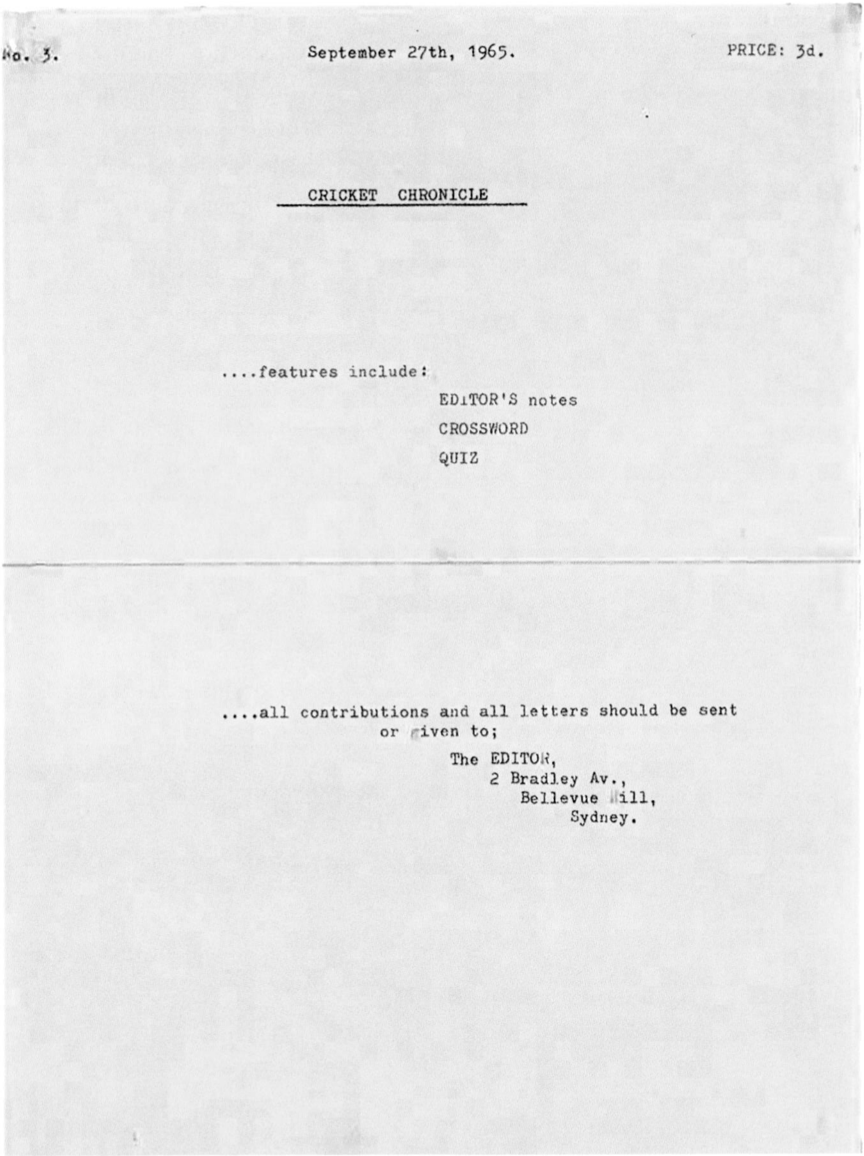

No. 3.   September 27th, 1965.   PRICE: 3d.

CRICKET CHRONICLE

....features include:

EDiTOR'S notes

CROSSWORD

QUIZ

....all contributions and all letters should be sent
or given to;

The EDITOR,
2 Bradley Av.,
Bellevue Hill,
Sydney.

An early edition of my home-made *Cricket Chronicle*—a taste of things to come. See the back of the book for a crossword and quiz, but you're too late to collect the prize. (Courtesy of Cranbrook)

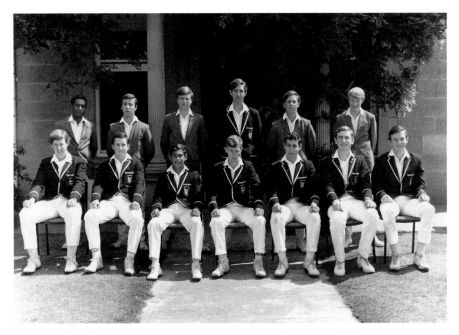

The Cranbrook First XI in 1968. I am sitting in the centre of the front row. To my right is Jerry Thiedeman, an exceptional junior cricketer, and to my left is my best friend Tim Cohen, who is sadly missed. (Courtesy of Cranbrook)

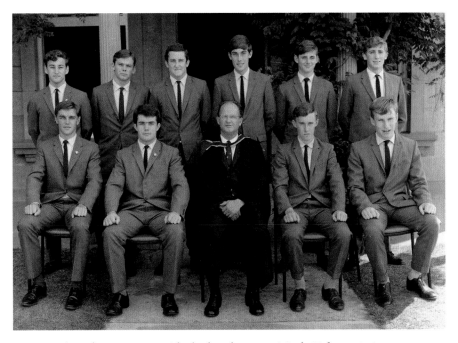

As second prefect in 1968, with the headmaster, Mark Bishop, sitting to my right. Alongside him is head prefect, Chris Leahy. (Courtesy of Cranbrook)

Still young and casting about for a career—just before my 21st birthday.
(Author's collection)

The 83-run partnership between Johnny Watkins (left), in his only Test, and
Bob Massie against Pakistan at the SCG in 1973 provided the excitement for
my ABC audition, which I called from the back of the Noble Stand into a
Nagra tape recorder. (Newspix)

The result was a turning point in the game for India and its supporters. On that day cricket became *their* game.

●

Alan McGilvray may not have been happy about a brash youngster usurping his place in the pecking order, but my bosses obviously were, because in 1984 they followed up by sending me to the West Indies. It was a five-Test series and Kim Hughes' first in charge after the retirements of Lillee, Marsh and Chappell.

Maybe they needed an impetuous new bloke to cover the impetuous new captain.

McGilvray had his nose out of joint about this and I should think he had every right to, after all he was 'the Voice of Cricket' and had been for almost half a century. It would have signalled to him that a new generation was taking over. He was in his seventies by then, and after the death of his wife, Gwen, calling cricket had become important in an otherwise lonely life at home.

In 1985 he published *The Game Is Not the Same . . .* , with a red and white ball on the cover. It's a good book that ends on a sad note as he bemoans the way commerce was robbing cricket of its higher ideals. You could add a pink ball to the cover these days, and a few extra noughts to the figures distracting modern players, but day–night Tests and T20 were a long way off as I started to feel my way as a commentator.

In his book he made it clear he was upset by the emerging larrikinism, particularly among the Australians, and yearned for the return of the gentleman's game. Those days were definitely on the way out and I'm yet to detect any comeback in that department.

He was not an old man out of touch—there were things going on that were unacceptable and I think players today would never get away with some of the behaviour they got away with then. There's far more scrutiny today, but greater rewards and exposure too.

Alan loved a drink and company. Looking back, it was incredible to think how much alcohol was consumed in the 1970s and 1980s. Mac, as we called him, had a constitution that defied logic. He would call you to his hotel room for what he called a 'prayer meeting', which basically meant drinking a six-pack to clear the head before heading to the ground.

He smoked like a chimney too. In those days you didn't have to go to a dark corner of the stadium; you simply sat at the microphone and lit one up. Then another. One after the other. At the end of each twenty-minute commentary stint he'd emerge from a cloud of smoke and hit the bar for a top-up.

It never affected his commentary. He was always razor sharp.

At the end of a day of clearing the head and topping-up, the drinking got really serious. In Sydney he'd hold court in his flat in Double Bay and you had to hang on for dear life. Around ten or eleven at night, when everyone was in fine spirits, he would produce a bottle of Black & White whisky, throw the top out the kitchen window and plonk the bottle down.

'Right,' he would say. 'No one's leaving until this is empty.'

The next morning everyone would tip-toe into the box, but not Mac. He'd have a fag or ten, a reviving high-cholesterol breakfast and call another prayer meeting.

He was a stern taskmaster, but as I have said we all took our cues from him. He was the template for all of us. When I had visited New Zealand before getting the job at the ABC, Peter Meares had schooled me saying 'this is what McGilvray said to me' and once I had got on the inside I watched him like a hawk.

If I had my time over I might have handled a few things differently. For a start, when I was asked at a Cricketers Club of NSW function around that time why I was doing the overseas tours, I might have been a bit more diplomatic.

'The ABC decided to send me not him,' I'd said.

It was too blunt and it got back to him. I should have said we were rotating tours or something like that, but it was an insult to 'the Voice'. He was really hurt and that proves how insensitive my remark was. Our relationship was pretty cool over the next few years and it made working together difficult at times. It wasn't until I approached Keith Miller that we patched it up. I had asked him how I should handle it and I don't know what he said, but after that Mac reached out at a lunch by offering a gentle compliment that broke the ice.

That was going on in the background when I headed off for my first Test series, but at the time I might have got a bit ahead of myself and not cared as much as I should have.

It was a big undertaking just to get to the Caribbean in those days. It involved about two days' travel, but I packed up my trusty tape recorder and off I went. To be honest, I would have rowed there if they had asked.

Radio stations have a reciprocal arrangement on most tours where the guest commentator from the visiting country sits in with the local team. I would work with the various radio stations on the islands and the ABC would take the commentary feed. We do the same with the BBC in the Ashes, but they have a lot more resources than us and will often have a full contingent of commentators and a producer out here to cover tours—that's the advantage of being funded by a licence system.

If I had to file back to Australia between Tests I used to record my piece and send it back by telephone. You used to have to screw the mouthpiece off the phone and clip onto the wires and play it back down the line. It was like something out of a spy movie. I used to ring Sydney and ask them to call me in my room because it was so expensive to call from a hotel with the rates they charged. The system worked fine in most places, but Guyana was dodgy. You struggled to make a call most days. It was 1984, but Guyana was a mess in every way after Prime Minister Forbes Burnham decided to kick the multinationals out and, allegedly, fill his boots on Guyana's rich resources.

From a distance the Windies looks all rum and parties and in the rear-view mirror it looks that way too, but when you are trying to work it can be difficult—and the rum and parties don't help.

My first full cricket tour was probably the best I have ever been on. And not always for the right reasons. I was still relatively young—well, I was 33—and I was single and there was a lot of fun to be had in the Caribbean.

I had a fairly eccentric collection of travel companions and they provided for some very memorable times on the tour, which stretched from February to May. This was when there were still afternoon papers and reasonable budgets for the print correspondents. All the morning and afternoon papers sent a correspondent. Rick Allen from the Sydney *Sun* was there, Phil Wilkins from *The Sydney Morning Herald*, Mike Horan from Melbourne's *Herald*, Greg Baum turned up on holidays, Peter McFarline from *The Age*, Jimmy Woodward from the *Daily Telegraph*, Frank Crook was there for a short time, and Evan Whitton. Ray Titus was the star *Adelaide Advertiser* photographer, but got himself into trouble parking cars. And the man with Marty Feldman eyes, Howard Northey, represented AAP.

It was a pretty entertaining group of reporters. McFarline handed out badges and hit us with fines for all sorts of stupid offences. He was the senior pro who'd broken the World Series Cricket story in 1977. My badge was Almost Famous. Yes, radio stole his thunder as the papers were coming out twenty-four hours behind at home.

It was in the days when newspaper men were hard living and genuine eccentrics. I remember Jimmy Woodward would stand on his head and sing songs after he'd had a couple. 'Good King Wenceslas' was a favourite. He'd served in Vietnam in conscription days and sometimes the darker side of his persona produced a more menacing, 'these hands are trained to kill'. Everybody seemed to be a little, well, different.

Newspaper companies don't have the money they used to. The afternoon papers are all gone and there are a lot fewer people on tour because of cost-cutting. Fairfax and News Corp each send one or two; *The Australian* will go to Test series and that's about it. Of course the internet correspondents have swollen the numbers a bit, which is good to see, and some of them are even paid enough to be able to book a room and eat the odd meal.

There are a lot of very fine young reporters making their way through the new media, but you worry about how they will ever make a dollar out of it. These days even the ABC has a social media reporter attached to our coverage at home, who tweets and blogs. It's a good innovation that ensures we stay part of the conversation on many platforms.

With the reduction in the number of correspondents and the increase in workload, the behaviour of the journos, like that of the cricketers, is a lot more restrained now. Partially because the office won't pick up the tab on the drinking sessions of the past and mainly because everyone has so much work to do. It might also be that people are just a bit more disciplined than they once were.

Anyway, it was a lively touring party in the Caribbean that year. A strong panel, as Mike Coward was wont to say. There was a lot going on away from the cricket and it was pretty wild at times. Wherever you went, on any beach, there was someone selling drugs of some description. There were lads there who would be selling trinkets, but it was really camouflage. They'd ask: 'you want some food for the brain, maan?' It was a constant refrain. Without giving too much away, it is fair to say that some showed more restraint than others when tempted in this manner.

The Australians were an eclectic bunch of cricketers led by Kim Hughes, who might have thought he was going to have an easier time of it with the old school having retired, but it wasn't to be—the Caribbean got to poor old Kim.

Dean Jones was on his first tour and made his debut along with Steve Smith, who opened the batting, but lasted only three Tests before being dropped. He ended up in South Africa on the rebel tour a year later, as did Hughes, Rodney Hogg, Carl Rackemann, Tom Hogan and Terry Alderman, who were all part of this uneasy squad. Maybe that tells you something.

The Australians played tour matches at St Kitts and Guyana then dipped their toe in the water with a one-day game back in Guyana. Desmond Haynes made 133 and the Windies won easily.

The first Test was in Georgetown and the Windies attack was pretty light on. Michael Holding and

Malcolm Marshall didn't play. There were some pretty gutsy efforts by a few of the visitors on that tour and on a rain-interrupted day it was the tail who showed some fight. Rodney Hogg came out to join the spinner Tom Hogan with the score 9–182. They batted for two-and-a-half hours and put on 97 runs with the ball whistling around their ears. Apparently 'Hoggy' had ignored a message from the captain telling them to have a slog. Big Joel Garner took six wickets in the innings. Australia was rolled in the end for 279.

Lawson, Alderman, Hoggy and Hogan did their best, but really weren't much of a match for the West Indies batsmen on their home turf.

The Windies were set 320 to win on what was a postage stamp of a ground. It shouldn't have troubled them, but Haynes and Gordon Greenidge seemed to be more focused on getting their centuries than winning the game. They were 0–250 after 61 overs, with Viv and Clive Lloyd having sat and watched from the dressing rooms, when time ran out. They had plenty of opportunity to increase the scoring rate, but they never got cracking.

The next Test was in Trinidad and Australia was in trouble, sent in on a damp pitch. Border scored 98 when nobody else could get going, and young Dean Jones, playing his first Test, made a 48 that was worth much more than the scorebook suggests.

The Victorian got a harrowing introduction from big Joel Garner. He copped one in the midriff and got his first runs when one bounced painfully off his bottom hand. He was having a hell of a time of it and 'A.B.' wasn't going so well at the other end.

Border had some sort of bug but batted for the best part of six hours—I think he threw up on the pitch at some stage.

Garner was ferocious. 'Deano' tells a story about being distracted while batting by Haynes, who was laughing while fielding at short leg.

'What're you laughing at?'

'You, you're shitting yourself, man.'

'Yeah, don't tell Big Joel.'

'I think he knows, man.'

The Windies did it much easier in making 468 and the Aussies were playing catch-up for the rest of the game. There was a bit of rain around and again the Australians managed to hold on for a draw, thanks to some good batting by the tail and an unbeaten 100 from Border, who was really coming into his own when they were never really in it. Viv's captaincy was bizarre, bowling himself and Larry Gomes at the tail-enders. I can see Tony Cozier making his way around the boundary from the Queen's Park Club end to the press box, trying to catch Viv's eye with a chorus of 'bounce 'em, ma-an, bounce 'em'.

A.B. had batted for ten hours in the match, made 198 runs and not been dismissed nor given a single chance that I can remember. The story goes that the side sang 'Under the Southern Cross' that night to celebrate his efforts. I don't know if that has ever been done before or since. That bawdy anthem is reserved for wins.

Border's efforts deserved to be celebrated in song. He showed something on that tour that no doubt suggested to the powers-that-be that he had the tenacity to lead this team through a tough period. Which was yet to come.

In truth the Australians were a rabble. Looking back on it now, some of the things that happened seemed so unprofessional that it is hard to believe they got away with it. As I said earlier, if those things went on in the modern game there would be all sorts of fines, suspensions and disapproving statements. Some things have been lost, some things gained.

Hughes had enormous problems with Rod Marsh and Dennis Lillee early in his captaincy. They were gone, but now he had to put up with Rodney Hogg, who was a cranky fast bowler and who may have had a problem with authority figures. His behaviour towards Hughes was pretty poor and culminated in him taking a swing at the skipper in the second Test when he didn't get the field placing he wanted. Ray Titus took an amazing photograph of the incident.

Can you imagine a bowler taking a swing at his captain in this day and age?

The tour had started on a bad note when Wayne Phillips and Greg Ritchie slept in and missed the bus to the ground for the first game at St Kitts. There are many stories around and one has it that they weren't actually at the hotel to catch the bus. Word was they'd gone on to one of those roundabouts where they have these rum parties. They are sensational affairs with breadfruit and a band playing and time can get away from you.

There'd also been trouble in the tour match against Trinidad & Tobago at the Pointe-à-Pierre ground, which was situated next to a big oil refinery. Some genius at the Australian Cricket Board had decided the players should wear whites made from wool thanks to a sponsorship deal they had with the wool board. They weren't to everyone's liking and were uncomfortable in the heat. The team was also dealing with a stomach bug that didn't lighten the mood.

So, maybe they had excuses for being so irritable, but Hoggy just walked off the field during the game without telling anyone what he was doing. Hughes sent Carl Rackemann to find out what was going on and the bowler returned to relay the message from Hogg that he had passed away and was unavailable for the rest of proceedings. Hughes sent Rackemann back to insist he reappear and the message came back that he had gone for a drive into town. He hadn't, but there you go; he was not an easy man to control.

Pointe-à-Pierre stank of rotten egg gas from the refinery. It might be the most fragrant ground in the world. It's certainly up there with Chennai in India, which used to get pretty heady thanks to a dodgy little waterway known as the Buckingham Canal outside of the ground.

I can still remember doing a commentary with Gerry Gomez on the local radio station at one corner of Pointe-à-Pierre. I have to confess I was suffering from a bad case of West Indian rum. I struggled to get to work that morning and while we were on air the smell of the egg gas hit me. I got up and said to Gerry, 'I won't be a moment' and I walked about five yards before having the biggest chunder I have ever had in my life.

The rum had ripped my stomach to pieces and whatever I'd eaten after lunch set it off.

That tour match included probably the worst day's cricket I have ever seen played by an Australian team. At least it involved the worst behaviour I have seen. It was embarrassing to be there. The game had dawdled along and Hughes obviously thought the T&T captain Rangy Nanan had dudded them by batting into the last day and giving them a few hours to get 180 odd.

Infuriated, Hughes padded up and went out there as opener and just blocked everything. Greg Matthews was at the other end doing much the same. At one point Greg had his pants down adjusting his thigh pad while the bowler ran in. He knew the captain wasn't going to call for a quick single. After an hour or so Hughes hit a spiteful six and later on he hit a four, but they were his only runs in the 24 overs the innings lasted.

Matthews got out and Wayne Phillips came in and things got even worse. Phillips actually sat down at the non-striker's end. They were lucky there was no television coverage back at home, but there was someone with a camera there. The team manager, Col Egar, was down town on some business, but the board found out about it and I think Hughes was fined for his behaviour.

Hughes even rejected an offer to call off the game and just stayed out there blocking the ball. It was very, very embarrassing, I thought. Today, it'd be serious, there would be profound repercussions for that kind of behaviour. I gave them a serve in my reports and I think the print guys may have too.

The backdrop to all of this was the Australian players were fighting with the board over contracts and pay— this had been and was the backdrop to so many tours from the early 1970s until there was a proper collective bargaining agreement in the early 1990s. There were meetings going on all the way through the tour and the number of guys in the touring party who ended up going to South Africa indicated just how unsettled everybody was.

Despite all that they got away with draws in the first two Tests when the odds and the game were against them.

In the third Test at Barbados Phillips made a brilliant century batting at eight, Graeme Wood and Ritchie got half-centuries and they did well to get 429 considering they'd been sent in to bat. Or so it seemed.

Phillips wasn't a good keeper, but I think they fancied his batting. Roger Woolley was the back-up keeper on that tour and he wasn't the best gloveman going around either. Anyway keepers didn't get a lot of hundreds in those days. Rod Marsh got three in 97 Tests and was considered pretty handy with the bat. Phillips was an opening batsman who was asked to try to revive a junior keeping career to fill the gap left by Marsh. He got 159 on debut in Perth against Pakistan at the start of the summer. Now he had another century seven Tests later.

The Windies made a strong start. The bowlers couldn't do any damage and they had to run Greenidge out to get the first wicket when the score was 131. Then Haynes and Richie Richardson put on 140-odd and the next thing you knew they had made 500. Hoggy got

6–77 but Alderman and Lawson went for a lot of runs. Hogan bowled 34 overs and couldn't get a wicket.

Forty-four overs later Hughes' men were all out for 97. Marshall had 5–42 and Holding, who had come back into the side from injury, took 4–24. Wood suffered a broken thumb, and that was that. For the third consecutive Test the Australians failed to take a second-innings wicket.

There was one amusing moment in the game when a peeved fast bowler cum optometry graduate, Geoff Lawson, good-naturedly removed umpire Lloyd Barker's spectacles, suggesting his prescription needed adjustment. It drew a laugh, in the spirit of the game, from Lloyd, and there was no match referee nor trial by wowsers that happens today.

That innings told you a lot about the gap between the two sides. The pitch had seemed chock full of runs and basically it was, but the Australians had been punching above their weight the whole series and they were overwhelmed when the West Indies scented victory.

After Bridgetown the side headed to the Antiguan Recreation Ground to start the fourth Test just three days later. Australia's disarray showed at the selection table as they tried their fourth opening pair, Ritchie and Phillips, who handed the gloves to Woolley. Hogg was injured and they brought in John Maguire and Rackemann. Another poor batting performance included one of those dumb Hughes dismissals when Marshall was posted on the long-on boundary to Roger Harper's off spin and Hughes holed out. Only Border stood up, making 98 out of a meagre 262.

The local blasters Richards and Richardson hoed into Australia's bowling after Woolley dropped a sitter from Richardson on 38 from Lawson's lively bowling. They plundered a 308-run partnership, Richardson hitting one extraordinary shot off Hogan. For most of the series the minor blaster had sat on Hogan, but he realised eventually that Tom didn't turn them much and worked out his flight. The ball disappeared over extra cover, out of the ground and down the street into St John's, allegedly just missing prayers in the church, and was last seen headed for a cruise ship in port to escape.

The West Indies won by an innings as Australia's batting capitulated meekly to Marshall and Garner, wrapping up the series two–zip. Haynes hit three centuries in the four one-day matches that followed.

Australia's dispirited band then hit Montego Bay for a four-day game against a Jamaican XI. The first two days were rained out and the game abandoned, so they decided to have two one-day matches on the last two days instead—they were washed out too.

The press pack had a day off for Easter Sunday. We had a driver called 'Brooksy' who took us to Rick's Café at Negril. When he came to pick us up his eyes were just rolling around in his head. I was amazed he could even drive. It was obvious he was up to his ears in marijuana, but for some reason we all climbed in and headed off for this lunch and a swim.

Everyone had a good time and we were in good spirits for the trip home.

On the way back things got really out of hand. Brooksy stopped in a field somewhere and came back with magic mushrooms. Things got pretty weird after that. Half-way home we ran out of petrol, which wasn't really a surprise, but by now it was pitch black and the back roads of Jamaica aren't really the safest place on earth. Brooksy disappeared into the night to get some petrol and we were left huddled in the car like a pack of scared kids.

Next thing you know, this gang of men comes towards us, which really got my heart pounding. I thought we were going to get mugged. Of course, it just goes to show how paranoid I was, because they turned out to be the friendliest people.

These locals decided to hang around and have a chat and of course out came the ganja again. One of them produced a joint that was so big I reckon it could have made it into the *Guinness Book of World Records*. It was massive, and his eyes were going around like one of those old-fashioned china dolls. He shared that with us while we were there by the side of the road waiting for Brooksy to return.

What could you do? It was a long way from Bellevue Hill.

Brooksy eventually returned and we got back to our hotels a little the worse for wear. The next day I went into the box to do a local broadcast and after five minutes someone just picked me up and took me away because I. Was. Speaking. Very. Slowly . . .

It took me days to recover. I remember having enough common sense not to do any reports back home. I just knew I wasn't right. That was something of a dereliction of duty, but it was probably better to not have gone on air than to have made stumbling utterances.

In Barbados we stayed at the Rockley Resort. We all had our own rooms, there was a nine-hole golf course and I was sharing with *Advertiser* photographer Ray Titus. We used to go and buy the flying fish at the fish markets and have a big cook-up for dinner at the resort with a few of the other guys. We drove around the 166 square mile island in our fleet of Mini Mokes.

One night Ray went out with Bob Radford, who was the chief executive of NSW Cricket, and when they got home they thought it would be a good idea to park the Moke in Ray's room. I woke up to hear all this noise and went out to find them pushing a car through the sliding doors into the room. They sheared the mirrors off on both sides, but managed to get it in.

It must have seemed like a good idea at the time, but it didn't the next morning. I remember a very shame-faced Ray trying to get it out before anyone woke up. It caused a fair problem with the hotel management, as you can imagine.

The press weren't the only ones misbehaving, but I am not about to start blowing the whistle on any players. You can probably connect a few dots yourself. It was a typical, old-style Australian tour. They played pretty hard off the field and they probably didn't play quite hard enough on it. After the 1991 tour Roland Fishman wrote a kiss and tell book, *Calypso Cricket*, that exposed dalliances and offended a number of players whose private conversations were quoted. Move on 30 years and players, wives and children are all on tour.

Towards the end of the tour, Kim Hughes had gone off for a rest, which he clearly needed. One day the boys came back from mucking around on the beach to find their captain drunk and watching television, but that wasn't the worst of it. He'd gone and had his hair braided. With beads and everything. It became apparent to everyone that he was really losing it.

Well, the tour was on the skids after that. After getting smashed in Antigua they got thumped by ten wickets at Kingston.

In five Tests Australia's bowlers did not take one second-innings wicket. That has never happened before or since in a five-match series.

You really wondered what was going on with Australian cricket at that stage. Rackemann had bowled himself into the ground in the fourth Test, taken five wickets and been dropped for the next match so they could bring in an extra spinner. Greg Matthews took Carl's place, but he bowled only two overs in the game. 'Mo' wasn't a bad bat and opened in the second innings because Steve Smith had broken his finger. So three openers—Kepler Wessels, his replacement Wood and Smith—succumbed to injuries. Kim was all over the place by now, at the end of his tether, and you couldn't blame him, but his batting was hard to fathom. He failed to get a start only once, but his highest score was 33.

They were the good days in terms of West Indies cricket. They were an unbeatable side, and the crowd support was fantastic. There were all these eccentric characters who just loved showing off. People like King Dyall in Barbados, a skinny, eccentric old man who smoked a pipe. The King would wear these bright suits, which he changed at every interval, reappearing to a rapturous reception wearing turquoise or vermilion. I believe his father was a tailor, so he had an endless supply of interesting outfits. He never worked a day in his life and was buried at sea when he passed away. The president of West Indies cricket delivered a eulogy at the King's funeral.

In Antigua there was a chap called Gravy (real name Labon Kenneth Blackburn Leeweltine Buckonon Benjamin), another character who liked to entertain. I remember Gravy used to dress up as a doctor and rush out with the stethoscope when someone got hit. Sometimes he would dress as Santa Claus and drag a big bag of trinkets out onto the ground to reward a 50 or 100.

Mayfield was another comedian on parade in Antigua. He was from Trinidad. They were all set on outdoing each other, and when Lara broke Gary Sobers' record for the highest Test score, Mayfield ran onto the ground with a load of LPs and began breaking them. It was his way of celebrating a broken record. There was a lot going on in the crowd. You were there for the show as well as the cricket when you went to the West Indies.

On one occasion the tea time entertainment featured a boxing bout. It was like watching a silent Charlie Chaplin movie. Mayfield was set to fight Gravy and in the preamble a chap appeared from the crowd with a large suitcase, dragged it onto the ground and flicked it open to reveal the unravelling Bernie, a rubber man. He was startlingly elastic as he flexed and cavorted to the cackle of laughter and hand-slapping high fives in the crowd.

Mayfield's massive gloves were examined by the referee, who pulled out a chain, handcuffs, a brick and a bicycle pump. A temporary ring had been created on the ground and the fight began. Gravy was swinging and missing, Mayfield barely moved, and then, as if on cue, Mayfield appeared to cop a punch to his chin, a miss in my view, but down he went. Stretcher bearers arrived and as they carted him off he said, allegedly, 'Don't tell anyone, but I'm knocked out.' It was hilarious and the crowd loved the antics and the theatre.

At Queen's Park Oval in Trinidad I had a bet with a spectator in the crowd. His name was Gabriel Belfon and he was the police constable from Blanchisseuse, the beach a few miles from the ground. He laid a conch shell against my bottle of Glenfiddich whisky that the Windies openers would score more than Australia's pair. He won (West Indies 35, Australia 4 and 1) and I had to head back to the beach after the game to pay my debt. He gave me the conch shell anyway, which I still have at home.

There were a lot more local fans watching the cricket than there are today because the game still meant something—and the West Indies were smashing us.

In that sense, it's the most stimulating—perhaps over-stimulating—tour I went on and there's never been one like it since. Even Tony Cozier said there'd never be a 'media' cricket tour like it again.

You had to feel for the Aussies. They played a lot of Tests against the Windies in this era. After the five Tests, they had the joy of hosting the Windies the following summer at home, Clive Lloyd's farewell series. In the end it was too much for Kim Hughes.

I flew home with Ray Titus and Jim Woodward and on the way we had a mad day out at Disneyland in Los Angeles. It seemed appropriate after the shenanigans on tour. I was still on a high when I arrived home and was in shorts and Caribbean shirt for some time.

6

Politics queer the pitch

I was never really that interested in politics but cricket has a way of demanding you pay some attention, because politics and international sport have a way of getting tangled up. The intermingled issues of South Africa, apartheid and sport caused a lot of angst throughout the 1970s and 1980s.

Ducking missiles on the sidelines in July 1971 during the controversial Springbok rugby tour was my introduction to the passions involved. A ball boy doesn't get much of a voice in the debate, but I had a good seat for the vigorous exchange of views. The protest leaders at the time said that while they wanted to disrupt the tour, the ultimate aim was to have the cricket series scheduled for the summer of 1971–72 cancelled—an objective they achieved.

The apartheid bans smouldered away in the background for decades to come.

In 1985, after I had dried out from my West Indies sojourn, I was playing golf with a friend of a friend who said there's something big coming up, that a lot of players are unhappy and are going to South Africa.

The Australians had returned from the Caribbean to be beaten around the ears again by the West Indies at home under Hughes and then Border, after Kim Hughes quit the captaincy in tears. There was a bit of talk of a rebel tour, but up to that point it had only been conjecture. This guy said he could show me an offer that had been made to Steve Smith and indeed, he came back with a photocopy of it.

I read it with interest. There was a $25,000 signing-on fee and the promise of $200,000 for two tours if players signed up. It was a lot of money. Smith was a talented young cricketer who had played three Tests for Australia and made a century early in his one-day career. He would finish his career in semi-exile in South Africa.

We ran a story on ABC news confirming the tour was on and naming a few who were in the touring party. It was the first public confirmation that it was going to happen. Back then Peter Wilkins and I were doing sport on the television news every night after David Hill, the then managing director, moved the 7 p.m. news bulletin to 6.30 p.m. and dubbed it *The National.*

Former Australian Test batsman Bruce Francis organised the tour on behalf of South African cricket board chief Ali Bacher and signed a fair roster of players, including Graham Yallop, Graeme Wood, Wayne Phillips, Andrew Hilditch, Dirk Wellham, John Dyson, Terry Alderman, Carl Rackemann, John Maguire, Rodney Hogg, Rod McCurdy, Tom Hogan, Murray Bennett, Peter Faulkner and Steve Rixon.

Faulkner, who is the father of the all-rounder James, was the only one who had not played Test cricket. They had also chased David Hookes and Jeff Thomson, but missed out on both.

Wood, Phillips, Hilditch, Wellham, Alderman, Rixon, Bennett and Rackemann had all been picked to tour England for that year's Ashes.

Breaking the story caused a bit of a stir. Kerry Packer and Cricket Australia had kissed and made up by now and the media mogul didn't like the idea of a second-rate side competing. The board used his money to woo Phillips, Wood and Wellham back into the fold, while Bennett had a change of heart. Hilditch also pulled out after being selected for Australia.

Francis then signed up Trevor Hohns, Greg Shipperd, Mick Taylor and Mike Haysman. Haysman, who was a first-class cricketer with South Australia at the time, enjoyed the experience so much he settled in South Africa, married Miss South Africa, and later carved out a career as a commentator.

Then the really big news broke. It was revealed on the eve of the tour that Kim Hughes, who had stood down from the captaincy, was going as well. His press conference announcing the decision was broadcast live from Perth and picketed by protestors outside. Nobody hid the reason they were going: money. They were going to earn enough from two tours to set themselves up for life. Rackemann bought his father a new tractor with the sign-on fee. They didn't know a lot about politics and, to be fair, at that stage the whole apartheid situation wasn't viewed with the universal condemnation it is now.

There was a lot of pressure on those who went, especially when Prime Minister Bob Hawke called them 'traitors':

> On the issue of South Africa and sporting contact with South Africa, I and this government will not change our view about that obnoxious system of apartheid. We will not change our position as to it being not right for people to collect themselves and deem themselves an Australian team, to give aid and comfort to that regime in South Africa . . .

which is so blatantly and desperately seeking international legitimacy via the medium of apparent international competition.

Anyway, the tours went ahead and the players copped three-year bans, but a few of them came back to figure large in future teams, notably Alderman, who was sensational in the 1989 Ashes. Steve Smith said later he thought that the tours would be good for his cricket and were worth a three-year ban, but as it turned out he never got back into the Test team.

In November 1988 I got an interesting offer from Ali Bacher, written on South African Cricket Union letterhead.

Dear Mr Maxwell,

It gives me great pleasure to write on behalf of the South African Cricket Union to extend to you a warm invitation to be the guest of this Union in March 1989. We are looking forward to celebrating one hundred years of Test/International cricket during that month—the first ever Test Match in this country was played in Port Elizabeth on 12–13th March 1889 between England and South Africa.

We are planning appropriate centenary celebrations and would like you to come out to South Africa . . .

I hope you do not think it presumptuous of me to enclose a video which is a summary of some aspects of an exciting grass-roots development programme that the South African Cricket Union is conducting.

We have introduced about 60,000 children—most of them from the Black communities—to cricket over the past two years in this programme, which has also seen the qualification of more than 1500 coaches of all races. Our development programme, we believe, is unique in its scale and technique and we also believe that its implications are wider than South African cricket. Certainly it has had a meaningful impact here for cricket and race relations. The programme is on-going and is conducted throughout the year and we would be very happy to show it to you at first hand should you visit us next year.

I look forward to hearing from you as to whether you accept this invitation and nearer the time I will let you have further details.

Yours sincerely

Ali Bacher

I chewed on it for a while and thought I should at least ask the ABC what they thought about it. Their answer was that they didn't think it was a good idea, so I didn't go. It was very tempting to visit and make my own judgement, but the sense that it was being paid for by the South African government for propaganda purposes left a bad taste.

The centenary Test never eventuated, but a rebel English side did tour the following summer and things did not go well. The African National Congress had just been 'unbanned' and this allowed the locals to launch protests against the games, which they hadn't during the two tours by the Australian rebels.

●

The World Championship Cricket was a two-a-side competition that visited Australia in 1968. I was leafing through the tour booklet recently and came across an intriguing passage beneath a photograph of an unidentified cricketer that reminded me of another international ban.

> It is probably [*sic*] that the world has never seen a better fieldsman than this cricketer from Rhodesia. Always superbly fit, he has been the fielding sensation of world cricket. His ability to hit the stumps from any direction or angle is phenomenal and during a television demonstration he knocked the

single stump out of the ground three times in a row (from thirty yards) when running at full tilt. He is also an outstanding batsman and many times rescued South Africa with hard hitting innings and revels in hitting the bowlers over the top into unguarded outfields. We knew you would want to see this outstanding player and so invited him to play in this tournament. Unfortunately, when he applied to enter Australia, he was refused a visa.

Even though he is unidentified it is obviously Colin Bland, a man they said was better in the field than Gary Sobers and Jonty Rhodes.

While the Pollock brothers, Denis Lindsay and Trevor Goddard all made that trip as representatives of the South African side, Bland was blocked because the British government was so angry with Ian Smith's minority leadership in Rhodesia and his decision to unilaterally announce independence.

Bland was Rhodesian and caught up in the mess, which saw bans imposed by the Security Council of the United Nations. Most of his countrymen got around the visa ban by using South African passports, which he had, but in this case I think it got too hard.

He wasn't the only one excluded, as a team of golfers were also blocked from coming out here.

I had already seen Bland play four years earlier when he toured with the South African side in 1964. According to my trusty scorebook, he made 51 and 85 in the third Test of the series and when they returned for the fifth Test he hit 126. Not a bad return for a guy remembered for his fielding.

The race issue is quite different these days.

In 2016 when the Poms ran all over the Wallabies in the rugby Tests, I caught up with Eddie Jones, the Australian coaching England, for a chat in Melbourne. He told me a story about his brief time at the Stormers in South Africa before he got the job as England coach.

Eddie told me he and the assistants picked fifteen players for their first match and thought that was that, but then the message came back that he couldn't have that side because there wasn't a Muslim in the team. It was explained to him that Cape Town has a strong Muslim community and they had to be represented. Eddie asked if they had a Muslim player; he was told they had one, so they put him in the side, dropped someone else and they were away.

In modern South Africa the issue of transformation (we would probably call it a quota system or positive discrimination) makes life very complicated.

In all sports there must be fair representation of black players and coloured players. It causes problems because that means some who might be more deserving of their place in a side are excluded. In 2015 the South African cricket side was preparing for its World Cup semi-final against New Zealand when, according to reports, the board stepped in and said Vernon Philander had to play in place of Kyle Abbott. It was publicly denied, but it was true—and the problem was Philander wasn't totally fit. The board, however, wanted a certain number of coloured players.

There are quotas at most levels now and you can understand why there are, but you can also understand why it causes friction when the best side is not put on the field. Part of the problem is that the black community in particular has not produced enough cricketers. Politicians, impatient with that situation, are forcing the sports sides to more fairly represent the country they represent.

South Africa is a great sporting nation and has achieved so much since coming back into the fold. It is not an easy situation to repair a country after the damage that was done by apartheid. It will take a long time, but hopefully they will get there.

Our old mate Tony Greig—another good man who is no longer with us—used to whisper when Australia played South Africa that it would be a fair contest if our board insisted on a quota system for Aboriginal people.

He had a point.

7

The day I took on Kerry Packer

I vividly remember being in Kerry Packer's office when World Series Cricket was announced. Paul Hogan, John Cornell (Hoges' sidekick, 'Strop') and Austin Robertson were all lined up with the big man, who was chain-smoking and blowing a lot of smoke about how special it was going to be. It was like a scene out of that television show *Mad Men*, although not quite as stylish.

It was 1977 and a man named Jim Bonner from ABC current affairs was there too. He was one of those wonderful reporters who knew how to get his man and after Packer had done with blustering about his intentions to put on this amazing new tournament that would be bigger and better than anything ever seen before, he asked for questions.

Jim had been waiting for his moment and piped up.

'Mr Packer,' he said. 'World Series Cricket has been compared to World Championship Wrestling. Is there any connection?'

Kerry exploded, as Jim knew he would. He was purple with rage and launched into one of his famous tirades, but Jim had his story for the night.

The ABC was the establishment and trenchantly of the view that this was exhibition cricket.

I was no foot-in-the-door man; I didn't ask a question. Kerry was too intimidating for a humble cricket broadcaster.

From that moment on there was clearly a line in the sand. There were a lot of us involved in the game who thought WSC would die and it nearly did in its first year. I remember, however, that Alan McGilvray warned Bob Parish, the then chairman of the Australian Cricket Board, not to close the door on the rebels. Of course that is pretty much what the establishment did, but eventually they opened it again.

Everyone got excited about the money the players were going to get, but we all knew that it was really about television rights. Nothing else. It was good that the players got more—they had been sold short for years, it was an absolute disgrace the way the board failed to look after them—but claiming that this was about improving the players' lot was rubbish.

Bradman was behind the players' impoverishment. I remember when Tim Caldwell was chairman of the board in the early 1970s and McGilvray suggested some initiative or other, Caldwell said, 'Oh, Bradman will never agree with that', even though Bradman was no longer officially involved. The Don was like one of those dictators who stands down from the official role but remains in charge of everything.

Not that things improved all that much for the players after World Series. All the trouble in 1996 when the side almost went on strike was about how they still weren't being looked after adequately. Now it's almost gone the other way. My old mate Malcolm Conn, formerly cricket writer for *The Australian* and also the fearless leader of the press corps for many a year, took to calling them 'million-dollar babies'. 'Connman', as he was known, thought the players were too pampered and precious in later years.

When the cricket war finally ended and Nine got the rights they were after it didn't really affect me. We were doing radio and TV, but what people forget is that Kerry couldn't deliver to the whole market in those days; we ended up using their pictures and our broadcasters to deliver it to large parts of Australia. I remember it was a ten-year deal, so not a lot changed. We kept broadcasting cricket and they started doing it.

There was a letter to *The Australian* in early 1994 asking why I wasn't covering the cricket for the ABC in South Africa, from a Rod Adams of the ACT. He also asked why I hadn't done the last two Ashes tours.

Thanks Rod, I was holding the fort at home, but at least I had the chance to be on hand when the Australian Cricket Board, as it was known then, announced its latest five-year exclusive deal with the Nine Network.

There had been a bit of angst around, as Nine had decided it was not going to show all of the 1994 South Africa series live. The coverage was beginning in the second session, quite late in the evening, and the public was pretty upset about this.

The rights' announcement was one of those self-congratulatory affairs, where Packer acted like he'd paid too much and the Australian Cricket Board crowed about the deal it had won for itself.

Everything was going well until ACB chief executive officer Graham Halbish asked if there were any questions.

I put my hand up and asked him if the ACB was upset that the series was not being shown live in full on Australian television. He said that it wasn't a matter for the board as the rights were owned by the host country and 'having acquired those rights, it is entirely up to the Nine Network when it decides to program them'.

There were a few journalists in the room who were reporting on proceedings.

One noted that Packer, who was sitting at the side of the room, 'fidgeted in the seat and looked annoyed'.

Kerry could never keep his mouth shut and despite having withdrawn somewhat from public life he wasn't going to let me get away with this.

'It *is* shown live. Or don't you notice that?' he bellowed.

He was quite the bully boy and never hesitated to intimidate people. I wasn't immune to that, but kept going. By now I wasn't as intimidated as I had been as a young man.

'Not all of it,' I replied.

'Well, what's going to air is live,' he spat back.

I countered that on the Sunday night cricket fans had been forced to watch *Dirty Harry* for the fourth time instead of a Test and asked if Nine was more concerned with ratings than cricket fans. That really got the big man riled up.

'We've just gone through the Winter Olympics, we've come through with cricket from South Africa, we are in the middle of the football season. What do you think— the only people who should see anything on television are people who want to follow sport? You don't think we've got responsibilities to anybody else? We have a responsibility under licence to bring a balanced coverage.'

I had obviously hit a raw nerve and that ended the press conference. The MC nervously announced that there were refreshments to be had.

When Kerry was leaving he stood over me and asked with some contempt if I was from the ABC. He knew very well that I was.

Daily Telegraph sports journalist Ray Kershler was watching the exchange with some amusement and summed it up best.

'Packer had lost the point but sometimes if you shout loud enough you can fool a lot of the people a lot of the time.'

Kerry had a strong Nine stable with him that day. Bruce Gyngell, Brian Morelli and son James were all flanking him as I recall.

The afternoon tea saw a strangely divided room. There were glares, and no conversation across the divide as the great and powerful gathered around Packer and the rest of us kept a safe distance.

I had recorded the whole event and with some technical help fashioned an audible rendition which I ran that night as ABC radio was leading into another day's play from South Africa.

I'd had a few encounters with Kerry over the years and most of them had been positive. Early on he stopped to give me a rap about what I was doing at the ABC in the days before WSC. And then there was the occasion of a famous and rare vote for the position of captain at the Royal Sydney Golf Club AGM and he turned up to support the eventual victor, who was a golf partner of mine. His thoughts on the rival candidate are not fit for print.

As it happens, Kerry too was an Old Cranbrookian cricketer. The big man approached cricket in the same way he approached business.

Brian Bavin wrote a history of the club called *I'll See You at Dangar*, in which he recounts one of Packer's innings, a 77 against the Old Sydneians at the Weigall Ground. 'The opposition was strong, the bowlers including Gordon first-grade leg-spinner Tony Wilson, but nothing mattered to Packer that day. At his heaviest around this time, Kerry hardly bothered to run, nor, in truth was there much need for him to do so. The factories which in those days were located across Neild Avenue took a battering; there were massive blows in the general direction of White City, and into New South Head Road. It was a quite extraordinary display.'

Kerry worked hard on his son James as a batsman when he was at Cranbrook. They had a bowling machine at home and Tony Greig was inveigled to give the young Packer some coaching. Former English Test batsman Barry Knight, who was also coaching James, tells the story of a trip to Barker College on the North Shore with Kerry to see James bat. Kerry growled and swore, 'I don't come this far on my holidays.'

Cranbrook won the toss, James strode out to open the innings and the first ball was short. An attempted pull went straight up in the air. Golden duck. Kerry's response is unrecorded—perhaps just as well.

8

A series box set

I've sat behind a microphone at many Tests over the past four decades, but I have never tired of the game of cricket. I can't say I haven't seen a bad day's play; I may have seen way too many, but the good outweighs the bad by a long distance. I have been blessed to be there at some of the great cricket matches and they are games I reflect on regularly, and will do so as long as I remain sensible and alive.

The thing about a Test match is it has five days in which to unfold. There can be a score of subplots and side dramas—and even more across the expanse of a series. Conditions shift as you move from venue to venue, players are dropped, their form fluctuates and in the background there is all the joy of travelling, catching up with friends, moving from one town to another.

I want to take you through three series that have provided me with some of my favourite memories.

Frank Worrell Trophy 1999

This tour of the West Indies wasn't quite as wild as my first visit to the islands. In fact, I was accompanied for most of it by my first wife, Madonna, and even Mum popped over for a time.

Mum was 86, but hadn't slowed down at all. She was in New York for a conference. I'd said to her she should come for a visit and she did, staying with us at an apartment we rented in Barbados. She absolutely loved it. One day I took her to a party at Tony Cozier's house on the other side of the island at Conset Bay. These events were always great fun. Tony was a wonderful host—he'd cook up flying fish, organise cricket matches and ridiculous party games, one of which involved dropping a coin clenched between your buttocks into a bucket. There was plenty of alcohol involved, as you can deduce.

Mum seemed to enjoy every minute of it, but not all the Australians enjoyed this tour.

Shane Warne figured large in most series, but in 1999 in the West Indies Brian Lara treated him with such contempt that the leg-spinner was dropped for the last Test. It was galling for 'Warnie' and I don't think he ever forgave Steve Waugh. In fact I am sure he never did. Steve had the job along with Allan Border and Geoff Marsh of selecting the team and they all knew what was coming when they made the call.

The three had it out in a room with Shane, who made an impassioned plea to keep his spot, but Geoff and Steve figured he wasn't fit and opted to go with Colin 'Funky' Miller. Warnie was still carrying on about it when he was doing some sad reality show in 2016. The leg-spinner doesn't forgive or forget, which is disappointing.

Warnie is a character, prone to narcissism. I think he would be first pick in just about any side and everyone knows how good a competitor he is, but over the years the team got a little uneasy about him and his behaviour. He was always an individual and I think in the end it grated a little.

Maybe this was the first hint we had about how difficult he could be.

Never one to take anything on the chin, he carried that contempt for Steve Waugh for decades. The World Cup followed this tour and Warne was magnificent, particularly in the semi-final against South Africa. Australia was losing that game until he got them back into it. I think you can actually see him convince them they are back in it. Then, when they won the trophy and everybody was celebrating how well they'd done to pull the series out of the fire, he drew all the attention to himself by announcing in the middle of the celebrations that he was thinking of retiring from one-day cricket.

Not all of his colleagues were impressed by him drawing all the attention back to himself.

It wasn't so much the swings and roundabouts of Warne as the swings and roundabouts of the cricket and Brian Lara that made this Test tour fascinating.

Lara was the captain at this time and he was under a huge amount of pressure, but like Warne he is a man of special talents, and they eventually came to the fore. When it mattered he was just so much better than everyone else.

Lara had just taken the team to South Africa, where they lost 5–0. The board appointed him captain for the series, but it was hardly a ringing endorsement of his leadership.

Michael Holding was not impressed and left nobody in doubt about his thoughts on the series.

'It was a shocking decision. Being captain of the West Indies is a huge honour and a huge job. It needs a big man to do it, someone well rounded as an individual; Brian Lara is not. He is a spoilt child.'

There was a feeling around at the time that Lara was a playboy who maybe did not put as much effort into his cricket as he should have. Yet I saw him make that 277 in Sydney in 1993 and that man could bat. I wasn't in Antigua for his 375 in 1994 or his 400 ten years later—both against England—but I can only imagine. Those lengthy innings take remarkable concentration and endurance.

This was the last time the Windies were seriously competitive and it was basically all down to him with the bat and Curtly Ambrose and Courtney Walsh with the ball. Of course they didn't have too long left in the game, which left just Brian.

He was a good man to interview. He wasn't one for deep analysis, but he had a laugh and liked to answer questions. I remember on this tour I was the only guy from radio and the print journos would let me ask my questions so I could record the interview, then I would turn it off and leave them to their own devices. I always enjoyed the chats with Brian on that tour, but he was a little down after the first Test.

The series didn't start too well for the home side. In Trinidad they made just 51 in the last innings to lose by 312 runs. Glenn McGrath and Jason Gillespie had bowled them out inside twenty overs and no other bowler got a look-in. McGrath took ten wickets and was man of the match.

The West Indies is a place riven by politics and there was an even louder cry for Lara to lose the captaincy after this. He was out of form with the bat and it seemed to have infected the rest of the side.

We went to Jamaica for the second Test and the locals were very parochial about a Trinidadian like Lara. These island rivalries make the resentments between states in Australian cricket seem trifling—which they are.

Australia won the toss and batted spasmodically, but a neat 100 by Steve Waugh took them to 256. It was Steve's first century as captain. I remember Mark Waugh was bowled by Nehemiah Perry with a 'rat' that pitched, turned and then scurried along the ground. That was a huge turning point in the game.

The West Indies were 4–34 when Jimmy Adams came out to join Lara, who was hanging around but not looking good. As I said earlier, games and series can hang on a moment and in this game it came when Mark Waugh dropped Lara at second slip. There are few men in the game with hands as good as 'Junior', but he just didn't hang on to this one. Lara was 44 at the time, McGrath was bowling. Sometimes you just know these things matter the moment they happen. On 99 Lara went for a cheeky single and Greg Blewett threw down the stumps. Out? Nobody will ever know. The crowd figured he was in and by this stage were out in the middle celebrating. It was one of many ground invasions on this chaotic tour.

It would have taken a brave umpire to give him out. Lara and Adams put on 344 for the wicket and that was the difference in the game.

Lara was 213 when McGrath finally got him. He was just in one of those moods. I remember talking to Gillespie about bowling to him later and he said that at times you just felt like you had no hope because when Lara was in form he could hit you anywhere. Gillespie had come up with this plan of coming around the wicket, a tactic McGrath used too. They would try to get the ball to move back in and hit his pads or hold its line so he might nick it. He told the story of bowling one that he tried to spear in and hit him on his pads; Lara saw it move at the last minute and flicked it through mid-wicket for four. Gillespie thought to himself that it wasn't a bad shot but if he could get a bit wider on the crease he might be able to get an inside edge and drag it on. So, he bowled the same ball from a little wider and Lara came forward this time; right at the last minute he flicked his wrists and hit it wide of mid-off for four. He'd basically played the same ball to opposite sides of the ground!

Perry got five wickets in the next innings, the Aussies collapsed, the home side won by ten wickets and suddenly we had a contest on our hands with the series level 1–1.

And then it was on to Bridgetown. Momentous things were happening. Real swings of momentum.

Blewett had been batting at six and he was dropped for Ricky Ponting, who'd been out since November. A lot of people forget that 'Punter' was in and out of the side a few times early in his career.

Ambrose and Walsh were unplayable early in the third game, and the Australians were 3–36, but the gritty Steve Waugh just managed to hang on with Justin Langer—who was showing signs of similar grit, and hit a good half-century. Given the conditions it was worth twice as much. Eventually the sun came out and batting got easier. Waugh and Ponting came together and put on 281.

Punter's century laid down a marker for the rest of his career. Perry ruined Steve's potential landmark by trapping him LBW for 199, but the Aussies posted 490.

McGrath and Gillespie bowled brilliantly when they got their chance and the Windies were 160-odd behind on the first innings, but then Walsh got a five-for in the second dig and the visitors collapsed to be all out for 146. Still, it was going to be hard to chase 311 in the last innings against an attack that included McGrath, Gillespie, Warne and Stuart MacGill.

Boy oh boy, what a chase it was.

Lara began the final day on two and showed the concentration he possessed by batting right through to the end of the innings. Ambrose came in with the Windies eight down and needing another 61. He held up an end for 39 balls while Lara plundered at the other end.

Ambrose was blocking with incredible flourish and the crowd loved it. He was out with nine needed. Walsh came in and had to face a whole over from McGrath. Every time he blocked a ball the crowd celebrated like they had won the match.

Warnie had already dropped a sharp return catch, but with seven runs needed Ian Healy dropped Lara off the bowling of Gillespie. That was a chilling moment and I reckon it spelt the end for 'Heals'. He knew he'd let the side down and he dropped his head.

Waugh said later he was disappointed with Healy's work ethic on the tour and felt 'let down' by him. Taking no prisoners, he also criticised his brother Mark for not helping out.

The Test, however, was a thriller. It was great fun and when Lara hit the winning runs it was insane. Steve Waugh said at the time it was one of the best matches he had ever played in and I couldn't help but agree with him.

Then Steve dropped Shane Warne for the last Test. Warnie had 2–268 to that point, he wasn't fit and it was the right thing to do. Colin Miller was brought into the team to partner MacGill.

The selectors also dropped the opener Matthew Elliott, who had not been scoring runs. Matty was a brilliant cricketer, as his best showed, but he was prone to self-doubt and could get into a pretty dark place. This was obviously not good for him, but it wasn't good for the team either. You don't want people on tour who are going to mope. They drag the energy down. This was in the days before they carried a psychologist with them. I know Steve Waugh thought a psychologist might have helped the Victorian play a lot more Tests.

Blewett was brought back into the side and opened the batting.

The Australians had to do something—they were 2–1 down and needed to win the last match, which was in Antigua. Things got pretty interesting with McGrath and Adam Dale opening the bowling—knowledge that can come in handy at trivia nights.

Almost inevitably, Lara scored another century. This innings, however, was in stark contrast to the six-hour effort in the third Test the week before. He got these runs in a frenzy, the second 50 coming from just 21 balls. He made only seven in the second innings and the West Indies collapsed after a gritty effort by Steve Waugh set the game up and the Australians won easily.

One of the sidebars in the match was Colin Miller's glittering innings of 43. He whacked a couple of big sixes over mid-wicket from the Windies quicks with a baseball swing that would have struck homers for the Yankees. One of them cleared the wall and flew into the jail next door to the rickety Antigua Recreation Ground.

The series ended tied 2–2. Waugh was pleased to win the match, but unhappy at not winning the series.

'What I saw as a drinking culture was affecting more members of the squad than I had initially thought,' he wrote in *Out of My Comfort Zone*. As I mentioned earlier, he went out of his way to criticise Healy and his own brother. 'I felt betrayed when later I discovered that secret pacts had been made by some of the guys to stay out past curfew . . . wasting opportunities and talent is a sportsperson's greatest crime.'

He was a hard man, our Steve, but he was nearly the victim of the bottle himself during the one-dayers that followed the Tests.

The Australians were 3–2 up going into the seventh match of the series, in Barbados. The fifth game had been posthumously declared a tie by match referee Raman Subba Row, after the crowd invaded the pitch at Bourda in Georgetown as Steve and Shane Warne attempted to run three to level the scores off the last ball. There'd been an invasion in the previous over as well. It was absolute chaos, but, in a way, that was the charm of West Indian cricket.

In the last game Sherwin Campbell collided with Brendon Julian and was run out. The crowd didn't like that at all and started to pelt bottles at the Australian fielders, who ran for cover. One narrowly missed the captain's head.

The match resumed only after the Australians decided to reinstate Campbell, and the Windies went on to win and level the series. Steve Waugh wrote later that they'd been told the police couldn't guarantee their safety if they didn't agree to resuming the game and while he didn't think it was right to put the batsman back in, there was no other option.

Mum was in town for the last match and I said she should come down. She hadn't been to a game since Wes Hall played for Queensland against NSW at the SCG in the 1960s and I think the last Test she'd seen was with Gerry Weigall at Lord's in the 1930s. Mum arrived just as the bottles started to fly, but took it all in her stride.

'It was the best day's cricket I've ever seen,' she said when we caught up that night.

India 2001

Cricket may have been born in England and it may find a certain creative freedom in the Caribbean, but in India it enters another dimension.

The subcontinent worships the game. Its people and their passion elevate it to something unique and exciting. Exotic. Some teams say Australia is the greatest challenge, but Australian cricketers will admit that India is the puzzle they cannot crack. Their spinners deceive our batsmen, but ours have no effect on theirs. Their weather withers our quicks and their crowds confound our fielders.

A number of elements converged to make the Australian tour of India in 2001 one of the most remarkable series of all time. Steve Waugh's team was in imperious form. The Australians hit the subcontinent having won fifteen consecutive Tests. This was heady stuff indeed.

The string of victories started with a ten-wicket win against Zimbabwe, three wins against Pakistan, a 3–0 defeat of India in the summer of 1990–2000, 3–0 against the Kiwis in a rare foray into that country and 5–0 over the once mighty West Indians in 2000–01. Then, in the first Test in Mumbai after the Australian summer, an easy victory against Sourav Ganguly's side.

Australia won that match by ten wickets to extend their streak to sixteen in a row and nobody could see how they could be stopped. The side's momentum appeared irresistible.

People had started to go on about how the dominance was boring, and I have to say it was hard to imagine them getting beaten, but cricket likes to make fools of us all. Not that the Aussies were laughing when the tide did turn.

I was well versed in subcontinental cricket by then. I was there in 1996 for the World Cup when Sri Lanka won in Lahore on a dew-soaked ground that made bowling impossible. In 1998 Sachin Tendulkar played one of his greatest Test innings against Warne, scoring a brilliant 155 in Chennai. Mohammad Azharuddin made 163 in the Kolkata Test as India won easily after making over 600, and another Tendulkar century (177) in the third Test wasn't enough to stop Australia winning with a Mark Taylor hundred, but Australia lost the series 2–1. Warne said he had nightmares about Tendulkar hitting him for sixes.

Taylor followed up in Pakistan later in 1998 by making 334 not out on a road at Peshawar. Local pundits couldn't understand why he declared when he had the opportunity to pass Bradman with the highest Test score by an Australian, but Taylor stuck to the policy of victory ahead of personal milestones. Walking onto the pitch before play on the third day a bubbly Gavin Robertson asked, 'have you paid?' Paid what, I replied. 'The toll . . . this is a freeway!'' So it was and Taylor scored another hundred after Pakistan had batted long enough to make the game safe.

The 2001 series in India had a certain tension about it. Steve Waugh had dubbed India the 'Final Frontier'. His all-conquering side had won every prize but was yet to take a series on the subcontinent. It was the one they wanted.

I flew out of Sydney on 23 February to Mumbai, and even though I had been there plenty of times before it amazed me all over again. Sydney might be Australia's busiest city, with its growing population and choking traffic, but it is a sleepy backwater by comparison with India's famous coastal city.

We arrived at 2 a.m. and even at that hour there is something frenetic about what was then known as Bombay. It's the heat, the traffic, the sounds of horns and dogs and humans and other mysteries of this fabulous country. None of this bothered the scores sleeping on the footpaths around the terminal while we waited for our car—human speed humps, covered by a thin blanket and totally unaware of their surrounds, apparently comfortable on the concrete.

I was tired and a bit anxious about preparing for the tour, but hopeful of getting at least one good night's sleep. We were booked in at the Oberoi, a reasonable place. Then, at 2 a.m., my phone rang.

'Bradman is dead.'

It was the office. They wanted live crosses, they wanted reaction from India, they wanted me to hit the ground running.

Naturally I was pretty groggy, but they asked me to come up with a two-minute piece on Bradman's life in cricket. Most media organisations have these pieces ready to go. Newspapers have obituaries of famous people written well in advance, and I had recorded a three-minute tribute with sound bites (actualities) sometime earlier, anticipating that the great man was not going to live forever—he was 92 when he died.

Of course they didn't want this. They wanted something fresh.

I shook myself awake and did my best to do something for the *AM* program. Bradman's numbers alone made it easy enough. His average, 99.94, was so famous that it is almost ubiquitous in Australian cricket. The ABC even adopted 9994 as the GPO Box for all its capital city stations. Of course nobody writes letters now, so that is of little relevance anymore.

John Howard, who was PM at the time and a self-confessed cricket tragic, provided a touching tribute from New Zealand. Bill Brown spoke of his memories of playing with Bradman. I did the numbers and tried to put some perspective on them: his average was 60 per cent better than anybody else who had played the game; he scored a century every third time he walked to the crease; only Bodyline had made him appear mortal (he averaged *only* 56 that series) and so on . . .

These were all things every cricket fan knew, but not everyone who listened to the ABC was a cricket fan and the hope was that nobody who knew minded being reminded. The trick was to give it a bit of a twist.

Doing the crosses was a bit difficult for me as were most things to do with Bradman, because it seemed that the first question was always: when did you meet Bradman? Well, you know, I never did. I did have the chance once or twice. The closest I ever got to him was when we were both sitting in a stockbroker's waiting room when I was about eighteen. He was a director of Kelvinator and a few other companies and must have been there to meet someone high up. It was Rene Rivkin's office. Rene was a young buck in those days and yet to make a name for himself. One of my mates worked there and I was about to splash a bit of money around during the Poseidon boom.

I should have put out my hand and said 'hello', just as I should have kept it in my pocket rather than forking out for those shares.

Actually, I had stood next to Bradman at the urinals at the SCG when I was about ten or eleven, but that didn't seem like the time or place.

I'd sat opposite him in the stands sometimes, and during those early years of my broadcast career he had occupied the row in front of our commentary box with fellow selectors Dudley Seddon and Jack Ryder. It just seemed that the time was never right to say, 'Hello, I am Jim Maxwell.'

Maybe it was better to keep The Don as one of those heroes I never met or became too familiar with. Like India did, I just watched him from a distance.

If any country adored The Don as much as his own it was India, which was strange as he never played a match there and only ever stepped a reluctant foot onto its soil. In fact, in 1948 when The Invincibles' ship had docked—not far from where the team was staying in 2001—he'd initially refused to come above deck to wave to the crowd chanting his name. A couple of the others disembarked and visited the local ground.

Journalism has no respect for sleep and I was forced to ring the Australian team media manager, Brian Murgatroyd, to find out what the side was doing. They were staying down the road at the Taj Mahal Hotel, opposite the Gateway of India.

It was breakfast time at home but still dark in India. Brian took the call and pointed out that the players were still asleep. He hadn't heard the news himself, but he knew that this was important and said he would put notes under the players' doors so they would know before they came down for breakfast.

When they did I was waiting with my tape deck to record their thoughts. Captain Steve Waugh spoke about a meeting with Bradman some years before. He talked eloquently about the historical context of Bradman and what he meant to Australia during the Depression and after the war. He said Bradman played the game in the right spirit and for the right reasons, which was a pointed reference to those who were in it for themselves in the modern era. Steve said he was worried about the game— and this was years before anyone had heard of T20, the Indian Premier League, pink-ball Tests or the Big Three.

Always competitive, he added that he hoped his passing would inspire the 2001 side to victory on the subcontinent.

Shane Warne spoke about how he and Sachin Tendulkar had travelled to Bradman's house on the great batsman's 90th birthday.

Tendulkar also spoke, revealing he had a framed photograph of that meeting on his wall at home. While watching Tendulkar bat on television Bradman had seen something in the young Indian that reminded him of himself, and had called his wife Jessie in to see if he was imagining it. She agreed that indeed the diminutive Indian had a very similar style to the man she married.

Justin Langer spoke about how so many of his Indian friends had rung up to offer their condolences and share his sadness.

Bradman's death had caused the cricket world to pause and reflect. It was strange to think that a man who had not played the game for 50 years could have such an impact on a group of players who so often seemed to be consumed by their own world and little else. Maybe we had them wrong.

Bradman was marked hard by a lot of people. I remember asking Roebuck about him a little later.

'Well, I don't know why everybody is getting so carried away,' he said. 'He was a great cricketer but that's all he was. He wasn't a Learie Constantine or a Sir Frank Worrell. These were great men who had a serious impact on society. All Bradman was, was a great cricketer. That was it.'

Typical Peter, blunt, unsentimental and contrary. Provocative? Yes. He liked to take down sacred cows. A bit later he took a set against Adam Gilchrist. Now everybody in the media and public thought the sun shone out of Gilly's cricket kit, but not 'Roebers', oh no. It was hard to work out why, but he wanted him taken down a notch or two. It was after he walked in the World Cup. Everybody thought this was one of the great acts of sportsmanship, but Roebers wasn't sure that he should be so revered. Eventually a baffled Gilchrist sought him out and they had a lunch and the obsession passed.

Anyway, there were plenty who lined up to criticise Bradman over the years. Bill O'Reilly, Ian Chappell and so on.

The ABC threw a lot of resources at that 2001 series. I was there with Glenn Mitchell and the hero of the tied Test, Greg Matthews. We also had Mike Coward and a young Harsha Bhogle to help us out. Peter chipped in a bit too, so we were well staffed and we did every ball of every Test (those were the days!).

The other person around was Mr Subramanian, who, despite conjecture to the contrary, is not a fictitious character. You couldn't invent him.

Mr Subramanian was a scorer for the India Cements team in Chennai, which would become infamous many years later for its association with one Narayanaswami Srinivasan, the controversial former Board of Control for Cricket in India and ICC boss. The company has eight teams which play full-time and its patronage has kept many an Indian cricketer afloat.

I'd first met Mr Sub in 1998 when we were in Chennai (it was still plain old Madras then). Somebody had asked us if we needed a scorer and the next thing you know this curious man showed up with his big scorebook and his eccentric way of relating what was in it.

Me: 'What are the details of Ponting's innings?'

Mr Sub, after some shuffling: 'Fifteen minutes, fourteen balls, six runs, no-o-o-o-o-o-o-o-o-o boundaries.'

It broke me up every time. He loved it. By the end of the tour we would anticipate that distinctive, rolling delivery. Sometimes we would go out of our way just to hear it.

He didn't speak much English, so it was very difficult to get anything out of him apart from the score. Sometimes he would just wobble his head.

We planned to pick someone else to score at each of the games as we moved about, but Mr Subramanian offered to follow us, so he got the job. We flew to the rest of the venues, while he followed us around on the magnificent Indian train system. We paid for his travel and a match fee. It was nothing by Australian standards, but a lot more than All India Radio was paying anybody who worked for that organisation.

Before the 2001 series a letter from Mr Subramanian (which must have been written by a friend) arrived at our offices offering his services again.

I take the liberty of writing to you, as one who has had the privilege of being your official scorer for the Australia–India tour of 1998. I sincerely hope you remember me. May I approach you again to offer my services to you for the forthcoming season? I would consider it a great honour to be associated with you and to take care of this area. Since you have already had an occasion to evaluate my services, I am sure you will be good enough to give me the opportunity again. I will naturally discharge my duties to your satisfaction. I would greatly appreciate your dropping me a line, so that I can get ready for the assignment, or meet you with a prior appointment as you may desire.

It was a relationship I was keen to renew. Mr Subramanian was one of those delightful old-world Indian cricket people who I suspect are becoming rare.

Mr Sub used to do puja (a sort of prayer ceremony) in the box. He would bring in religious idols, build a little temple in the corner and burn incense. It was while dealing with technical frustrations on this tour that I decided myself to adopt some of the local religion.

I had learnt that Ganesha, the elephant-headed deity, was renowned for clearing obstacles. India had plenty of them, so I invested in a small statue and would put him on top of our equipment in the box. From that day things got better, so he accompanied us everywhere. A few years later the Channel Nine cameraman Ilankovan Frank, who was born in those parts but is based in Sydney, bought me another Ganesha, which still sits on my desk. Colleague Mike Coward has one in his home, with a cricket bat in his hand, which I have always admired.

'Unprepossessing' was a term Mike was fond of and one he used in relation to our broadcast facilities at Wankhede Stadium for the first match. I don't pretend to understand the politics of Indian cricket, but this particular venue was constructed close to the Brabourne Stadium, owned by the Cricket Club of India.

This beautiful boutique ground with its old-world Deco stands, sweeping patios, overhead fans and gentlemen's accommodation above the dressing rooms is one of the delights of India. In the evenings members walk the perimeter of the field, or enjoy a gin and tonic in a wicker chair nearby. It is British Raj India, but it was pushed aside in some dispute or other and the less elegant Wankhede was built next door in 1975.

At the 'new' venue radio was squeezed in above the television broadcast boxes on such an acute angle that it was impossible to see the entire ground.

We saw enough, however.

We had arrived the day before expecting, optimistically, that an ISDN line would be waiting in our 'box' as we had been promised. What we found instead was two solitary wires protruding from the wall. I sought out Mr Patel from All India Radio and he told me not to worry, that a man from the MTNL, Indian Telecom, was on his way and it would be sorted. Mr Patel used the phrase 'man come, man come soon'. It was one we were to become quite familiar with.

We waited and waited and waited. The players trained and went home. We continued to wait. Eventually we gave up. Someone reassured us that 'the man' was working on our problem and everything would be fine when we arrived tomorrow to call the game. I had been around long enough to know this was almost certainly untrue but also been around long enough that day to not care.

We arrived the next morning to find the two wires protruding from the wall and nothing else. What to do? You can only do your best, so we jerry-rigged some equipment. IMG (the TV rights holders) very kindly let us piggyback on their power as the local source was a tad unreliable, and we were away. After a fashion.

The ISDN line we'd rigged up operated well for a couple of hours and then went dead, forcing us to use our back-up, which was a standard old-fashioned telephone connection. The quality was pretty poor, but to make matters worse it was a crossed line and I could hear people babbling away loudly. I felt as if I were speaking over a crowd.

It was like being on a party line, but fortunately I was the only one who could hear it as it wasn't being picked up back in the studio. It was great to have Glenn Mitchell on this tour. He is a thorough professional and a good mate, and he helped hold it together. We were going alright for a while. Well, we were until we asked the technicians who were scrambling around if they could do something about the crossed line. They were pretty good these guys and fixed the problem in an instant—by cutting off the line completely.

Now our ISDN line was down, the telephone line cut off and there was only one thing to do—use a mobile phone.

We were patched in like callers on talkback radio and proceeded to call the game. I would call an over and then hand it across to whoever was doing special comments for their take. It was the sort of thing that used to happen when the family had to get on the phone and take turns talking to a distant relative.

Naturally the sound quality was marginal and it wasn't helped by the incessant din of the crowd.

Everyone kept saying 'man come, man come soon' but no man ever came. We became quite fond of that saying actually and used it a lot. If you don't find some humour in these situations you can find yourself getting overwhelmed by frustration. I am not sure how well this would have gone down at home. Strangely enough we received lots of feedback from people telling us how much they enjoyed our rudimentary coverage—apparently it reminded them of the old days of listening via short wave. Others said it sounded so authentic it gave them the feeling of being there.

The game began with a minute's silence for Bradman. It was touching and solemn to commemorate his passing so far from home with a foreign crowd who clearly respected the old Australian. It was also one of those rare moments when an Indian crowd is quiet.

The only other time silence could be detected at a game was in the shocking moments after Sachin was dismissed. If you had been momentarily distracted when the event occurred, you didn't have to run to the window to find out what had happened. That disappointed hush meant only one thing.

The Mumbai Test was an amazing game on a turning pitch. Steve Waugh won the toss and defied the old maxim oft quoted by Ian Chappell: nine times out of ten you win the toss, bat first; the tenth time you think about it and still bat first.

Steve decided to send the Indians in. Opposition captain Sourav Ganguly said he would have done the same.

Australia's bowlers tore through the Indian top order, which limped to 4–62 at lunch. Tendulkar staged something of a comeback, but silence descended when he was removed on 76 and the innings ended well before stumps with the home side out for 176. Waugh had obviously made the correct call.

'Keep it disciplined, keep it tight, dry them up and wait for mistakes,' the captain had said in that inimitably dry way of his. McGrath did exactly that, sending down nineteen overs and taking 3–19. It was an extraordinary spell of bowling from one of the best in his trade. He was never express, didn't swing the ball much, but worked with the precision of a Swiss watch.

The game was full of twists. Resuming the following day Australia got to 1–71 when Harbhajan Singh dismissed Langer and Mark Waugh with consecutive deliveries then Ponting for a duck. At 5–99 the Australians were in trouble when Gilchrist joined opener Matthew Hayden at the crease. What followed was to become commonplace, but never dull.

'Gilly' counterattacked. How many times would we see the Australians in strife one minute and out of it an hour later thanks to the wicketkeeper, who lived by the old adage of 'see ball, hit ball'? The locals missed a chance when they dropped him early and he made them pay.

He was incredible, moving from 50 to 100 in the blink of an eye (29 balls the scorebook tells me). His 84-ball century was the quickest by an Australian at that point in history.

Checking into the hotel a few days earlier a young fan had asked Gilly for his autograph and he obliged.

'You are my favourite batsman,' the fan said.

'Thank you,' Gilchrist replied.

'But you cut too early in your innings,' he was told.

He certainly cut early that day.

Years later Gilchrist wrote in his book *True Colours* about having an 'epiphany' the night before. He was extremely nervous before that innings; Harbhajan was turning the ball square. Then it occurred to him to go out there and bat like he was already fifteen or twenty runs. It obviously worked. To that point Gilchrist had played fourteen games, all of them victories.

Hayden had prepared himself an Indian-type pitch in Brisbane before leaving and spent hours down on one knee practising the sweep. In fact he'd practised so much before the game that he'd worn out all the net bowlers and recruited a good friend of mine, Darshak Mehta, who was the liaison officer on tour.

Darshak is a businessman, philanthropist and club cricketer from Sydney (born in India). He fancied himself as a spinner and sent down many overs to the big man, who noted later that 'the fact that many of his offies were off target was almost a bonus, because I perfected the art of sweeping balls from anywhere'.

'Haydos' could have swept all the sand out of the Rajasthan desert the way he went about batting. He and Gilly put on almost 200 and that was that; India couldn't catch up and the game was over on the third day, but there were a few interesting moments before it ended— as would become standard for Australia–India clashes.

Two catches were memorable. Tendulkar was going along nicely when Mark Waugh bowled him an old-fashioned long hop that should have been hit out of the stadium. The batsman pulled it straight into the back of Langer, who was making himself as small a target as possible at short leg. The ball flew off Langer into the air and a quick-thinking Ponting swooped. Cue the silence.

In a way the catch wasn't the fluke it sounds. Langer had worn a lot of balls at short leg. Sometimes they hit him, other times it was obvious he was willing to stand there and be hit if it stopped runs. It takes a certain kind of crazy to do that and J.L. was a certain kind of committed crazy.

The other 'catch' was taken by a diving Michael Slater off a mistimed pull shot by Rahul Dravid. The batsman stood his ground, the third umpire gave it not out and 'Slats' lost it. It was an ugly scene.

Steve Waugh copped criticism for not dragging his player away, but said later he was worried that would further exacerbate the situation. Slater was going through a marriage break-up and was not in a good place. He was let off with a warning by the match referee, but that was upgraded to a suspended one-match ban and fine because he had gone on radio claiming he'd done nothing wrong.

I had got a call from Sydney telling me that there was a wire story saying he had been banned for a match and asking me to file an update. I did so on the spot and sent it through. I should have checked first. I had a nagging feeling that something wasn't quite right and rang media manager Murgatroyd, who told me it was a suspended ban. It was still early in Australia and I managed to get the story pulled before it went to air. It was a good lesson: always check your facts!

These days the team has a psychologist among its staff when overseas and it's probably a good idea. These blokes can be under enormous strain at times and it takes its toll, as we have seen, with a few suffering breakdowns in recent times.

Poor old Slats was in a tailspin and it wasn't a good look that day. I'd first met him when he was just a teenager and Bob Radford gave him a job at NSW Cricket while he found his feet. He was a very sound opening batsman and could pin the ears back on occasion. He had a habit of making a statement at the start of a series. In Brisbane in 1994–95 he hit Phil DeFreitas for four first ball and proceeded to run away with the match against a very ordinary attack. In 2001 in Birmingham he hit four fours off Darren Gough's first over.

Slats was always an affable guy and has managed to carve out a great career for himself on commercial radio in Sydney and as part of the Channel Nine commentary team, having started his commentary career with one season on ABC radio.

At the end of the Test Sourav Ganguly was booed off the ground by the Mumbai crowd, who didn't appreciate the efforts of the Kolkata captain.

The Australians had sixteen wins in a row. I'd had a few bets on the series and I had them at 2–0 and 3–0 and I was thinking that it was looking pretty good. Not that I usually bet on cricket series, but I thought the way Australia was playing, there was every chance of those results.

Before we left Mumbai the local technicians had the last word. After the match finished Mike Coward and I were doing our summary when this man walked in and unplugged us. Just like that. I have to admit I lost it. The shamefaced bloke beat a hasty retreat. It was so ridiculous we all fell about laughing after he left. What else could we do?

It just so happened that Kim Hughes and another bloke were in town at that time and had arranged to do an auction of Bradman memorabilia at the Oberoi, which is a pretty fancy pub. Their timing seemed perfect—after all, you would think that this stuff had multiplied in price with the death of the greatest batsman of them all, but it seems they were in the wrong place with the wrong crowd. All these Bollywood people showed up and they just didn't seem interested in The Don.

Item after item was passed in.

To be honest it was not that surprising; it was 'created memorabilia'—basically a collection of things signed by Bradman over the years. I've known a lot of people think that because there is a lot of money in India there is a lot of money to be made there, but nobody ever got rich giving their money away and Indians aren't about to be the first.

The team marched on to Kolkata, a city that is Mumbai multiplied. Its intensity is insane. So many people doing so many things. In some ways it was an appropriate place for the game we had.

Eden Gardens is an amazing place for cricket. The commentary position is in the open on a small balcony behind the wicket and just above where the players hang out. It's a great spot from which to call a game. The stadium holds 100,000 people and when they get so many in its terraced stands the atmosphere is incomparable.

Naturally our equipment wasn't set up before the match and no matter what we did we couldn't get any joy. It didn't help that it was Holi day, a major religious celebration. Everyone in town was busy throwing coloured powder on each other, which is part of the tradition.

Quite a few had been indulging in the local bhang lassis (marijuana drink), which added to the carefree nature of the celebrations.

We were further frustrated by an extraordinary security set-up at the match. There'd been crowd problems at previous matches at the ground, so they despatched 8000 police officers of various descriptions to ensure it wouldn't happen again. Getting in and out of the venue with our equipment was hell. The local authorities also decided that the media passes we had been issued were no longer valid.

Again we covered the first day of the match handing a mobile phone back and forth.

Back in Australia our bosses announced they'd had enough and threatened to pull the coverage unless the Indians got their act together. You can imagine how well this would have gone down. And again, listener feedback was positive.

With fast bowler Javagal Srinath out of the game and former players like Bishan Bedi bemoaning the awful state of Indian cricket, nobody really gave the local side a chance. They had even less reason to after the Australians reached 1–193 at close of play on the first day. I remember walking back to the hotel through the din of the city with Glenn Mitchell discussing the possibility that we were in for another three-day Test.

The home side looked cooked, but Harbhajan and the strange game we love had other plans. 'The Turbanator' picked up a hat-trick on the second day with Ponting, Gilchrist and Warne gone in consecutive balls. Gilchrist smashed it onto his pads but was given LBW. That's the way it goes . . .

Harbhajan took seven wickets, but even then the Australians weren't in any real trouble and they managed to get to 445. You can't lose from there.

Well, especially not after India was rolled for 171 and forced to follow on. They were 3–115 and even deeper in trouble in the second innings when Ganguly joined V.V.S. Laxman at the crease.

The home crowd was not happy. When Tendulkar (LBW to McGrath for 10) walked off, a member of the crowd threw a water pouch in his direction, which caused a flurry of activity. Everyone was on edge, including Harsha, who was so uptight he was commentating with both hands around Ganesha in the hope the idol could do something to save India.

Mr Subramanian daubed the statue with the same colour he wore on his forehead to further expedite divine intervention.

On the field Steve Waugh set up all his fielders on the off side to Ganguly. It was an overly aggressive move that showed little respect for the Indian captain and might have stiffened his resolve somewhat.

The pair didn't like each other and had a private war bubbling away. Ganguly had a way of getting under people's skin. He would be late for everything, a situation that became ridiculous in Australia where he would leave the opposition captain and match referee lingering in the middle before the toss. Told he needed to lift his game by one official, he replied he had many matters to attend to.

'He's a prick—and that's paying him a compliment,' Waugh said at a Cricket NSW presentation night sometime later.

At stumps Laxman and Dravid had advanced the score to 4–254 with Laxman 109 not out, but they only appeared to be delaying the inevitable.

Slater was so confident he packed cigars in his kit the next day in anticipation of the party that night.

Laxman made 281, Dravid 180, Warne took 1–152, poor old Michael Kasprowicz had 0–139 and the Indians pulled off one of the most remarkable comebacks in the history of Test cricket. Tendulkar chipped in with three wickets in the second innings, including Hayden and Gilchrist. After his triumph the match before, Gilly walked away from the game with a king pair.

There is a perception that Australian captains have been shy about the follow-on since and it may or may not be true. It certainly places a strain on the bowlers and that seems to be the prime concern when captains make the call, but it is rare for a follow-on to be in play and Kolkata to go unmentioned.

In that Test the follow-on was the obvious thing to do. Australia had India on the run, they made 445 and they were bowled out for 171 in 47 overs, so the bowlers hadn't done too much work. They were still 40-odd behind with four wickets down going into the fourth day, which was the most amazing day with those two guys batting.

The Australian bowling was shredded by Laxman in particular. If Warne came around the wicket to get into the rough, he hit him through extra cover or he opened his front foot and hit him wide of mid-on. Warne was powerless to stop him no matter where he bowled. That didn't happen too often. Although if it did it was either in India or against them. He was mauled for 1–150 against them at the SCG on debut. Ravi Shastri took him apart on his way to a double century and was his only wicket for the day.

Warne just never really clicked in India. His figures were 0–147 on his previous visit to Eden Gardens. The leggie took 34 wickets at 43 from nine matches in India. He struggled bowling to Indians, picking up 43 wickets at 47 against them.

The Indian batsmen know how to play spin bowling: their footwork is decisive, they wait for the ball, they don't often go down the wicket, they wait and they play late. Tendulkar was a master of it. Hayden, Slater and Langer all bowled; that's how desperate they were.

The closest Australia got to breaking the partnership in that innings was when Ricky Ponting bowled the last over before lunch from the pavilion end and I reckon he hit Dravid absolutely plumb in front, but umpire Bansal gave it not out. Other than that we never created anything that looked like half a chance—it was complete domination. Bansal gave a lot of LBWs against the Australians, and apart from the Gilchrist one I reckon they were all okay. There were some unpleasant stories at the time pointing out that he had officiated in six Tests and the Indians had won all six, but that can happen.

There was no television monitor in our box for the match, but there was one next door, which meant we could see replays if we craned our necks and squinted a little. And then, quite suddenly, our neighbours didn't have one either.

At tea the bracket holding the television up gave way and it dropped like a stone into the crowd, catching a policeman on the shoulder on the way down. It was amazing nobody was killed.

Perhaps it was another omen.

The Cricket Association of Bengal announced on the scoreboard during the tea interval that it was donating

200,000 rupees to Laxman for making 200, a further 1000 rupees for every run up to 236 and then 2000 for every run after that. He made himself 312,000 rupees, which was about $13,000. Not to be outdone, the government chipped in 100,000 for Harbhajan and Dravid.

In the twilight after the match the Indian fans rolled pieces of newspaper and burnt them like torches, holding them above their heads in the stands. It created a magic atmosphere that was fitting after such a brilliant win.

After our visits to India's two biggest cities (we'd even squeezed in a tour match at Delhi, the third biggest) we went off south to Chennai, a fishing village that had turned into another thriving metropolis. The ground is close to the sea and the beachfront is quite a place in the evenings. There's an enormous stretch of sand; it seems to take half an hour to walk from the footpath to the water. Everybody flocks down there when the temperature drops a bit and the day's work is done. There are old-fashioned carnival rides and food stalls selling fruit drinks and fried fish. It's quite a place.

There was a bit of tension in the lead-up to the match when John Buchanan said in an interview after the Kolkata Test that he thought Shane Warne was unfit, which seemed like a hint that he might not play the third Test.

Steve Waugh laid that to rest and put the coach back in his place when he observed on the eve of the game that some things were better kept 'within the team than outside it'.

Australia, thanks to Hayden, made a good score, reaching 3–362 at the end of the first day. The big opener was in imperious form again and was the last man out, gone for 203. Unfortunately the rest of the batsmen had shown no intention of hanging around. Harbhajan was the chief destroyer again. He finished with 7–133 and Australia had lost 7–51 after a good start.

The Indians got a first-innings lead thanks to a century from Tendulkar and Australia took up where they left off, struggling to play the turning ball. Harbhajan took eight wickets, fifteen for the match. Chasing 155, India steadily lost wickets and in a tense finish it was Harbhajan who hit the winning runs. They won the Test by just two wickets and the series, miraculously, 2–1. The cigars remained unsmoked and the champagne undrunk.

The Final Frontier had remained unconquered and Steve Waugh's hopes of success there would have to remain unfulfilled.

I remember interviewing Hayden after the match and putting to him that the recently departed Don would be appalled at how many lofted shots he played. Bradman had always said that if you didn't hit them in the air you couldn't get caught. The Queenslander said there was 'a lot more room in the air', which summed up his approach.

He'd had quite a series, scoring 549 runs at an average of 109. Only Laxman came close with 503 at 83.

By far the most impressive performance of the series was Harbhajan's 32 wickets at 17.

All three players had really compiled some amazing numbers for a three-match series.

The series was bookended by Bradman. On returning home I was called up and asked to do the ABC television commentary for his memorial service at the Adelaide Oval. Tim Lane had been asked to do it for radio and I was paired with Tony Squires to put words to the pictures for the TV. It was a wet, windy day, and Richie Benaud gave a memorable eulogy that finished with the simple accolade: 'Bradman was a great sportsman.'

In 2004 the Final Frontier was conquered, for the first time since 1969, when the Australians won 2–1. I was there and it was an impressive effort for a side led by Gilchrist in the first three Tests, memorable for Michael Clarke's 151 on debut, Damien Martyn's string of centuries and a herculean effort by McGrath, Gillespie and Kasprowicz. The trio bowled lines so dry even the Indians lost patience.

The other event of note in that series was a political fight which saw the cricket association that looked after the Nagpur ground prepare a green top to upset the BCCI and captain Ganguly.

Ganguly withdrew from the game, which eventually granted Australia the series.

2005 Ashes

My first full Ashes in England and what an introduction! Of course I had spent plenty of time in England and played cricket there with the Old Cranbrookians, but arriving for what is without doubt the ultimate cricket contest in the home of the game was exciting.

I was there in 1972, 1975, 1978 and 1989 with the Old Cranbrookians. In 2001, after India, I was given the one-day series and the first Test before Tim Lane came in to replace me.

In 2005, my youngest son, Oliver, flew over and I met him at Heathrow on the morning of the Champions Trophy final. He was eleven years old and a passionate cricketer. When he got off the plane I said to him, 'fancy a game of cricket?' Brian Scovell, a legendary cricket writer from the *Daily Mail*, had a team called the Woodpeckers and they were playing at Kent that afternoon, so we raced off on the M25 to the ground. Oliver got to bat, bowl and field before we drove north to stay with a friend of mine, Richard Hunter, the Regius Professor of Greek at Cambridge and one of the smartest men I know. He was a fine sportsman in his days at Cranbrook, where he was dux of the school and the number one student in NSW in the HSC. Oliver slept for the next 24 hours, but it was an introduction to England he would never forget.

Ponting's side arrived in England for these Ashes with the sort of expectation Steve Waugh's team had when they arrived in India in 2001. They were, in all respects, the dominant side in world cricket. They had wiped the floor with England in the past eight series. The poor old Poms had lost at home and away and not won an Ashes series since they beat Australia on our soil in 1986–87.

Oh, they had a few good bowlers in Steve Harmison, Andrew Flintoff, Simon Jones and Matthew Hoggard and they had shown some form in the lead-up, but nobody could see Australia being beaten. How foolish that seems when you look at the names in that sentence now.

Lord's is the most genteel Test ground in the world. The cathedral of cricket with its army of eccentric gentlemen in their striped blazers, bacon-and-egg ties, and their refined female companions. The members in their orderly queue that stretches down the road. Inevitably letting you pass with a 'there you go, old chap' as you squeeze through the 'tradesman's entrance'.

You will know our press box—it is that monstrous thing that looks like an alien landing craft at the Nursery End, and is unkindly referred to by some as Cherie Blair's mouth. It has an amazing view of the sloped ground, but the windows don't open, which always makes you feel a little cut off from the play.

The Australians had been a bit off in the lead-up to the Tests. They'd infamously lost a one-day match to Bangladesh in Cardiff with Andrew Symonds showing up to the game straight from the pub, but it hadn't seemed *that* significant at the time.

There was certainly no hint at the start of the 2005 Lord's Test of what was to follow. Match referee Ranjan Madugalle met the two captains, Ponting and Michael Vaughan, in the middle for the toss. Ricky won and chose to bat. As you do.

And then it was on.

Harmison came steaming in and Langer let the first one go. The second one bounced a little more than the left-hander was prepared for and cannoned into his arm. Now 'Alfie', as they call him, is a tough fellow and loves a scrap, but that one hurt. The bruise grew into an egg as team physio Errol Alcott made his way to the middle.

It was Ponting's turn next. He got hit on the face and a nasty cut opened up on the skipper's cheek. Blood trickled down his face and after the series the skipper had plastic surgery on the scar, but you can still see it if you look closely.

It was a brutal start and it was obvious that the Poms were up for this. On neither occasion did a fielder come in to enquire about the wellbeing of the batsmen. They stayed out in their circle. Indifferent and hostile.

It was as if they had adopted the approach of Allan Border in 1985. Back then A.B. had decided he had been too friendly with the Poms when Australia had been beaten in the previous series and so he resolved not to make the same mistake twice. On the next tour he point blank refused to engage with the other side, even his old mate David Gower. He knew a lot of the opposition well from playing over there and they were good mates, but A.B. stuck firm. They were the opposition, if not the enemy, and he was going to treat them that way. There's a story that at the toss at Edgbaston it had become so ridiculous that he had to be encouraged to actually call heads or tails in the Englishman's presence. A.B. admitted later that he might have taken it a little bit too far.

Australia made only 190 in that first innings in 2005 and England must have thought 'here we go, we're away', but for all the drama of that first innings Ponting's men won comfortably in the end. England might have had all the fire power in its bowling attack, but they did not have McGrath. 'Pigeon' loved that slope at Lord's and in no time at all he had taken 4–7—he finished with nine wickets for the match.

Clarke, Martyn and Simon Katich batted beautifully in the second innings, each scoring half-centuries, and that was that. Australia won by 239 runs. Only Kevin Pietersen had shown anything with the bat for England.

Everyone assumed, as they had in India four years earlier, that it was all over. McGrath, then Brett Lee, had cleaned up England's captain, Vaughan—the Poms just didn't look like they knew what to do.

I remember before the Test a certain casino was a sponsor of the cricket that year and invited us out to a function where they gave us free chips. We were playing roulette. Late in the night this punter yelled out to Merv Hughes that he had got 33–1 on Pietersen, who was just about to play his first Test, being the top scorer in the series.

Merv looked at the bloke and said, 'Mate, you have wasted your effing money, he will be dropped after the first Test.'

In Merv's defence the big South African import had looked like more of a one-day slogger than a batsman.

I was staying at the Marriott and after the game I ran into Rod Marsh, who at that stage had been coaching the Poms at their academy. I said it looked like business as usual, but he was very cautious and said not to underestimate this England side, that they felt their bowling had the measure of these Australians and that they would be back.

I remember talking to Vaughan sometime later and he said that they felt the Australians were vulnerable and they took heart from the early bruising they had given them at Lord's. They just had to get their lines right. Harmison had been a bit wayward in that first spell, but they felt they weren't far away.

A series has a lot of moving parts, but there are little trigger points you can point to in most of them where things change course. They're often around an injury, a dropped chance or a crucial toss—and in the second Test at Edgbaston there were some triggers.

I was in the commentary box preparing for the day's play when word came through there was a bit of trouble. McGrath had stood on a ball before play. He was out and Kasprowicz was in.

Ponting put England in to bat despite having lost his strike bowler. Everyone thought 'Gee, that's dangerous.' I remember talking to John Inverarity in the car park after practice in the lead-up to the Test. He was coach at Warwickshire, he knew the ground and said how important it was to bowl if you won the toss. That was in Ricky's mind too, because he had done his research and all the talk was about sending them in.

Of course to this day Warne is adamant Punter made the wrong decision.

At lunch the score was 1–132. Marcus Trescothick flayed the Australians, 'Kasper' was underprepared, Gillespie had shown signs of losing it and the attack was pretty lacklustre.

Warne got us back into this game, but England made 407. Then Flintoff and Jones showed what they could really do. They were absolutely stunning. Australia still managed to get to 308, thanks to half-centuries from Langer and Ponting.

The Poms led by 100 but then Warnie got 6–46, including the most amazing ball I have ever seen from a spinner.

The leggie pitched one a metre outside the left-hander's off stump and Andrew Strauss moved across to cover the ball, but it spun viciously, taking out his leg stump. Absolutely incredible. Lee picked up the other four wickets and the Poms were all out for 182. It was game on.

Flintoff was having a huge game; his 70-odd in the second innings kept England in it and he bowled like a man possessed. He was Ian Botham for a new generation. A big man with a big heart who could take a game by the scruff of the neck and turn it his way.

The Australians started the run chase well enough, then wickets just started to fall. 'Freddie' came around the wicket and had Ponting feeling at one. It was the seventh ball of the over. He'd bowled a no-ball with his sixth delivery and had to repeat it. Wickets began to tumble regularly after Ponting was out. Clarke got knocked over by a Harmison slower ball in the last over of the day and Australia was 8–175, basically 100 runs short.

We arrived on Sunday morning expecting it all to be over pretty quickly, but Warnie was going well and got to 40-odd when he missed a full ball from Flintoff down the leg side. Most of the time you would just curse yourself for not putting it away for four. The problem here wasn't that he'd missed out on easy runs, but that he'd stood on his stumps. It was absolutely bizarre. Things just seemed to be falling England's way.

The Poms had the Australians 9–220 and they needed another 61 to win. The game was over. Or so we thought. Lee could bat a bit, but 'Kasper' was unlikely and there was no way the two tail-enders could hold out this attack.

It would be fair to say that Birmingham is a fair distance from London and Edgbaston a world away from Lord's. At the home of cricket almost everybody whispers; at the venue for the second Test the crowd was more like what you might find at a soccer game. The atmosphere was fantastic, the noise something else.

That morning things started with a great sense of celebration as the locals could sense victory, but you could hear the crowd getting quieter as every over passed. It was like a blanket of doubt had doused the fun. I don't know if I have ever been involved in a more exciting match. Kasper and 'Binga' just kept batting and batting and the crowd was absolutely stunned.

It is tradition in the broadcast box that when a country looks like winning their commentator gets the honour of calling the final overs. BBC producer Peter Baxter made the call and I came on air. Lee played a blinding drive to deep-cover off the first ball of Harmison's over that should have gone for four and won the match but Ashley Giles, who had taken a few key wickets but was not flash in the field, stopped it, bringing Kasper onto strike.

He blocked the next one and then tried to get out of the way of the third delivery, but was tucked up and it came off his glove to the keeper. He was out.

The previously silent crowd went insane. England had won. It wasn't so much that they had pulled off a miraculous victory, more that they had stopped Australia snatching a miraculous win.

Of course replays showed that Kasprowicz's glove wasn't on the bat when the ball hit it, but I don't care. All I can say is thank god there wasn't any DRS. It would have destroyed one of the great moments if we had gone through all that nonsense about whether he did or didn't have a glove on the bat.

It was all over before lunch on the fourth day. To be honest I don't think anyone could have endured another session. It had been a remarkable Test and was reminiscent of the time Jeff Thomson and Allan Border came together at 9–218 chasing 292 to win the Ashes in the 1982–83 Boxing Day Test. They fell four runs short after one of the more amazing sessions.

●

Next it was in the car for the three-hour drive north out of the Midlands and up to Manchester.

The Australians were lucky to get away with a draw. McGrath had somehow got fit, but the bowlers were starting to have problems with no-balls and it was costly. Vaughan got clean bowled by McGrath in the first innings but the bowler had overstepped. Lee had a couple of these moments too.

The main reason they got away with a draw was Ponting's lone hand in the last innings. The skipper shouldered all the weight and made 156 in 411 minutes. Nobody else went with him. Hayden, Clarke and Warne had scores in the thirties but nobody hung around. It was a fair knock. Maybe one of his best. Punter was the ninth man out with four overs to go and McGrath had to hang around with Brett Lee. It was another gripping finish, but they were just hanging on.

171

This Test also provided one of the most enjoyable things I have ever done on air—and it had nothing to do with the game unfolding. The BBC runs a feature on Saturdays called *View from the Boundary*, which involves getting in somebody of interest, a cricket fan from another world, normally a celebrity, for a chat during the lunch break. At this match it was a woman called Michele Verroken, who was in charge of the anti-doping program for the UK. I was asked to interview her as I was the only person around who'd actually worked at an Olympics and allegedly knew something about the subject.

Michele explained that these days they had to have a line of sight on people giving urine samples. I asked her why and she said that they found that many of their male athletes were testing positive to pregnancy, so they knew they had a problem with people switching samples.

She said she could show me how they did it if I liked. I agreed and so live on radio I gave a urine sample.

Or that's what it sounded like. In fact, we'd set it up the night before. It sounded to the world as if I was peeing into a test tube, but in fact I was pouring a glass of wine.

I then asked her if there was anything she could detect from my sample before it was sent to the lab. Michele was a very good operator and she replied that while she could tell I was obviously not on performance-enhancing drugs, I certainly had a drinking problem.

That little episode highlights the magic quality that radio has, which television can't produce. The whole performance was an illusion. A radio play with sound effects and rehearsed lines.

And then it was back down the road to Trent Bridge in the rather unremarkable town of Nottingham (although we took up residence at a hotel called Langar Hall, out in the countryside). The BBC had lined up a bloke called Hugh Cornwell to do *View from the Boundary* at that match and he stayed out at the hotel with us. Hugh was the lead singer of a band called The Stranglers and had a fascinating story. He has written a number of books, including an autobiography, which is a great read. He and I got chatting one night and hit it off very well and have stayed in touch ever since. If I am in London I will have dinner with him and when he's out in Australia we catch up. Hugh even came and sang his famous hit 'Golden Brown' live on air for us during an Ashes tour Down Under. It's funny the way cricket brings people together and it is one of the things I cherish most about my time with the game.

Australia was in trouble before the Test match even got started. McGrath's ankle was no good again and Gillespie was obviously out of petrol. He was well down on pace, a shadow of the bowler he once was, and his return of 3–300 from the first three games told you all you needed to know. So, the tearaway Shaun Tait was brought in to make his Test debut. Lee and Kasper took the new ball. The attack looked insipid without McGrath.

Now we had a cricket series on our hands. That man Flintoff knocked up a century and Jones—Geraint not Simon—made a few too. The Poms put up a very good 477. Simon Jones and Hoggard then tore through the top order in a brilliant display of swing bowling. Four of the top five batsmen were out LBW. Jones took 5–44.

An attempt at a middle-order fightback was ended when Strauss took one of the greatest catches of all time to get rid of Gilchrist. He was standing at second slip and I reckon he took it to the left hand side of where third would be. That and the Warne ball were made for the highlights reel.

So that was that really. The Australians trailed by plenty on the first innings and had to follow on. Punter was famously run out by the substitute fielder Gary Pratt and completely lost it with coach Duncan Fletcher, who was leering from the balcony.

Ponting had been complaining that England had been abusing the spirit of cricket by resting bowlers and bringing on specialist fielders such as Pratt. He was right about that but, no matter how you looked at it, it was a poor run by him and Martyn.

The two sides may have had equal batting line-ups but the real difference was the bowling. England was better at swing bowling in their own conditions than Australia. When McGrath was out of the team the gulf between the two sides was vast.

Ponting's team made enough to make England bat again, chasing 129. Australia made the mistake of not opening the bowling with Warnie. Kasper had two overs and went for nineteen runs.

Warne was brought in and England started losing wickets everywhere. They lost Trescothick, Strauss and Vaughan to the leggie and when Lee got Ian Bell they had gone from 0–32 to be 4–57. Pietersen and Flintoff got them back into the chase, but when they lost another three quick wickets to be 7–116 a win still seemed possible. It was all very giddy, but Giles and Hoggard got them over the line. It had been another dramatic last session.

•

It was back to London for the last Test at The Oval, with the series 2–1 in England's favour.

There was nothing in it after the first two innings. Strauss got a hundred for England, Langer and Hayden did the same for Australia, but the match ended in a draw. Kevin Pietersen killed us in the last innings, after Warne dropped an absolute sitter off him in the slips. Talk about Herschelle Gibbs dropping the World Cup—Warne'd dropped the Ashes.

It was cruel in a way. Warne was so good in that series it seems hard to believe a side with him in it could lose. He took 40 wickets at an average of 20 and he scored two half-centuries.

I remember interviewing Ponting in the dark after the game. He was always very straight up and honest and I asked him if he took personal responsibility for Australia losing the Ashes and he gave a very good answer. Essentially he said yes.

I flew out of London as Flintoff was taking a leak in the garden of No. 10. I remember how drunk he was on that double decker bus as they drove through the streets. My old mate Jonathan Agnew—known to all as 'Aggers'—was on the bus covering it live, which would have been amusing.

The Australians really should have picked Michael Hussey in that series. He was in great form in the one-dayers, but they had made the mistake of selecting the Ashes team beforehand. Yes, it is easy to see these things with hindsight.

As far as cricket and Ashes history is concerned, Australia losing that series was the best thing that could have happened. After years of England being hopeless and whitewashed, they were back.

Of course that was their last free-to-air series on television in Britain. It is tough for cricket in a competitive market not to be on free-to-air television and it has to be damaging to the game. Can't see it happening in Australia. Cricket *is* our national game.

I often wonder how much that punter had on Pietersen, because the South African was the highest scorer of the series with 473 runs at an average of 52. No doubt he would have loved to rub Merv's nose in some of it.

9

Captains

When I started at the ABC, Ian Chappell was the captain of the Australian team. It seems like a different world altogether: the cricketers weren't earning much money and were all but amateurs, there were no ODIs, no coloured clothes, certainly no T20, no flashing bails when someone was bowled or fireworks when someone hit a six. Not that there were too many sixes back then.

There was a lot less cricket too and when it was played it was a much more austere occasion. When they travelled the cricketers stayed in mid-range hotels, they drank at the bar, they smoked cigarettes and carried on like club players—during and after Tests.

There were no media managers or coaches or any of that stuff. You look out in the middle now and there seem to be more people in team uniforms than there were helping Tenzing and Hillary get up Everest. It's getting ridiculous. Once upon a time there were two captains and a match referee at the toss, now there can be more people on the field than in the crowd.

When the Australian side left Cardiff for London during the 2016 Ashes there were more than 100 people in the tour group. Admittedly a lot of them were family (something else you didn't see much of in the past), but a fair chunk were staff filling various roles. The ever-expanding number of employees is an indication of how much money Cricket Australia has these days.

Ian Chappell basically ran the show himself in the 1970s and that was the way it was for many years. Managers were present but not always accountable. There was no coach. These days there seems to be a coach for every element of the game and even the team managers have support staff.

I can't imagine a team ever again running itself like they did in Chappell's day, but of course back then they didn't have all the interviews, appearances and scrutiny that there is now.

Michael Clarke stepped down from the captaincy during the 2015 Ashes. It wasn't unsurprising; he didn't go out on a high, but not many of them do. When he finished I thought he'd scored every run granted him, but as I write this he is contemplating a comeback of sorts. I was there for his first Test when he got the 151 in Bangalore and I was there for his last when he got 15 and wandered from the field at Trent Bridge. In total he played 115 Test matches and I saw a fair proportion of them. I probably witnessed quite a few of his 245 ODIs as well, but they all blur into one. It's amazing how a Test can stick in your memory but the 50-over game is mostly a forgettable experience. I don't think I am alone in saying that.

Clarke's exit got me thinking, I've seen a few Australian captains come and go in my time. Australian captains as a rule have a steady and extended tenure. They certainly last longer than prime ministers have in recent years, although there was a period there during the World Series Cricket and rebel tour chaos that saw a bit of churn.

A captain is always defined to a large extent by the quality of his ammunition. Skippers lucky enough to have a Warne and a McGrath or a Lillee and a Thomson don't have to do much other than make sure that they stay fit. Captains unlucky enough to see their best players run off to join a circus or their best bowler tread on a ball before an Ashes Test find life a bit more difficult.

Ian Chappell came to the job when the board dumped Bill Lawry, and he brought a swagger and attitude that possibly made Bradman and his yes men wonder what they had done. He took over when there were grumblings about the amount of money going into the players' pockets. It was a destabilising narrative that lasted for decades, right up until Mark Taylor's time.

The oldest of the three Chappell brothers led Australia to a famous victory at The Oval to square the 1972 Ashes, thanks largely to Lillee, Bob Massie's sixteen wickets at Lord's, his own batting and that of his brother Greg.

Ian Chappell's first full series at home was against Pakistan in 1972–73 and he was in full pomp. I was, as I mentioned earlier in this book, at the back of the Noble Stand auditioning for a job at the ABC. Pakistan only needed 150-odd runs to win in the fourth innings and really were only chasing that many thanks to an unlikely partnership by the Australian bowlers Massie and Watkins.

The visitors fell 50 runs short. We thought nothing of it. Innocent times. Four decades later the Australians won a match against Pakistan at the SCG in almost identical circumstances. Pakistan had the game under control, with Australia struggling in its second innings, but a 123-run partnership between Michael Hussey and Peter Siddle gave Clarke's men a lead of 175. That partnership alone should be enough to end the folly once and for all of giving the 'batsman' a single in order to attack his tail-end partner. The home side won by 36 runs and we were all wondering what the hell was going on. There had been enough going on between bookmakers and cricketers in the intervening years to cast a shadow across what may well have been an entirely clean match. We will never know.

Chappell's Australians were a formidable outfit. He was smart enough to realise that with a team like that all you needed to do was give them their heads. Some might argue he was too liberal, but so be it.

It all came together for him in the Ashes summer of 1974–75 when Lillee and Thomson destroyed the English batsmen while Doug Walters peeled off a century in a session at Perth. There was a ruthlessness about the cricket which was in part a reflection of the captain. That said, Chappell has a reputation as a hard man and I think people believe the 'ugly Australian' side started in this era.

Ian approached the game in the right spirit and does not think much of the sledging and carry-on these days. Rod Marsh gave the MCC Spirit of Cricket Cowdrey Lecture in 2015 and said this about his old captain:

Ian Chappell is mistakenly labelled as one of those players who didn't necessarily abide by the spirit of the game. I can promise you Ian played the game hard, he was uncompromising, but I never once heard him abuse an umpire or an opposition player. I did hear him say on many occasions after we'd appealed for an LBW and the batsman indicated he'd hit the ball that the said batsman should leave the appealing to us, the decision making to the umpire and that he should concentrate on his batting. (Expletives deleted!)

Ian was also quick to put an end to any of his teammates' misbehaviour on the field. He saw this as his responsibility and this is very much what this law, the Spirit of Cricket, actually means.

Ian didn't have it all his own way. Against the Kiwis in 1973–74 they won easily at home, but only managed to square the second half of the series across the Ditch. Glenn Turner got a century in both innings of the match New Zealand won at Christchurch, and it's one Kerry O'Keeffe brought up once or twice in discussion over the years.

Ian asked me a couple of years back about how his old leg-spin mate was travelling and I joked that he was alright, but he still says he would have got Turner out with a 'soggy tomato'. Ian was a bit perplexed until I explained that despite the side bowling 150-odd overs in the game he hadn't given his leggie a bowl. Ian had no idea what I was talking about, which was strange, because he has great recall and jumped straight onto Cricinfo to look at the scorecard.

Ian and Greg hold strong opinions on the game and sometimes their brotherly relationship can veer from the respect and loyalty you would expect. They are passionate men, you might even say a pair of competitive bastards!

Some years ago we were in Cairns for a Test match against Sri Lanka and as it happened Ian was on duty for Channel Nine and Greg was in between jobs and working for ABC radio. At dinner one night I raised the subject of the Dennis Lillee/Javed Miandad kick-in-the-bum incident at the WACA in 1983–84, when the Pakistan batsman waved his bat and the Australian bowler swung his foot. After an hour of debate neither Ian nor Greg would make any concession.

Ian was in the commentary box, Greg was in the thick of the action. Here's their respective takes reviewed and not forgotten 30 years later. Ian:

Javed had been doing what he always did: standing out of his crease and inviting a throw at the stumps (which he could always beat home) and Dennis had been trying to get the better of the battle. Prior to the incident Dennis threw at the bowler's end stumps from mid-wicket while looking in another direction and had hit umpire Tony Crafter in the shins.

Dennis always liked to have the last say in these situations and when he came on to bowl Javed played the ball in the direction of fine leg and took off for a run. After running a few paces he decided there was only a single in the shot and began walking to the non-striker's end, but kept an eye on the fielder at fine leg. While he was looking at fine leg, Dennis moved off his line to get into Javed's path and this in my opinion makes him the instigator. I think Javed was surprised when he found Dennis in his path and threw up his hands and probably hit him with his bat.

I have always said that if I found a bowler moving off his line to try and get in my path (in other words attempting to make running between the wickets difficult and perhaps cause a run-out), I would have dug him in the ribs with my bat handle. Glenn McGrath would have received a few bat handles if I played against him.

What followed between Dennis and Javed was comical. I think Greg's main bone of contention was that Dennis got punished and Javed didn't.

Captains

As they say in tennis, fifteen–love to Ian.

Here's Greg's take:

I remember the night well. I was on D.K.'s side. I stood up for him because he responded to Javed making contact with him first. Ian would not see it.

Have a look at YouTube. It is not obvious unless one watches closely, as I did on the day. As Dennis moves back towards Javed to have the last word, as was his wont, Javed, who is carrying his bat in two hands across himself, makes a small movement with his arms, following which, Dennis, all 100 kilograms of him, is thrown back off balance. After he gathers himself he goes after Javed and kicks him up the bum. I had no doubt then and I have no doubt now, that had Javed not struck him first, Dennis would not have laid a hand or foot on him. How Ian refuses to see that Javed made first contact is beyond me. One can argue that Dennis should not have got close to him, but Javed still had no right to hit him in the ribs with the bat. That is why we refused to give Dennis matches and fined him instead. If Javed had been man enough to put his hand up and take 50 per cent of the blame, I would have had no trouble giving Dennis games off, but I wasn't going to see him take 100 per cent of the blame.

Fifteen–all? I think in the spirit of the game we can sort this out over a few more drinks . . .

Ian had taken a step back from the game and handed the captaincy to Greg, who inherited an outfit that was running smoothly, but times were set to change. In the background Ian had been agitating, demanding the players be paid fairly. The board wouldn't hear a word of it.

When Thommo got injured in the first Test of 1976–77 the side began to lose and the strain began to tell. Greg was as uptight as Ian was laid back and there was a strange feeling around the team. By the time of the Centenary Test in 1977 deals were being done. They went to England, lost and thirteen of the eighteen-man squad would go off to join Packer's mob.

With an almost en masse defection, the board was left with the impetuous Kim Hughes and the inexperienced Graham Yallop as potential leaders. Both were outcasts from the boys club that was World Series Cricket.

There were all sorts of agendas going on. Things were unsettled and it took years for it to calm down. Bob Simpson was a major force in making sure that Australia started to play cricket that would be respected. He gave them some confidence, not so much when he returned as captain after Greg went to WSC, but after that, when he came back as coach. He too fell foul of the board despite doing a sterling job, including leading the side to the West Indies when in his early forties. Simmo resigned after the wise men in Melbourne refused to guarantee they would back him for the whole of the 1978 Ashes tour.

When the board looked at what it had left, they found Yallop and handed him the job of leading the team in the 1978–79 series against England. He wrote a book about the tour called *Lambs to the Slaughter*, which tells you all you need to know about the team's 5–1 humiliation. He didn't make it through the next series as he got injured and the job was handed to Hughes for the last Test of the summer.

These were the lost years for Australian cricket; there was a dislocation in the game and the board weren't on the case. Packer shook it all up and it stayed shaken.

The board sent Hughes off to the World Cup then announced peace with Packer. Most of those tourists knew that when they returned they would not be playing the Test series. Greg Chappell walked back into the captaincy the following summer, Lillee and Marsh were reunited with Thommo, and Hughes found himself in the side, but on the outer.

It was a confused time highlighted by the fact that at one stage Greg captained a team that contained two former captains: Yallop and Hughes.

The job got to Greg, and it showed at the MCG when he refused to accept Kiwi Martin Snedden's word when he claimed a catch. And then the infamous underarm bowl . . .

The day Trevor Chappell bowled *that delivery* to Brian McKechnie is etched into cricket history. Most people remember where they were when it happened. I know I do. The Old Cranbrookians had just played and we'd headed to the Four in Hand in Paddington to rehydrate. For some reason there was no television in the bar; why that was the case in 1981 I have no idea, but we ended up watching the game outside on the street on a television that was perched on somebody's car.

It was quite a moment and just so unnecessary. The Kiwis needed fifteen to win from the last over. Trevor took 2–8 off the first five balls and the game was in the bag. Back in those days at the MCG the pitch was a shocker and the ball rarely got above knee height anyway. The Kiwis needed a six to tie and there was no way McKechnie could have got under a ball to hit it that far.

We all know it became an enormous incident. Our old mate Richie Benaud gave a scalding to Greg that probably smarts to this day. New Zealand Prime Minister 'Piggy' Muldoon said something about how he now knew why the Australians wore yellow.

I was working at the next match when the crowd applauded Greg as he led the side onto the field at the SCG. It had become an issue of national pride and people decided they were standing by their team and their captain. He had made a mistake—they weren't denying that—but they were rallying around their man.

He became an occasional captain, picking and choosing his tours, with Hughes taking over for the 1981 Ashes. The young skipper had a bad tour, the team lost and the pressure built on him and kept building. He was replaced by Chappell again for the following summer and on it went. Back and forth.

Greg and I had an email exchange about it recently and I asked why he wasn't keen to tour. This was his explanation:

Cricket still wasn't a great paying pastime. I had three young children and businesses that were paying me much more than cricket was and which needed some more time from me. My partners and my family needed me around more. We had no family in Brisbane so Judy was bringing the kids up on her own. Ideally, I would have retired fully, but I wasn't ready to do that and so I decided to confine my cricket to playing in Australia, which meant no overseas tours, to have winters at home.

Each time I stood down as captain I expected it to be permanent and I was comfortable with that, but each time I made myself available they made me captain again. When the first tour to Sri Lanka was confirmed, [cricket board chairman] Phil Ridings prevailed upon me to relent and lead the tour. As it was a short tour and somewhere I had not toured before, I was happy to accede to their request.

Hughes finally got some clear air when Chappell, Lillee and Marsh retired after the game against Pakistan at the SCG in 1983–84, but it had already got too much and back-to-back series against the brute force of the Windies broke him.

He resigned from the job after seven harrowing Tests away and at home against the West Indies, in which his top score was 37.

I was sitting in the front row at the Gabba in the room next to the dressing rooms the following November when Hughes walked in to address the media. He was looking pretty shattered. Team manager Bob Merriman was with him.

'The constant speculation, criticism and innuendo by former players and sections of the media over the past four–five years have finally taken their toll. It is in the interest of the team . . .'

He couldn't finish reading and handed it to Bob to finish.

Hughes went to South Africa in the following summer as captain of the rebel team. It was a disturbing time in Australian cricket. Australia was vulnerable in every sense and it was going to take an extraordinary force of will to get things back on track. Hughes was only 30 at the time and could have been a great contributor under another skipper, but it just didn't turn out that way.

That force came in the shape of the stubble-jawed Allan Border with the backing of Bob Simpson as coach. A.B. was a little reluctant to take the job and you couldn't blame him, given what he'd seen happen to his predecessors.

Winning the 1987 World Cup was a dramatic turning point for Australian cricket. Mike Gatting's team had beaten them in the 1986–87 Ashes and nobody expected this inexperienced squad to have any impact. The selectors embarked on a stick-and-pick policy and held their nerve on Steve Waugh, who took four years to score his maiden Test century. They also backed players like Dean Jones, Craig McDermott, David Boon, Geoff Marsh, Bruce Reid, Mike Veletta, Simon O'Donnell and Tom Moody.

Border had already served under Chappell, Yallop and Hughes in his brief career and knew how destabilising the whole issue had been when the position was being rotated about, writing later in his autobiography about the 'divided dressing room, with all sorts of under-currents and dramas'.

When he took over from Hughes the side was in turmoil in terms of discipline. It was lacking the rigour to make it successful and that is why Simmo was so important in reshaping the side. I heard journalist Robert Craddock once say Simmo was perhaps the best cricket coach of all time and it would be hard to argue against that. There was a good decade there that started with the World Cup in 1987 that he can take credit for.

Border was the most resilient of players without ever being an outstanding tactical captain. The selectors gave him a settled team, which made a big difference. For example, there was only one change to the personnel during the 1989 Ashes series.

You had to admire Border's passionate commitment. He was determined and dogged, no matter what was going on around him. He is a bit unrecognised when pontificators nominate the great teams of yesteryear. It was a rough period but he kept performing.

I first came across him when I went out to the SCG to interview him in 1977; he was in a Colts team playing against Victoria. He was the up-and-coming batsman for Mosman and on the verge of playing for NSW. The interview was hard work—he just didn't have anything to say and it was a long while before he did. He did most of his talking with the bat even when he was captain. They were quiet years for the media in terms of getting a line that you could run with.

Although taciturn, Border was not unfriendly—he is just quiet. I suspect that is why his relationship with Simmo worked so well. The skipper concentrated on batting and what happened on the field; the coach took care of everything else.

Captains all go a bit mad in the end, however.

Border hung on too tightly and lost the plot when his deputy Geoff Marsh was dropped. He was booked for dissent in the 1992–93 series against the West Indies, which was a bad look. He and Merv Hughes blew up when Richie Richardson wasn't given out. They were both reported but at least Hughes turned up to the hearing. The fast bowler was fined something like $400 and A.B. was hit for $2000 for his impudence. He then struggled to contain his own and his side's frustrations in South Africa.

Border finally quit in the middle of a round of golf. He'd played 153 consecutive Test matches and gone on 29 tours. He still had enough legs to play out a couple of successful seasons in the Shield after that, but he'd had enough and it was time.

A thick-set lad from Wagga Wagga by the name of Mark Taylor had made stacks of runs in the 1989 Ashes. What's more, he had a level head on his shoulders and was the obvious next choice—although others might have been hoping for a different outcome. I remember my phone ringing the day before the board was set to announce Border's replacement. It was Steve Waugh asking me if I knew what was going on. Even at that stage he had ambitions towards the captaincy. I told him I hadn't heard anything apart from the obvious and that was that everyone seemed to think Mark Taylor would get the job. Which he did.

The new boss moved in and put his stamp of authority on the position by staring down Simmo and instituting a change of coach. He established himself very quickly and had the good fortune to have McGrath and Warne as his main weapons. He inherited two smouldering issues from his predecessors: the desire to win against the West Indies in the Caribbean and the festering unrest around player payments.

Taylor's captaincy began with a series against Pakistan in Pakistan in 1994, which they lost narrowly, and then a home Ashes they won easily. They then set off for the Caribbean.

Taylor's side came undone on a dodgy pitch at Trinidad but pulled off a remarkable series victory, winning 2–1 despite losing Craig McDermott before the series began. Steve Waugh had a great tour with the bat, but an unhappy one with crowds after claiming to have caught Brian Lara in Barbados. It looked to have bobbled out of his hand on the replay, but he insisted that it had bounced off his wrist and never touched the turf.

The board and the players entered into another tense pay dispute, but with Taylor's guidance and some flexibility (finally) from the board, an agreement was reached and strike action averted. It was, however, a close-run thing and Taylor blamed the negotiations when he was given out padding up for a duck in a Test against the Kiwis around that period. It had taken decades to settle the pay issue. In fact, it spanned the reign of seven captains.

Taylor then had to deal with his own loss of form in 1997, but the team kept winning so it was little more than a personal distraction. He was a very solid, composed leader of a good team. He lost the one-day job, which was the first time they split the captaincy. There was a need to do something after losing the 1996 World Cup. Australia did well to get to the final but along the way it was clear that Taylor's style at the top of the order, when he wasn't influential, was not sustainable in 50-over cricket.

Mark went on to be a board member at Cricket NSW and then at Cricket Australia, where he is so respected they had to do some fancy footwork to get him a directorship. These days he is our most prominent elder statesman. Mark has played the game and it is good to have people like him steering it now. He is a sincere, honest person who is easy to like.

Taylor's captaincy record stands up well: finally beating the West Indies, winning the Ashes and getting to the final of the 1996 World Cup—a big improvement on 1992.

And then Steve Waugh got the job. He was another strong captain who placed a lot of faith in his troops, who it must be said deserved that faith: they were pretty good. He was as tough off the field as on it, as he demonstrated by dropping Shane Warne for the last Test in the Caribbean in 1999, and some of the things he had to say after that tour about Ian Healy and his brother Mark.

Dropping Warne was entirely justifiable. Lara was killing the Australians and someone had to go. It was a big call and some thought they should have dropped MacGill, but Waugh was firm: MacGill had out-bowled Warne in the series. I don't think Warne was at his best in that series, as he was coming back from injury. They replaced him with Colin Miller and it won them the Test match.

Waugh's finest moment might have been the 1999 World Cup after Australia got off to such a bad start.

You have to say that he got the best out of the boys until maybe 2001 in India when it all went off the rails at Eden Gardens. To that point the side had sixteen consecutive victories. Not even the Windies in their prime had achieved anything like that.

If there was any criticism of Steve it was that at times he was too attacking. He infamously enforced the follow-on at Kolkata in 2001, but it is only with hindsight that was proved wrong. He certainly was over-attacking in 2003 in Antigua when the Windies chased down more than 400 to win. He had this extraordinary belief in his bowlers. It is the Australian way, but I think sometimes you have to back off and control the game. He might say he was let down by his bowlers.

Waugh was a good captain, very analytical and with a keen understanding of people's personalities. And he was such a bloody-minded competitor himself, which was a significant factor in the way Australia played their cricket. He was in the middle of it again when they dropped Michael Slater in 2001 and picked Justin Langer for The Oval Test. It was a hard call and it was tough on Slats, because they won the toss and batted on what was the best pitch of the series. As it turned out, picking Langer signalled a new era in Australian cricket.

I liked Steve as a cricketer and a competitor. He showed that very early, first with the ball, not the bat. In the 1987 World Cup it was his bowling at the death that was so important. He was an illustrious Australian cricketer in many ways, particularly his take-no-prisoners combativeness. It was no easy feat to get a team to win that many Test matches in a row—the great West Indies teams never bettered eleven on the trot. I think his teammates fed off his hunger.

Waugh had an honesty about him in the way he dealt with people off the field. He was easy to deal with, like Taylor before him and Ponting after him, because everything was up front. No spin. They were direct men. Steve was uneasy socially, almost nervous; it was hard to get him to relax. Taylor was easygoing off the field, but Ponting was a non-event as far as I was concerned. He wasn't rude, he just didn't give you anything. He lived with his game face on and built an exclusion zone around himself. Border became very good in his later years, you could have a chat with him, but it was another era and socialising was still an important part of the game.

Steve probably stayed on too long, but he managed to organise that well by announcing it was his last season. He was like a Pope, celebrated at every Test match venue that summer. His form had fallen away, but that sheer bloody-mindedness got him through—it was his trademark.

And then came Ricky Ponting. A man equally as flinty as his predecessor.

It might have surprised some that the Mowbray boy with the goatee and the black eye from a fight in a Sydney nightclub ever got the captaincy, but he was probably always going to be the one.

Back in 2001 I wrote in the *ABC Cricket* magazine that he had problems against the Indian spinners but commended Steve Waugh for sticking with him. I wasn't totally convinced myself and was proven wrong on that front, as he went on to become one of the era's best batsmen. I also had doubts about his character, saying at the time, 'I don't think it's too harsh to say that on occasions, like Shane Warne, Ponting has shown a streak of immaturity. Maybe they have both been indiscreet, picking the wrong place to have a good time and perhaps losing control—notoriously in Ponting's case in a night club in Kolkata in 1998 and later in an incident at a drinking spot in Sydney's Kings Cross. Now, in another era . . . these lapses probably wouldn't have mattered, but today it's hard for the players to get away with any social misbehaviour. Not that they should, but they're still only human after all.'

At the time I think he needed a bit of guidance and it looks like he got it. Unlike Warne, Ponting grew up. The only other candidate for the job at the time was

Gilchrist, but they don't make wicketkeepers captain as a rule. Warne thought he should have got the captaincy, but he had too thick a file at headquarters from his past misdemeanours. Warne did a good job on those occasions when he got to fill in, but I don't agree with those people like Ian Chappell who say he would have been a good captain. He was always too concerned about his own interests. I think he would have got distracted on tours, but who knows because it never happened. Before 6 p.m. he would have been fine, but it was his night-time dalliances that would have been an issue.

I remember Ponting's first series against Sri Lanka over there. They dropped Simon Katich for Andrew Symonds, they were behind in the first innings of all three Tests and they won them all, which said a bit about the side. They didn't have a great pace attack, but they had Warne. Darren Lehmann and Damien Martyn were both outstanding. Murali was always a threat, but Lehmann just walked down the pitch and bashed him, which was quite something to see.

I wouldn't rate Ponting as highly as Michael Clarke or Mark Taylor in the captaincy stakes. You have to have some anticipatory nous out there—you can't just work out a plan and stick to it, which he appeared to do too often. Captains need to respond to what is happening in the game and I don't know if he always did. Taylor was the best of them when it came to that.

What Ponting did have was a greater rapport with his players and perhaps greater respect over the course of his captaincy than his successor. The strength of a cricket team is based on having them all with you in the rooms. Michael Clarke would argue that he did, but I don't know about that.

There is a strange mix of personal achievement and corporate responsibility that goes into making cricket work. It is essentially a game where you can get away with some selfishness. You spend so much time together as a team, but a lot of the game is up to the individual.

The blow up with Katich in the dressing rooms in Sydney probably said something about the way Clarke was seen by the players, even if he wasn't captain at the time. I think it demonstrated that he was a bit more out for himself in those situations. He certainly didn't seem to have much love for the old-school dressing room culture—but more on that incident later. Lindsay Hassett said that a captain only comes under notice when the team is losing. Clarke won more than he lost and scored significant runs.

There is one jarring note on Ponting's resumé and it occurred in 2008 during a Test at Nagpur at the end of what was clearly a frustrating and unsuccessful stint for him and his side. He got behind in the over rate and was widely criticised for bowling part-timers rather than chasing an advantage in the game. He would have been suspended if they didn't make up the overs, but you would have thought the main aim would have been to win.

In the end they lost and lost badly and Ponting copped a lot of stick. I think Michael Clarke might have been one of the ones making noises around those decisions at the time, but he wasn't alone.

Mohammad Amir dropping Ponting before he got off the mark in Hobart in 2010 was a moment that resonated. Ponting went on to score 209 and it was two years before he got another century. If Amir had taken that catch that may have been the end. As it was, he played for another two-and-a-half years.

Ponting was one of the great batsmen of his era and a highly respected cricketer—and another one who hung on too long. I remember thinking he would probably quit when he handed the captaincy over to Michael Clarke, but he didn't. He stayed for another eighteen months. He got away with it, but it was ugly at the end. Ponting isn't alone in that. It is sometimes hard to know when you are finished—and let's face it, batsmen never willingly leave the crease. Those are the times people in charge need to be a bit more hardnosed.

There is a tendency to let veterans linger beyond their due date. Greg Chappell always said he would rather see a player given one too many games than one too few, but I am not sure about players who hang around for one too many series. Since the central contracts were introduced, some players, such as Steve Waugh, Ponting and Hayden, have lingered. Hayden was talking up the 2009 Ashes tour, supported by the chairman of selectors Andrew Hilditch, when he realised that his form had waned and retired after the SCG Test match in January 2009.

Michael Clarke hit the captaincy at a hundred miles— or runs—an hour. Much as Ponting had and Steve Smith was to do. The job inspired him to achieve the best form of his career when he scored a triple century and three doubles in 2012.

He had his ups and downs of course. I wasn't all that surprised that he announced his retirement during the 2015 Ashes. The game at Trent Bridge was obviously the final straw—he was second guessing when he was batting. As hard as he'd worked to get on the field, his body was letting him down and in many ways a better outcome for all concerned would have been for him not to get fit for the World Cup and been cut by the selectors.

There was a case to be made for the selectors telling him that they didn't think he was fit enough and that they needed to move on. They were close to doing it until Phillip Hughes' tragic death, which put everything on hold.

A couple of nights before Phillip was struck that blow, I had been at a party in Sydney that was promoting Michael as an ambassador for a watchmaker at the World Cup. There were a few media types there and Mark Nicholas did the spin with Michael. A bit later a guy in a suit asked me what I thought of the captain and I said 'he needs to be very careful because he has got himself off side with a lot of people and he needs to pull his head in'.

When he left I asked Andrew Webster, a journalist for *The Sydney Morning Herald*, who I had been talking to. He said it was Jim Kelly, Clarke's manager, and sure enough ten minutes later the Australian captain came over and said 'we need to talk later'.

I thought to myself: 'what are we going to do here?' Anyway, I eased onto the front foot and told Michael he had the most important job in the country after the prime minister and everybody had an opinion on how he was doing it. He said he was totally dedicated and would do only what was best for the game. I asked him why he wouldn't go to Adelaide for the tour game against India that Cricket Australia wanted him to play and he said that flying was bad for his back.

It was all going to blow up the next day. The press boys were writing stories that were becoming more

I made my debut calling Test cricket at the SCG in January 1977, while Imran Khan's prodigious swing destroyed the Australian line-up. He took six wickets in each innings. (Newspix)

Commentating in the early 1980s at the SCG, backed by stands that have long since been torn down. (Australian Broadcasting Corporation Library Sales)

BBC *Test Match Special* colleagues, from left: Don Mosey, the bespectacled Christopher Martin-Jenkins, who could not distinguish a remote control from a mobile phone, Henry Blofeld (in the cap) and Brian Johnston, who caught me out with his ice-cream trick. (Patrick Eagar/Popperfoto/Getty Images)

The ABC's Geoff Mahoney (left) with the Voice of Cricket, Alan McGilvray, who started the day with a 'prayer meeting'—a six-pack of beer shared in his hotel room—and smoked like a chimney in the commentary box. Yet he never missed a beat. It was absolutely extraordinary how much alcohol was consumed in the 1970s and 1980s. (Author's collection)

India, led by Kapil Dev, won the 1983 World Cup in England—watching the Indian team play, you could see a new era was dawning. (Bob Thomas/Getty Images)

My first tour to the West Indies, in 1984. Here, I'm watching the Test match at Georgetown, Guyana, with Phil Wilkins, from the *Sydney Morning Herald* (centre), and Howard Northey, from AAP (right).

(Author's collection)

My tour to the West Indies was fun for me, but not so much for Kim Hughes. As if he didn't have enough to contend with, Rodney Hogg tried to punch him out during a Test in Port of Spain. The image was captured by my boisterous roommate, Ray Titus. (Newspix)

Looking over Mark Waugh's shoulder at an ever-present form guide, in Barbados, 1995. (Author's collection)

Dealing with the technology in the 1996 World Cup in India, alongside Tim Gilbert, then of 2UE, now of Channel Nine. You had to laugh. (Author's collection)

Calling the hockey at the Atlanta Olympics in 1996. (Author's collection)

Interviewing Shane Warne during the second Test at Kolkata in 1998. The subcontinent was tough for everybody; Warnie returned figures of 0–147 in India's only innings. (Author's collection)

Cricket has taken me to some amazing places. Here, I'm in Pakistan, on Australia's last tour there, in 1998–99. Behind me is the Khyber Pass; beyond lies Afghanistan. (Author's collection)

Steve Waugh congratulates teammates at Antigua in 1999, having just won the fourth Test to draw the series 2–2, thus retaining the Frank Worrell Trophy. It's one of my all-time favourite series. (Tom Shaw/Allsport/Getty Images)

'Gravy', one of the eccentric West Indian cricket fans, had all manner of costumes, including a doctor's gown and a Santa Claus outfit.

(Author's collection)

Brian Lara is mobbed by fans after his unbeaten century secured the Windies a victory in Bridgetown, Barbados, in that extraordinary 1999 series. (Ben Radford/Allsport/Getty Images)

In Mumbai in 2001 Ricky Ponting (left) celebrates catching Sachin Tendulkar after the ball ricocheted off the body of Justin Langer. The crowd went quiet. (Hamish Blair/ Allsport/Getty Images)

By the next Test in Kolkata it was a different story, as V.V.S. Laxman (left) and Rahul Dravid (right) piled on a game-changing, series-defining 376-run partnership, much to the dismay of Shane Warne. (Shaun Botterill/Allsport/Getty Images)

pointed. It was going to be a huge story, but when that ball hit Phillip things that seemed so important suddenly seemed trivial. Michael had been at the ground and left just before it happened. When he got the call he rushed to the hospital.

You have to say credit to Michael to get himself back from that injury, but there was a question mark about his ability to face quality bowling and unfortunately in the Ashes series that followed that Australian summer he came unstuck.

Clarke's inability to play anywhere near his best cricket arguably cost Australia the 2015 Ashes. It might be harsh, but he admitted the team was playing with just ten men half-way through the series. If they were playing at home you wonder whether he would have played all five matches.

Clarke was an imaginative captain, bold too; he produced victories like few other captains were able to. Think of the game in Barbados in 2012 that looked like fizzing—he declared when Australia was almost 50 runs behind on the first innings and with just over four sessions to play. The declaration manufactured a close victory, turning what could have easily been a dull Test into a thriller, Australia getting home with three wickets in hand.

There were times, though, that he didn't know how to defend. In England in 2013 Ian Bell got the easiest runs of all time to third man, but Clarke would not put a fielder there. There were times when he over-attacked, the classic case being in his last series when Stuart Broad and Moeen Ali put on that partnership at Edgbaston in 2015. If Australia had dismissed either one of them early they might have been level on the first innings and stayed in the game. Clarke had Mitchell Johnson bowling without anyone between square leg and extra cover, so every time he pitched one up it got pushed for four straight down the ground. They were trying to get Moeen out on the short ball with two men behind square. Some of his captaincy in that game was bizarre and I wondered if his woes with the bat affected him tactically.

The real strength of Clarke was that he was such a positive captain, just as he was a positive batsman, but at times it needed to be tempered.

One of the more extraordinary examples of Australia's resilience was that short series in South Africa in 2013. Having been rissoled for 47 at Cape Town it took a pretty good side to come back at Johannesburg and level the series. That was a great effort, especially as Johnson was struggling so much and Pat Cummins was on debut.

It wasn't surprising that the lowest moment under Clarke—the ridiculous homework scandal that saw four players sidelined for a Test for not completing a written assignment—happened under duress in India, a place that can bring out the worst in people.

I didn't really get to know Michael off the field. He was always professional and polite. He got a bit prickly with me towards the end with some of the interviews before and after a match, but then again I think he just became more worn down and less cheerful.

He could be a generous person. I remember doing a breakfast function for Western Suburbs and University NSW Cricket on day three of a Sydney Test. He was captain of the team and he turned up and spent twenty minutes answering my questions before the day's play. He did the right thing by the club.

He was a good spinologist, if I can invent a term, but he wasn't alone; this is the modern way. Ponting was more direct and honest, but Michael knew how to spin a line.

I think Michael batted in much the same way he captained. He liked to take the game to the opposition— he was positive, his running between the wickets was first rate and his footwork against spin bowling left most of his teammates for dead. You rarely saw him playing a laborious innings. He took risks, which is the way the game is these days, batsmen don't sit back and wait. He was a classic stylist; in his pomp he was one of the most attractive batsmen we have seen. When he was going the game was moving. He finished with an average just under 50—lower than what it was for much of his career. He was critical to so much of Australia's success before and after he assumed the captaincy.

The Clarke efforts that stand out for me were both in Cape Town: the innings in 2011 when he made 151 in the first innings of that extraordinary game where all eleven of them could only cobble together 47 in the second knock.

Then, during the last tour in 2014, an innings that highlighted his bravery *and* his skill. He was bruised from head to toe by Morne Morkel and batted through a lot of pain, but he refused to buckle. I don't know how many times the physio and doctor ran out to treat him— he had taken blows to his forearm, his elbow, his helmet and his shoulder—and I don't know how many times Morkel bounced him and he wore the ball rather than swinging at it and risking getting out. He was undefeated on 161 when the Australians were finally all out. Ryan Harris then showed the same pluck to bowl through the pain barrier and get the wickets needed for a win.

It was only later we learnt that Clarke was in so much pain he could not sleep after that pummelling—and days later that we learnt his shoulder had been fractured. Clarke was a lot grittier than people gave him credit for. He never lacked courage.

10

Peter

*'Cricketers are vulnerable because the game
attracts sensitive men of aesthetic temperament,
the very men who are, in the end, least well
served by it.'*
PETER ROEBUCK, IN DAVID FRITH'S *BY HIS OWN HAND*:
A STUDY OF CRICKET'S SUICIDES

Seventeen November 2011

I have lost count of how many times I have cleared my throat and welcomed people to a Test match, but that morning at the Wanderers Stadium in Johannesburg I struggled. It was the most difficult broadcast of my life. I can turn on a microphone and talk for hours when the covers are on and the rain is falling, but this was a situation I had never encountered before.

I'd lost one of my best friends. Colleague and commentator Peter Roebuck was gone. He'd jumped out the window of our Cape Town hotel a few days before. Jumped just moments after I had left his room.

I took a deep breath and this is what I said.

Normally at this time Roebers would be hovering with a cup of tea and a biscuit, telling Princess Grace—Caroline Davison our producer—that because of his various deadlines he could do the hour before lunch, nothing after tea and so on, but always let's see how it goes.

Peter's gift of language, ideas, knowledge of the game, his self-deprecation, occasional intensity and downright contrariness made for stimulating, often brilliant, broadcasting.

He loved to challenge everyone . . .

I was doing okay, but it was a battle. I tried to shut out emotion and concentrate on the job at hand. He'd have scoffed at me for being so maudlin. I got on with the show.

Ever the internationalist, he disliked nationalism and cheerleading. He was judgemental and decisive in making a point.

He took up Australian citizenship. I remember asking what it was like being an Australian. He said 'being Australian is sitting up the front of the taxi cab, never taking the back seat'.

He saw Australia as a country that was striving, vibrant and challenging.

We have all been lucky to share his wisdom, sense of humour, sense of justice . . . he was complex, caring, brilliant . . .

And then it was time for the toss and the cricket started again. As it always does.

You might remember that series against South Africa. Michael Clarke's second as captain. I know I will never forget it for obvious reasons.

In the first Test at Cape Town the Aussies had been bowled out for 47 and handed a fearful flogging. I don't know if I have ever witnessed anything like the second day of that game. Clarke's team resumed on 8–214 and at the close of play South Africa was 1–81, which doesn't seem so strange until you realise that we have travelled from the first innings to the fourth at warp speed.

A total of 23 wickets fell that day. When South Africa were batting in the morning one of the support staff went into town. When he returned later in the afternoon he looked out and saw the Australians in the field and assumed the first innings was still going.

Australia battled on the first day, led by a fighting 151 from Clarke. They made 284 and South Africa had progressed to 1–49 when someone flicked a switch and wickets began to fall at a hectic pace. It's hard to remember chaos like it on a cricket field. After getting to 1–49 the home side lost 9–47 and were all out for 96. The Australians were 188 in front on the first innings and in complete control of the game.

There was an unfit-looking bowler by the name of Vernon Philander playing his first Test alongside Dale Steyn and Morne Morkel. He got a few wickets in the first innings but didn't seem to do much. Wobbled it around a bit. In the second, he did most of the damage, taking five wickets.

I had never seen a procession like it: Watson 4. Hughes 9. Ponting 0. Clarke 2. Hussey 0. Haddin 0. Johnson 3. Harris 3 . . .

Australia was 9–21 after fourteen overs and eighteen wickets had fallen for just 68 runs. At Cape Town they have a big electric scoreboard with Table Mountain behind it. It told a surreal story that day.

And then the wickets stopped tumbling as quickly as they had started.

South Africa chased down the 236 required and won with eight wickets in hand.

The game started on Wednesday and ended on Friday. We were stunned, but at least we had Saturday off. Cape Town is a magnificent place to spend a bit of time. The scenery is stunning and the wineries of Stellenbosch are a short drive inland. It's beautiful up there and the pinotage goes down alright.

We were all staying at the Southern Sun hotel in Newlands. It's nothing fancy, just a short walk to the ground, and we had got used to it over the years. Drew Morphett and Geoff Lawson were working for the ABC on that tour and we all got along well. We are easy in each other's company and have been tight for decades. Glenn Mitchell had popped up too. He had been with me on the 2009 tour of South Africa, but had been derailed by mental health issues and wasn't with the ABC anymore. It was terrible for him; I knew he struggled with depression and he just reached a point where it got too hard and he had to leave. Glenn was trying to get things back on track and was over working for the South African Broadcasting Commission, which wasn't going so well. They kept changing their mind about whether they wanted him or not.

Peter was at breakfast on the Saturday morning after the Test with a young lady, a Zimbabwean girl I think, who was engaged to one of the students from his house in Pietermaritzburg. He was in a strange mood, somewhere between excited and agitated. I didn't think too much of it at the time; you were never sure what you were going to get from Roebers, but on reflection it is possible he did have something on his mind. I told him we needed to catch up for ten minutes to record something on the game and he said 'that's fine, that's fine, that's fine', but didn't commit to anything.

Roebers headed out to watch cricket with a friend from the University of the Western Cape, Nic Kock, an Afrikaner from Stellenbosch who did a lot of charity work with a cricket team at the university and who had a bit to do with Peter in this area.

The next time I saw my friend things happened very quickly.

One moment things were proceeding as planned, the next there was chaos. A little like the Test match.

Peter and I were great mates. He was a curious, intelligent, eccentric Englishman, a solid county cricketer who started to come to Australia for the summer and found himself helping out at the Cranbrook School as a tutor and cricket coach. That's where I first encountered him. I have a long association with the school and its cricket. Naturally he was wrangled into playing a few games for the Old Boys. He made an impression on and off the field.

After a few years he started writing for *The Sydney Morning Herald*, columns that were picked up by the other Fairfax papers. At the ABC we were looking for someone to spice up the coverage, to bring a point of difference, and I suggested we try Roebers. At first we used him once, maybe twice, a day during Test matches and then it became a bit more regular. Essentially he was there for the occasional spot to bring a different perspective. The longer it went, the better it got and the more confident Peter became about what he could deliver.

He set us apart from what anyone else was doing; the television basically calls the game, they were not really editorialising. Peter would dive into an issue. Sometimes he would get his teeth a bit too close to the bone or get too excited, and sometimes we would say 'wait and see what happens in the game, don't go too early', but he could get a bee in his bonnet and usually couldn't be stopped. The time he called for Ricky Ponting's sacking after the so-called Monkeygate Test was a perfect example.

That was the price you paid. Peter was great, but he was complicated and could be difficult.

Roebers brought a level of erudition, a breadth and perspective to the coverage that we had never had before. He had an outsider's take that could provoke listeners, make them reassess what they had always assumed to be true, because Australia was a novelty to him. You needed people like Peter to point out that riding in the front seat of a cab was a reflection of national character.

His work was outstanding. That period was fantastic for us. It made the whole broadcast great to listen to and contributed to people turning down the sound on the TV and listening to us.

I became very good friends with Roebers as we spent more time in each other's company. He had a house in Bondi that was not too far from mine and we knew the same people, but ultimately I was forced to admit that I didn't know him as well as I thought. That is something I wrestled with a lot after his death.

Cricket is a game of rituals and we had ours. Every morning I would arrive and he would be there. Peter liked to get to the ground early and the conversation at the start of every day was almost always about the financial markets. That was his fascination more than anything else. He loved following financial markets, all the movements and intrigue of business. He was always tipping me into something, telling me to get out of something else.

Peter was definitely a strange character. Unique. He wasn't like anyone else you met and he was, well, socially awkward.

Overseas we went out for dinner a bit, but at home he had his own company and people he knew in various cities as the cricket caravan moved around the country. He wasn't a great one for food or wine. It was all a little bourgeois for him. It was one of the things that held him apart from the rest of the pack.

Yet I do recall one great dinner with him, in Barbados in 1999. That was some night. The solid Labor Party men, John Faulkner and Robert Ray, were in town and they invited us out to dinner with Steve and Lynette Waugh. I think they were half thinking they might be able to lure Steve into politics. The most unusual part of the night was, however, that Roebuck paid. It was one of those rare acts of munificence—and typical of him.

Roebers shared everything he had, but he didn't have much and never paid much mind to physical possessions, apart from real estate and shares. His clothing was, well, unique. He would arrive in India with a battered empty suitcase, collect his pay from the Indian newspaper that owed him some rupees, find the cheapest tailor in town and get a couple of pairs of trousers and jackets made, which would soon be torn, stained and ragged—but they would last him much longer than they should have.

We had dinner together occasionally, but he liked his own space—or you could say that he was uncomfortable in other people's space. He used to come around when we had dinner parties at home and his behaviour was extraordinary: he would get up after the main course and say 'I have got to go now, I have some work to do' and he would just leave.

He was more comfortable when it was just me and my first wife, Madonna. He would get into her ear about something and chew it off for hours—sometimes you couldn't stop him. He was very intense. If there was a big crowd, he wasn't there. He had to find someone he could talk to, but in a larger group he would go missing.

I didn't know all of him; I knew only some of him, and maybe some of it was a bit superficial, because you could get only so close.

Remember that Donald Rumsfeld line? 'As we know, there are known knowns; there are things we know we know. We also know there are known unknowns; that is to say we know there are some things we do not know. But there are also unknown unknowns—the ones we don't know we don't know.'

What I am getting at is that I knew there were unknowns with Pete, but maybe there were bits I didn't have a clue about.

I can only conclude now he was a disturbed person; he wasn't at ease with himself. Kerry O'Keeffe had a good description of him—he said he was a fumbler, and it was true. He sort of bumbled through life, juggling things. He was brilliant, but never urbane or assured.

You only got so far with Roebers and then he wouldn't let you any further. He was quite open about his frustration with vague things that were going on in his life, without being literal about what brought it on. He could get into a tizz about little things, like crowds or queues, which he didn't like at all. Things that seemed inconsequential would upset him and he would get anxious. He was appallingly impatient and that's why he was always the first person to the lunch room at the cricket. It was quite a skill, nobody knew exactly how he did it, but if he was held up and a line formed he would bail out.

In all honesty I knew him but I didn't know him well. On reflection, our friendship was a bit superficial, and that hurts a bit. I don't think I got inside his head, but he probably got into mine. We used to talk a lot about aspects of living, we used to talk a lot when I was going through my separation and divorce. He was very good at counselling—that was the schoolteacher in him. He couldn't form a relationship himself, but he seemed to be wise from a distance.

In the last four or five years of his life he took to calling me for no reason at all, just to have a chat. I guess he was lonely and wanted to have a sounding board for what he was thinking about. He would talk about cricketers or the life he had with all the students he was supporting in South Africa. It was almost as if you were listening to a conversation he was having with himself. He had usually made his mind up about what he was going to do. He just liked to talk.

I knew he had family, but he never talked about them. I thought his mother had passed on. He would say 'my family is in Africa'. Those students he supported there— and there were scores and scores of them—became his life and he was in constant contact with them. Organising their courses, paying for this or that, dealing with their dramas, usually via Facebook or the like.

After he died we learnt he did genuinely communicate with his mother, his sisters and brother, but you wouldn't have known that there was any relationship at all. I remember asking about his parents and he just fobbed it off and started talking about something else. After you have known most people for a while you will find out something about their family and ask after them and they will fill you in, but you didn't get much— if anything at all—out of Peter on that topic. He didn't want to go there; it was like a denial, but I don't know why he was in denial. Having spoken to his mother recently I now know there was a strong bond there and they communicated.

And then he jumped out that window.

He did give warning of it many times. He said he would never again go through the humiliation of what happened in England, where he had been charged with common assault in 1999. The details of that case have always been murky, but it seems he had beaten some young men with a cane as part of some strange disciplining. They were staying in his home and playing cricket. He was their coach.

He said the lawyer told him he had to plead guilty to the lesser charge and he probably wouldn't have a conviction, but the judge came down on him like a ton of bricks and gave him a suspended sentence, saying his evidence wasn't to be trusted and there was a sexual element to the beatings. From that day on he became the person who jumped out the window. He was, sadly, a ticking time bomb.

That whole situation was classic Peter. He would show charity and support to these young men, open his house to them, then go too far. Overstep the boundaries by disciplining them with a cane. He just didn't conform.

It was typical of Pete—a man who was a brilliant scholar and one who had studied law—to not bother with the detail of his own case. I can just see him now dismissing it and hoping it would all go away.

In Sri Lanka a month or so before his death he was full of regret that a friend—an African student—had committed suicide. He thought that if he had read the tea leaves, been in the right place at the right time, he could have stopped it. That was preying on his mind.

Anyway, it turned out that in Peter's final days he knew that a young man had gone to the police alleging he'd been sexually assaulted by him in the hotel where we were staying. This had been going on behind the scenes for a few days, but none of us knew anything about it.

I just think when the police came to arrest him he had one of those moments. I don't know whether he wanted to kill himself, so much as he just thought 'I am out of here'. Unfortunately he was on the sixth floor. He was like that. He just wanted things to go away, like he wanted the earlier court case to go away.

There are scenes that I have kept rehearsing in my head since that time. It was an obsession for a while, but it's a lot better now.

After I saw him at breakfast that Saturday morning I went for a drive with Drew Morphett and one of the locals down to Hout Bay, a beautiful little spot about twenty kilometres to the south of Cape Town. We got back to our hotel around dinnertime.

I was in my room when the phone rang. 'You have to come, you have to come.' It was Roebers and he was in an absolute state. His room was down the corridor from mine.

There were two policemen in the room. The chronology of events is confused in my mind. I think one of the policemen, a detective, Mr McDonald, met me at the door, told me they were taking Peter away to charge him with a sexual assault, but he let me in for a minute or two.

Peter was sitting in the corner by the window, away from the door. He was beside himself. In an absolute state. Agitated and alarmed. Talking rapid fire about meeting people at the airport the next day and that I had to ring them to let them know he wouldn't be there. I asked him for the number and he didn't have it because his phone was broken or some bloody thing—his phone and computer were always broken. Contacting Roebers was always interesting. He told me I had to look up these people on Facebook. He was just blithering. It was awful. I asked him if he wanted me to call someone back at home, *The Sydney Morning Herald* or somebody, and he said 'they'll know soon enough'. I can still remember him saying that. This whole exchange had taken maybe a minute when Mr McDonald said 'you will have to go now' and we walked out of the room together. He then described in detail what was happening and would happen. He said that Peter had been arrested, he would be taken to the lock-up and he would face court on Monday. I asked what it was about and he said he couldn't give too much detail but there was 'an incident in the room' or something like that.

I asked the policeman for his number. He gave it to me and went back to Peter's room and I walked down the corridor. I was only six or seven rooms away.

I was a bit shaken by the whole thing and I went to Drew's room, which was near mine, and was telling him about it in the doorway when McDonald walked into the hall again. He was on the phone and then I heard him say there had been an incident, that someone had gone out the window and then he broke off into Afrikaans. He couldn't see us because we were in a space between the door and the hallway, and he was walking down to get into the lift.

Drew and I just looked at each other. I didn't want to believe it was true.

And it went from there.

It took a while before we actually learnt what had happened, but we suspected the worst. 'Henry' (our nickname for Geoff Lawson) rang and said he had heard a thump. He was a couple of floors below us on that side of the building.

For a long time after that I kept thinking that I shouldn't have left the room. All sorts of things go through your mind when something like that occurs, but that was the thought I kept having.

It was such a strange night. What do you do? I rang his colleague from Fairfax, Greg Baum, who was at a restaurant at Sea Point with fellow cricket writer Peter Lalor, and he said they would come straight over.

At first the police couldn't find Peter's body, because it had landed on an awning above the entrance of the hotel. Then the paramedics were working on him.

At one point I remember they asked me to come up to the landing and help them with some information. His body was still on the awning and that was how they were accessing it.

I think that was when we found out Peter was dead.

We all sat downstairs in the lobby of the hotel, all five of us—me, Drew Morphett, Geoff Lawson, Greg Baum, Peter Lalor—just trying to sort this out in our heads. There was a police counsellor, who was very nice and helpful. Everybody was. We sat there until the early hours of the next morning. The hotel manager offered us drinks, but for once nobody had much desire to drink.

It was late in South Africa but early in the morning in Australia. We tried to work out what to do. It was one of those situations where nobody was sure how to proceed. We didn't know his family. He had no partner or children. We rang various people, including Mike Coward, who was close to Roebers, and then spread the news a bit further.

The night seemed to go on forever, but in the end we had to return to our rooms. By now the news was filtering back to Australia.

The police had said to take my time and give a statement when I needed to. I rang them that morning and
said 'I want to do it now', so they came and picked me
up and took me to Claremont police station. I took
Henry with me as a witness. The bloke wrote it all down
long hand and the first question was: 'Did you know that
Mr Roebuck was a homosexual?' I was a bit thrown by
that. What did that have to do with anything, whether
or not it was true? I didn't know, and in my mental state
I wasn't sure what I knew anyway.

After I'd done that we all met up at a hotel nearby
and had lunch with some old-fashioned psychological
counselling via a few red wines.

They were difficult days. Two days later in Johannesburg I remember I did a piece with Ginny Stein
on *The 7.30 Report*, because this was big news in
Australia. That interview must have been one of my
better moments, because the managing director and the
head of radio took me out to lunch some months later to
thank me.

I listened back to it recently. I held it together pretty
well until Ginny asked me how I would remember him.

'There was a sense of justice about everything he did
and that was the sort of world he was trying to ensure.

That's how I am going to remember him. And as a friend unfortunately I no longer have.'

You could hear the emotion in my voice as I spoke that last sentence. I was struggling and to this day I still battle with my emotions over what happened.

And then we moved on and were a man down and I had to get back on the horse for the start of the second Test. I wasn't sure if I could do it. I knew I had to do something to mark Pete's passing, but what was I going to say and how was I going to get through it? There was a bit of shock and I was struggling. I rang the Cricket Australia psychologist, Ross Chapman. They had offered his services to us, which was very kind of them.

I was somewhat traumatised as it was all sinking in. I still get upset when I think about it. When people ask me about it I don't want to go back there, I don't want to think about it, but it's not going to go away.

At the time my head was spinning. Ross was fantastic in helping me get on air and pay tribute. He talked me through it, he was very good, very reassuring about how I needed to be positive, speak the truth and let myself go. I think that's what he said.

South Africa won the toss and chose to bowl. We were short-handed, so the television guys jumped in and helped out with the commentary, which was fantastic of them. The whole cricket community was extraordinary the way they helped us out. There's not many of us on tour and we all know how hard it can be even without something dreadful like this happening, so we stick pretty close.

When we all got back to Australia we had an official memorial service at the SCG and I spoke. This is what I said:

Good afternoon and thanks for sharing in this tribute to Roebers.

You have each made a connection or a friendship with Peter that has left you inspired. By his counsel, his wisdom, his knowledge, his commitment to you, the fact that he cared.

Sorry Roebers, but that's enough of the sentimental bullshit.

And of taking advice.

Remember that Devonian who was in your charge . . . well he was in the house at Bondi some years ago in the passing parade of proteges. After another of the lad's hungover awakenings you asked him, 'So how many women have you slept with and how many times have you been drunk?'

'I think I've slept with uh two women and been drunk . . . five times . . .'

'Well reverse that!!!!!'

Roebers was at his best engaging, or perhaps informing/lecturing a tyro about who, when, why and what . . . it was his signature tune and when he couldn't do one-on-one he was apt to pick up his kit and move on.

He was the envy of those of us who find it hard to say goodnight at a dinner party and depart, because he'd simply announce his retirement and be out the door before dessert had hit the table.

I met him when he was coaching cricket and teaching English at Cranbrook in the off seasons of county cricket 30 years ago.

Occasionally we'd ring him in for a Sunday match for the Old Cranbrookians cricket club; the understated Aussie in us would have said, yeah he can bat a bit, and he's not a bad judge of a run.

The friendship grew when he started writing occasionally then regularly for *The Sydney Morning Herald* and as a result of our discussions between overs in the press box he was flung into occasional then regular summarising stints on ABC radio. The scope of our discussions broadened from analysis of tactics and character to more weighty issues about social justice, Zimbabwe, Cricket Australia, ICC, SCG Trust and/or greencoats, Zimbabwe . . . and his growing commitment to enriching young lives.

Roebers was also consumed by the markets, applying his unique intelligence abetted by former students who'd become stock pickers to the business of making money . . . or losing it as every fisherman cum investor won't tell you. Not a day seemed to pass without a tip, a phone call, an email, that made both of us victims of the bourse. Hopefully the students, the family he supported, will be beneficiaries of his investing.

In the early 1990s he became an Australian citizen and was proud to be an Australian, stating that this was a country where people were striving, unlike England, which he had turned his back on, and that was before the unhappy court case in 2001.

One day in our radio ramblings I asked him what it meant to be an Australian. He said, 'being Australian is sitting up the front in a taxi cab, never taking the back seat.'

I have received many letters about Peter and here's the best of one of them that hits the mark.

'As a schoolboy rower and rugby player I have never had the slightest idea about what is going on during a cricket match. This probably never changed but I became a committed Roebuck reader in the 1990s when I came across one of his columns. It was a revelation to me; beautiful writing and that it was about cricket held no consequence. Roebuck wrote about life, personal choices, character, moral positions. That he could do so hiding it in the sports section was his exquisite skill. The ABC cricket commentary is good, but Roebuck's commentary was something else again.'

During a lunch where he was the guest speaker, he gripped the lectern for dear life and the whole time he spoke his legs contorted, twisted and shuffled while above the lectern he spoke with enthusiasm, clarity and authority.

In a short time I got such a clear picture of the outward authority but inward uncertainty.

While most of us whisper of the world's corruptions and injustices, Roebuck exposed them with the searing authority of an unshakeable moral resolve. If he saw injustice he exposed it. I hope that he will be remembered for this.

He loved to challenge us with his gift of language, his ideas, his knowledge of the game, downright contrariness . . . all made for stimulating broadcasting and brilliant writing.

At times he could be intense, broodingly introspective. I knew him well enough as friends do, to draw a halt: 'You're the most self-absorbed, obsessed person I've ever met . . . pull your head in and get on with it.' At least I got a smile, a laugh from him and, as he wrote, yes sometimes I forgot to laugh.

So it's hats off to Roebers and the challenge continues . . . I would like to present a cheque for $3000 to the LBW Trust and hope that you too will play strongly in giving what you can.

Peter had been close to Ed Cowan, who would break into the Test side that summer. Ed donated his match fee from a Sheffield Shield game to the Learning for a Better World Trust as well. When he made a century in Brisbane the next year—on the first anniversary of Peter's death—he dedicated it to him.

Roebers had an odd group of admirers. Somebody organised a wake at an art gallery in Collingwood and the singer Paul Kelly showed up. He was a fan. That turned into a riotous night. There was a table for about a dozen booked at a nearby Greek tavern but I think 30 of us went. Peter would have hated it!

I read some of the book that came out on Peter in 2016 by Tim Lane and Elliot Cartledge, *Chasing Shadows*, and I am sad to say the more I learn the more it seems clear there was a sexual assault. The book made sense of the line Peter said to me—'they'll know soon enough'— when I asked if I should ring his employer, Fairfax. It was basically saying something had taken place and it will be out there.

There were a lot of stupid, if not slanderous, suggestions, from people who had no idea what was happening, suggestions that Peter's colleagues protected him or excused his behaviour, and that we were somehow to blame. We didn't know. We probably all felt that he had homosexual proclivities, but there is nothing wrong with that. He didn't talk about his private life; he just didn't go there. I didn't know him well enough to talk with him about relationships of that nature, whether they were with males or females.

I want to have more clarity on all of this. I've tried to stop thinking about it because it has all been so messy, not just with the circumstances of his death but also with his business affairs, as he died intestate. Dealing with the estate and the lawyer appointed by the family was a saga that felt like it would never end. His executor and Peter's family had all these ideas about trying to clear his name, of reopening the inquest into Peter's death, and I advised that it was best to move on, with Roebers' impatience ringing in my ears from another place. Hopefully a scholarship fund or foundation in the Roebuck name will be created when the estate is wound up.

There has been ongoing conjecture about a conspiracy and suggestions he might have been thrown out the window, but I never ever had any doubt that he jumped. I am absolutely convinced. We'd had many conversations where he'd said he would never be able to get through a similar situation to what had happened to him in England.

If he had written a will I'm sure he would have wanted all his assets, mortal and tangible, to reside somewhere, somehow, in the country he loved, Africa.

11

Commentators

When I started at the ABC as a specialist trainee
I was given outstanding training and joined a
great broadcasting tradition. We had mentors at every
turn and it was a time when young people got to learn
the ropes while actually being paid. Today it seems that
every second aspiring adolescent in private enterprise is an
unpaid 'intern' being strung along on the promise of a job.

Still, no matter how much training you have and
how good you are, there will always come a time when
your foot lands squarely in your mouth. If you talk long
enough you are going to make a fool of yourself.

I remember the morning in Melbourne Allan Border
and Jeff Thomson mounted that rearguard rally and
almost got the 70 runs needed to win against England at
the 1982–83 Ashes.

The game had crawled into the fifth day and because England needed to take only one wicket nobody was expecting much action, so admission was free. Thommo and Border needed another 37 runs for the last wicket to pull off a remarkable victory. It was consuming cricket and had attracted a crowd of 20,000 enthralled spectators.

'The crowd that's been let in for free are really getting their money's worth,' I told the listeners.

The phone lines lit up and nobody let me live it down for a long, long time. If social media had been around, then it would have gone viral.

There was another afternoon in Hobart where I amused my co-commentator Kerry O'Keeffe and a few others. It was December 2012 and Australia was playing Sri Lanka.

Me: Rangana Herath, over the wicket. Wade swings. BOWLED! (pause, hasty retreat) Oh, no he's not. He's caught in the deep.

Kerry: Ha ha ha ha ha ha . . . (yes, that maniacal laugh again . . .)

Me: He's out anyway. (sheepishly) Gee, that was a beauty . . .

Kerry: Ha ha ha ha ha ha . . .

Me: He swung at that and I swore I heard a tinkle,

but the ball went down long-on's throat. He's out. There you go: 5–181.

Kerry: Ha ha ha ha ha ha . . .

Me: I will have to go and see Geoff Lawson, no doubt about it.

Kerry: Ha ha ha ha ha . . .

You can imagine how embarrassing that was and can see the sort of support I was getting from Kerry. Geoff, if you don't know, is a qualified optometrist.

Unfortunately, our commentary box is very close to where all the print journos sit and I had been so loud they'd heard every word. When I finished my session on air and went out of the studio to get a cup of tea they stopped work to give me a round of applause.

The print mob are hard markers.

My comedic lapses aren't quite up there with the line that is attributed to Brian Johnston: 'the bowler's Holding, the batsman's Willey'.

It's not so formal in the box these days as it was when I began, but a tradition has arisen that means we usually have to be on our best behaviour for at least one session of the summer. Back in 1988 when Bob Hawke was the prime minister he decided to visit us in the commentary box. The knockabout PM loved his cricket and famously had his glasses smashed playing a hook shot in a press match in Canberra. He fancied himself as an all-round sportsman.

After a few pleasantries about his cricket career at Oxford and playing in Perth in his youth, I suggested to him that he might try his hand at ball-by-ball commentary. Of course he was up for it and while he may have made something of a hash of it, he managed to call the second wicket of Merv Hughes' hat-trick (Merv took the wickets across three overs in two innings).

Ever the politician, Hawke saw the political capital in this and announced that he had got the wicket for Australia. When Hughes dismissed Gordon Greenidge with his first ball in the West Indies' second innings to claim a remarkable hat-trick, Hawke's fame as a commentator was established.

That visit established a precedent and I think almost everybody who has been prime minister or coveted the job has tried to find their way on air during the summer. It means for one day of the year the corridors are crowded with security guards in good suits and fretting media advisers—and it makes for an interesting session of cricket.

Some are better than others. Paul Keating was not interested in cricket and not interested in pretending he was, so Opposition Leader John Hewson saw an opportunity. Or his advisers did. Anyway, he came into the box at the Gabba when Angus Fraser and Devon Malcolm were bowling and I made some joke about how he would feel right at home with this bowling attack. He had no idea what I was talking about. I explained that the bowlers were *Malcolm* and *Fraser*—it was excruciating radio. He was sweating, clearly uncomfortable about being behind the microphone and could not wait to get off air.

Mark Latham did the same thing when in opposition and had the misfortune of being teamed with Tim Lane, who was very sharp on his politics and grilled him about his party's position on Australia touring Zimbabwe. Latham was lost and like Hewson squirmed through it.

'I don't know what our bloody policy on Zimbabwe is,' he hissed as he left the box.

Julia Gillard did a couple of stints and usually arrived armed with some other issue to talk about because she wasn't going to pretend to be across the cricket. I remember one year we talked about the Brisbane floods.

I made the mistake of telling Kevin Rudd about Hawke getting a wicket for his country and inviting him to try. No wickets fell and we couldn't get him off air because he was determined to make a name for himself.

It dragged on and on and on. At one point, to break the tension, I brought up time zones. As you do. I said, 'How come we have five time zones for 24 million people in Australia and India has one for a billion people—surely you can do something about it.' He thought about it for a while and told me that there was some old Labor Party wisdom he always fell back on in situations like this: If there are no votes in it, don't worry about it!

Like Hawke, John Howard was a true cricket fan. He is a great supporter of the game and can often be found at Test matches. I've run into him in 2005, 2009, 2013 and 2015 at the Ashes in England and was on a panel with him after the Lord's Test in 2015 debating the topic 'Culture Wars, The Ashes and National Character' alongside Gideon Haigh at King's College in London. He is, as Mark Taylor famously pointed out, a genuine cricket tragic, which Howard said he regarded as a 'great term of endearment'.

In 2016 he was walking around Hyde Park, London, for his early morning constitutional in a rather dated Australian team tracksuit. Team management noticed his outfit and saw to it that an up-to-date version was quickly despatched.

On one of John Howard's visits to the SCG box during the New Year Test, Kerry O'Keeffe suddenly announced that the PM had a very good bowling action. People don't realise this, but my colleague is one of the better-prepared commentators. He arrives at the ground with a folio about an inch thick filled with background notes on each player. One of his habits was to record any cricket footage from the news, so he had footage of Mr Howard and Mr Hawke from matches against the press. It was obviously not the embarrassing footage of Mr Howard bowling with a papier-mâché ball to the troops, when he struggled to get the ball to the other end.

'You are bio-mechanically very sound,' Kerry told him. 'Your arm angle at release is outstanding, you have a balanced upright head position, you tuck in beautifully with your left arm and your front leg is braced nicely.' I think he called him the best off-spinner to live at the Lodge since the war.

Mr Howard was absolutely chuffed, but not as much as his advisers. Kerry got a lot of calls from his ALP mates howling him down, but he was serious. The next day one of the papers had a picture of the PM bowling with pointers to all the technical strengths that had been highlighted.

Kerry was an enormous hit during the thirteen years he commentated for *ABC Grandstand*. People loved his maniacal laugh and unique observational humour, but he was not just the court jester; in fact, I think that he might have been frustrated by that perception at times. Kerry has a very sharp cricket mind and was an analytical commentator who understood exactly what was happening in the game.

He came on board in the early 2000s after a discussion between the ABC's head of radio sport, Peter Longman, and myself about spicing up the coverage. Around that time Kerry had started appearing on *The Fat* on Monday nights with Tony Squires and it was obvious that he had a presence about him that people liked. He'd also done some work with 2UE in the 1990s when they had a fling at doing cricket as a rival to the ABC. We'd used Greg Matthews a few times, but he wasn't always available as he was still playing, so we gave Kerry a shot.

Kerry was a phenomenon: he had that rare gift of being very funny, he was unpredictable and he could go close to the line on a number of subjects. I remember our producer Caroline Davison, a wonderfully caring person, spent a bit of time gently admonishing him to get back on topic, but if Kerry launched into a story there was no stopping him. His frog joke is famous and his story of almost getting lucky with Jerry Hall is a classic.

I used to say to him that he would not have lasted five minutes with McGilvray and it was true. It took me some time to loosen up and get used to working with him. I came from the old school where the scores and the game were the core of the coverage, but he was out there and he took us with him.

It was a great journey. O'Keeffe and Roebuck were chalk and cheese, but it worked. Kerry would torment

Harsha Bhogle. He loved involving the crowd and it was extraordinary to watch them from the box when he was working the audience. You could see ripples of laughter go through the stand as he told his stories, or took the mickey out of Harsha. At the SCG and other places where we were accessible, the crowd started to pass items through the window. Shirts and cakes were popular, and one time these naga chillies made their way to the commentary box when Harsha and Kerry were on air. Apparently they are the hottest chillies. The challenge was on and the crowd was urging it on from the stands. Harsha remarked at the time 'this is the first time I have been on radio and felt like I am working with a live audience'.

Kerry kept demurring and the crowd kept urging him on. It was extraordinary to watch and to listen to. At one point the crowd started a slow handclap to urge Kerry to eat the chilli. Michael Clarke was 258 not out and he must have been completely baffled by the sounds making their way out to the middle. In the end Harsha sampled some naga chilli and immediately regretted it.

I think it takes a lot out of you to work like Kerry does and he retired at the end of the 2013–14 season. It probably didn't help that the ABC couldn't really pay him more generously, which was a shame. We are poorer for his absence and fans still hanker for his return.

Harsha was a great find and has probably turned into the biggest media star the game has known. The ABC can take some credit for giving him a start. I think he had done some work with All India Radio and he sent a tape of his work to us before the 1991–92 series, which coincidentally was Sachin's first. *Grandstand* founder Alan Marks thought he was worth a shot.

Harsha is very eloquent, has a very refreshing style and would always be positive about the game; he always found a silver lining and that Indian smile of his came out in his voice, which made people love him. People identified with his warmth and enthusiasm—there was rarely a dark edge to anything he said.

Whenever we went to India he was our co-commentator and now is part of the family. He loves a practical joke—I remember on one trip Glenn Mitchell got a call from a BCCI official who informed him on the eve of the match that we had lost our commentary box. If true, it was a disaster, and he ran to my room in a very agitated state to tell me the news. Neither of us were happy so we stormed off to find Harsha, who could often help in these situations. He answered the door and began to speak in a strange voice. I had no idea what was going on, but Glenn realised immediately he'd been had.

We have always valued having commentators from the touring team's country on our broadcast to widen the scope of our coverage. It is something our friends on television could think about returning to. You need a different perspective.

With Harsha the cultural differences always made for a bit of good-natured byplay. I remember once we presented him with a large jar of Vegemite on air by way of thanking him for his help. He thanked us and asked us if it was something Australians used to clean their shoes.

As I said, Harsha is a superstar now. In India he is Oprah Winfrey meets Eddie McGuire. He has 3.4 million followers on Twitter, which is just phenomenal.

It shows how long I have been doing this that I started work with Alan McGilvray, who was basically a pioneer of the medium, and I have been lucky to last long enough to have fun with Kerry, Harsha and a whole new school of commentators.

Back in the day Mac ruled the roost and if he editorialised about anything he would usually throw to Hassett with the line, 'Don't you agree, Lindsay?' Of course they always did, because everyone was reverential towards Mac.

I got to work with some outstanding people and quite a few of them aren't with us anymore.

Christopher Martin-Jenkins became a good friend and for a long time was a brilliant BBC commentator before moving on to become the *Telegraph*, then *The Times*, cricket correspondent. All the stories about 'C.M.J.' were about his eccentricities and accidents. He was always falling over or knocking something over in the commentary box. A cup of coffee stood no chance with him around. He attracted calamity and chaos.

There is a story about him getting frustrated by a mobile phone that refused to work. Somebody had to point out to him that the fault was with the user. Apparently he had left his hotel room in a flap and picked up the remote control instead of the phone. He was very absent-minded, but when he was broadcasting he had a great feel for the game, a real passion for it, and timed his work beautifully with the summariser working with him.

C.M.J. would infuriate McGilvray because he was never on time. Alan was a stickler; you didn't want to run over your shift by more than a minute or he would berate you, and the same when he finished and expected you to replace him. If you weren't there, god help you. McGilvray was obsessed with the disciplines and C.M.J. was not.

I didn't work on air with C.M.J. because we were both ball-by-ball callers, but there was a great sense of camaraderie among the commentators, particularly if you played golf and/or liked to socialise.

When C.M.J. was in Australia I would take him out to play and he would return serve when I was in England. We would often go to his house in Sussex and he would take his dog Pepper, a collie, along with him when we played at West Sussex Golf Club. In England they let dogs on the course if you keep them on a leash, but of course after a few holes he would say 'I think it's time to give Pepper a run' and this dog would take off like a mad thing. It would be alright if it retrieved balls or something useful, but Pepper just went crazy chasing birds and distracting other golfers. It was madness, up and down the fairway, and happened every time.

Then there was his language on the golf course. C.M.J. had the most proper way of cursing. If he missed a short putt he would stamp his feet and exclaim, 'Fish cakes and buttercup pie!'

We were quite competitive and played for a fictitious trophy we called The Ash.

We had a lot of fun. He was an extraordinary after-dinner speaker, an accomplished mimic who was just very funny. I will never forget his habitual start to his routine by saying, 'Isn't it interesting that in this marvellous, wonderful world we live in, that we can put a man on the moon but we still can't put one on Martina Navratilova.' You probably couldn't get away with that now, but he did. C.M.J. sadly died in 2013 of cancer.

He was president of the MCC at the time, which gives you some insight into his standing in the game.

I couldn't get to his memorial service, but it is worth quoting some of the article by Derek Pringle in *The Guardian*.

> You have to be a colossus in your field to have a service at London's most famous place of worship, which is no doubt why Baroness Thatcher's funeral is there on Wednesday. That C.M.J. managed to nip in ahead of her would have seemed entirely right to him as he never wavered from his belief that sport should come before politics.
>
> Botham did not attend Tuesday's Memorial Service, being in Spain, but at least six England captains—Andrew Strauss, Michael Vaughan, David Gower, Michael Atherton, Mike Gatting and Chris Cowdrey—turned out to pay their respects to someone who had described their careers in far greater detail than they can ever hope to recall.
>
> They were accompanied by scores of Test players from across the generations as part of the 2000-strong full house that filled Sir Christopher Wren's magnum opus. There, with the whispering gallery enhancing acoustics, the congregation listened to moving readings from his two sons, Robin and

James . . . The one thing that all the orations agreed
upon was that C.M.J. was a thoroughly decent man,
a rare virtue in these times.

C.M.J.'s eccentricity might have come in a direct line
from Brian Johnston, who he'd gone to for advice about a
commentating career while still at school. A war veteran
who was awarded the Military Cross, Brian was a radio
celebrity who hosted a number of popular programs and
brought a wicked sense of humour to his cricket work.
It's debatable if he ever uttered the Holding–Willey line,
but during the 1961 Ashes Test at Headingley he did say
'There's Neil Harvey standing at leg slip with his legs
wide apart, waiting for a tickle.'

Johnston was famous for dissolving into uncontrol-
lable laughter at his own jokes. Perhaps he was England's
Kerry O'Keeffe. He saw the lighter side, which was fine,
and he always drew a response from the audience with
his talk of cakes and pork pies and god knows what.
He came from a different broadcasting background.
I worked with him only a bit, but soon learnt he was
a practical joker, always putting you on the spot when
you had a mouthful of cake (or eating an ice-cream that
he had just given you). I think that working with Brian at
the World Cup in 1983 made me realise you could loosen
up. Until that point I had sat nervously by the senior

guys and stuck rigidly to the script. I was too uptight. I left any editorial, humour or observation to the doyens.

Jonathan Agnew took over from C.M.J. He played cricket at the highest level, including three Test matches, and had a background in journalism. I think Aggers is the best cricket commentator the BBC has ever had. Saying that, no one could ever match John Arlott for his imagination and poetry, but in terms of being on the game and bringing together everything that is relevant and delivering it in such a precise and informed style, Aggers is the best. All his editorial pieces are spot on too. Again, the social dynamics of our relationship have been wonderful. We are good friends and he often puts me up at his house in Scalford, a village in Leicestershire. He has or has had an army of dogs: Hoggard, Curtly, Klusener and Brackin. His wife, Emma, is delightful and the time spent at the local pub next to his house is always a highlight.

The English do a fine line in eccentric commentators and Henry Blofeld is the prime example. One of the original red trousers brigade, he is full of old world, private-schoolboy mannerisms. 'Blowers' calls everyone 'my dear old thing', primarily because he can't recall their names. He was actually a very good schoolboy cricketer, a wicketkeeper and batsman at Eton. Unfortunately, he was hit by a bus when riding his bicycle and was forced to give up playing the game. Blowers has a devoted following in England and Australia and knows the game intimately.

The bond between the BBC and ABC remains strong. Unfortunately other countries don't quite have the traditional relationship between the public broadcaster and the game.

Tony Cozier was for many decades the voice of West Indies cricket in much the same way McGilvray was the voice of Australian cricket. A great broadcaster, he was part of the revolution on Channel Nine when the Windies were the biggest thing in cricket, and was a formative influence for me from his first visit to Australia in 1968–69. As I said earlier, television doesn't seem that interested in picking up touring voices, which I think is a shame. Tony didn't come to Australia for the Windies' more recent tours as the work just wasn't there and that is a shame, although at least he was spared the ignominy of watching what has become of his team.

He had a great passion for the game and had a love of what the West Indies were doing in that fifteen years when they were trampling on everybody, but he was always very fair and had a good sense of humour. He was an outstanding commentator, and the moral conscience of West Indies cricket. Tony, sadly, passed away in 2016.

Nowadays Fazeer Mohammed has slipped into the role Tony had and he is very good too. He is extremely well versed in the politics of the game in the Caribbean and a forthright man, so much so he upset the West Indies when they were here in 2015–16 and was banned by the team from doing interviews. It was a ridiculous situation and blew over.

Bryan Waddle is the voice of New Zealand cricket and a staunch supporter of the same. He is great company and has to suffer a lot of barbs when things aren't going well for the Kiwis, mainly because he gets a bit prickly. He can get a little sensitive at times but he is a fair commentator and it always amuses me when Australians accuse other country's commentators of being biased. Again, we have played golf and I have to say that he is up there with the worst. I remember he hit the ball into the same pond in front of a hole ten times one day, but he kept trying.

I admire Bryan's work. I have seen him carry the entire commentary by himself on tours and that is an extraordinarily difficult thing to do. Like his country, he punches above his weight.

He eventually got a ball on the green that day.

South African broadcasting is a moving feast these days. They have people working in six different languages on six or seven different outlets and the South African Broadcasting Corporation is driven by political agendas that make it difficult to find any continuity. Neil Manthorp is one of the best of the contemporary callers and he's been a regular voice on *ABC Grandstand*.

There is no cricket like Indian street cricket. You can't walk anywhere without stumbling across the national obsession. (Author's collection)

With my commentary-box colleague and social media superstar Harsha Bhogle. The quickest way to get through security in India is to follow in Harsha's wake. (Author's collection)

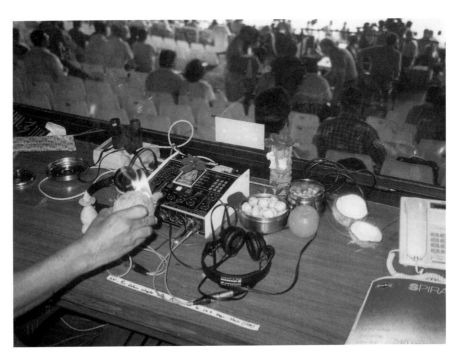

Pictorial proof that Mr Sub—Mr Subramanian—is a real statistician and not a figment of my imagination. The temple on his desk, and his puja before a day's play (below), didn't always help to overcome technical difficulties in India, but who's to say. (Author's collection)

Phoning it in. (Author's collection)

The Jim Maxwell ABC Stand in Antigua, 2003. There is no explanation for those shirts. (Author's collection)

Another one of my favourite-ever series. Steve Harmison's opening spell in the first Test at Lord's in the 2005 Ashes, in which he struck and dismissed captain Ricky Ponting, set the tone for what was to follow. (Alessandro Abbonizio/AFP/ Getty Images)

In the next Test, at Edgbaston, Shane Warne was up to his old tricks, bowling Andrew Strauss with a ball that pitched a metre outside his off stump. One of the best deliveries ever seen. (Tom Shaw/Getty Images)

With great mates Kerry O'Keeffe (centre) and Jonathan Agnew at the Boxing Day Ashes Test, 2006—my 200th Test. We had a lot of fun in the commentary box. (Nicki Connolly/Newspix)

The 'Monkeygate' racial sledging of Andrew Symonds (right) by India's Harbhajan Singh (left) in Sydney in 2008 led to a major falling-out between the two teams. It was the cause of much controversy in the commentary box as well. (Ezra Shaw/Getty Images)

Peter Roebuck brought clout and authority to the ABC commentary box—as well as a contrarian edge. His suicide in South Africa in 2011 deeply affected me and the cricket world in general. (Patrick Eagar/Popperfoto/Getty Images)

With Aggers and the chirpy Phil Tufnell (right), both of them former Test cricketers, at Lord's, 2013. The Queen was about to stop by, so we're looking our best. (Gareth Copley/Getty Images)

With Henry Blofeld, the famous BBC commentator known to all as 'Blowers', at Lord's, 2013.

(Gareth Copley/Getty Images)

Michael Clarke's undefeated 161 at Cape Town in 2014, when he was battered and bruised by Morne Morkel, exemplified his courage and skill, in my eyes.

(Morne de Klerk/Getty Images)

Tony Abbott is just one of the prime ministers (and would-be prime ministers) to visit the ABC commentary box over the years. Some show more aptitude than others! (Mark Nolan/Getty Images)

The colour, noise and excitement of the Big Bash League has got the crowds in. It will never replace the contest of a Test match for me, but cricket is ever-evolving, and that's a good thing for the game. (Matt King/Getty Images)

Gerald de Kock was another South African commentator who did a lot of work for us in the past and was
very professional and fair. Unfortunately he too is not
with the SABC anymore, I assume because of the politics
and better-paid opportunities at SuperSport, where
Gerald is an all-rounder, specialising in cycling.

At home the ABC has been blessed to have a number
of outstanding commentators. When I started, the Test
panel consisted of McGilvray, a visiting commentator and
one ABC caller from each state. So there was a variety
of voices including Graham Dawson, Peter Meares, Alan
Symons, Bob Bower, Jim Fitzmaurice, Peter Ewin, Dick
Mason and Alan Marks. After WSC, Dennis Cometti—
which might surprise some AFL fans—came on board,
and for a series without an overseas commentator both
of us joined McGilvray. Over a period this format varied
as I was also working on golf tournaments and until
McGilvray's retirement the team was more flexible than
permanent.

From 1985–86 Neville Oliver joined up, and then Tim
Lane later on, so in some matches we had four commentators sharing the duties. This continued through the
1990s until Neville's departure and then Tim's after
2001. Since then Glenn Mitchell was a regular with me
and we blended with Mike Coward and Roebuck on
tours to India and South Africa. More recently Drew

Morphett replaced Glenn and the two of us covered South Africa in 2011.

In 2014 the budget-cutting began as I did South Africa on my own, picking up locals like de Kock, Manthorp and Michael Abrahamson alongside Barry Richards, Peter Kirsten and Cricinfo's Jarrod Kimber. Luckily I stayed healthy, as the brief involved technical production, commentary and filing reports/previews for TV and radio.

Subsequently the ABC continued its commitment to the Ashes coverage from England with a co-BBC production, but for the first time since New Zealand became a Test match regular in 1973–74, there was no coverage of the away series there in 2016.

Tim Lane was the best all-round commentator the ABC has had, adept at calling track and field, AFL and cricket. We shared tours to India and Pakistan, and Tim's cross-examination of Percy Sonn, the president of South African cricket, when he overrode selectors and insisted on Justin Ontong over Jacques Rudolph in Sydney in 2002, endures. Percy was reduced to a blabbering wreck.

Glenn Mitchell replaced Tim, bringing energy and accuracy to the call, plus a swag of stats that Bill Frindall, the doyen of English cricket statisticians, would have tripped over. Our tours to the subcontinent and South Africa were memorable. Once we visited Darwin and Cairns for an out-of-season Test series against

Bangladesh with Kerry in tow. Kerry said that we had refreshed ourselves so generously at our Darwin hotel bar that they might now be able to build a foyer. It was an unprepossessing two-and-a-half star establishment.

Inevitably the match finished quickly and we decided to hire a car and drive out to Humpty Doo, home of rice-growing experiments and a population not necessarily diligently engaged in 9–5 labour. Kerry noted women in leotards at our watering hole and concrete stools in the bar. Glenn teetotalled while we cordialled up until the barman told us to leave so that they could hose down the bar for the evening entertainment. Cricket does take you to some strange places.

•

I sat down the other day and figured that I have covered 285 Test matches. It's a fair number when you consider McGilvray did 219—and he was going until he was 75. I also noted that 426 Tests have been played by Australia since my first Test commentary in 1977, far more than would have been played during McGilvray's 50-year span. In fact McGilvray's career spanned 292 Australian Tests, so it's a high percentage given he was still running the family business until he sold it and became full-time at the ABC in the 1960s. I've lost count of one-dayers, but including World Cups Australia has played more than 850 since the mid-1970s, so I must have broadcast 300 at least.

At the end of the 2014–15 season there was a meeting of cricket-connected people in the ABC. The purpose of the meeting was to try to find a way to improve our cricket broadcasts. It was initiated by Mark Scott, the then managing director of the ABC.

To be honest, we had not had our best year in 2013–14. The boss felt that what we had been doing was not good enough. In recent years we had lost some senior people. Kerry had left, Glenn Mitchell quit, Drew Morphett was pushed into retirement, Roebuck was gone and there was a hole in our coverage. We organised to use different commentators in different places that summer, including Allan Border, but when Phillip Hughes died and the cricket calendar was disrupted, our roster was thrown into chaos.

Mark was always of the belief, or so it seemed to me, that replacing Roebuck was more important than replacing Kerry; he liked the clout and authority that Roebuck brought to the coverage. That's where Gerard Whateley came into the picture; Mark had so much respect for him as a journalist and broadcaster, it was important to bring him on board and put people around him who would add thrust to the coverage.

So in the makeover the ABC employed Simon Katich, Chris Rogers and Dirk Nannes. We were initially aiming for Katich, Mike Hussey and Damien Fleming, but 'Flem' was getting well paid elsewhere and Hussey fell through as he was committed to Channel Nine.

While we didn't get who we hoped for, I think the way it turned out was fantastic. Nannes was the last to come on board. It was disappointing the Hussey deal didn't come through, but sometimes you get lucky. Dirk turned out to be quite direct and penetrating in his views and I am not sure Hussey could have equalled that because he didn't have that distance from the players, as he was still playing BBL. When we missed out on Fleming we went for Rogers, who was fantastic. It was great to have a cricketer who had been opening in an Ashes series only a few months earlier.

It turned out then that we had those three, along with Fazeer Mohammed for the West Indies and Bryan Waddle for New Zealand for their respective parts of the summer.

Adam White came on as a full-time producer for the Test matches, and we engaged Geoff Lemon and Adam Collins to write around the game and do social media.

Together I think we created a coverage that was as good as anything I have ever been involved with in 40 years at the ABC. I thought what we achieved was outstanding.

The program before and after play was well worth hearing. With the former players doing most of the interviews on the ground, we were able to tease things out of the current players in a way that I don't think we could have if I was doing them. The former players had them relaxed and joking, which helped extract some humorous asides.

The continuity was something we had never had with Kerry, because we were always chopping and changing our expert commentators. That meant we lost a few regulars—Quentin Hull and Geoff Lawson in particular—and it was hard on them as they had been committed contributors.

I have to admit I was anxious about the changes. I think I have episodes of insecurity, and in part I trace it back to Roebers' death and some inconsistent decision-making at the ABC. Prior to 2005 I had never done an Ashes tour in its entirety. Yes, Tim Lane and Glenn Mitchell have moved on, and although I've been regarded as the voice of ABC cricket for the last decade, it's never been official. As per public service jargon, I am a designated Content Maker at the ABC and am expected to be versatile, not just a cricket specialist in the fashion of McGilvray.

In fact, when Mac retired any expectation that I would take over from him was hit on the head when I was usurped by Neville Oliver, who became the head of

ABC radio sport. It smelt like a deal had been done. He took on the big tours himself.

It was demoralising.

Some years later I applied for another job and was ready to walk out on the ABC.

When I was overlooked for the 1989 Ashes I fired off an angry memo that stated in part: 'While I have always believed that broadcasting is a privilege and not a right, after 12 years of Test match commentary, without a hint of displeasure from ABC management, I am disillusioned, demoralised at your decision. Selection for this job is surely a recognition of performance in a specialised field. If there have been any shortcomings in my performance, now is the time for those to feel so to say so.'

At the time there were a number of messages of support, and Jack Gibson, the legendary rugby league coach, best summed it up when our paths crossed. 'What's goin' on Jim? You always go first in the commentary in every Test and then get dropped.'

As it turned out ABC TV covered the Edgbaston Test because Channel Nine was covering Wimbledon—the dates of the events clashed. So while on holiday in Europe I received a call from producer Max Donnellan to get to Birmingham in time to join up with Roger Wills and Keith Slater to cover the match. In 1993 and 1997 Neville was the voice of the Ashes, and continued to be the departmental head. In 1996 I applied for a job as media manager for the Sydney Olympics, but was unsuccessful. Yes, you can say this is sour grapes, just cop it and move on. Which is pretty much what happened until Oliver overstepped in 1998 and took a redundancy.

A valedictory decision organised by Oliver saw Tim Lane and me go to India in 1998. It was the first time two commentators had been sent overseas for Test match commentary. When Peter Longman replaced Oliver he sent us to the Ashes in 2001, but he wanted me to do half and Tim to do half.

Since 2005 I have been lucky enough to do all the Ashes tours and the patience, passion too, has paid off. Sometimes you need to heed your own advice; as I told Quentin Hull when things turned sour, nothing is permanent, and there are times to just strap yourself in with the seatbelt and wait.

12

Richie

If cricket had ever anointed a Pope it would have been Richie Benaud. He has been the most influential, revered and respected person in the game for 50 years. As Australian captain he never lost a series. As a commentator he was precise, authoritative and deliciously understated.

Richie was the master of the pause. Silence marked him as the best exponent of television's essential craft; let the picture tell the story, then utter appropriate gravitas, a memorably droll bon mot.

If you ran a poll today on the most popular cricket commentator in Australia, Richie would still be number one.

He is immortalised in beige, that prominent lower lip, acute analysis and the 12th Man parody recalled by the fan's refrain: two for twenty-two.

As a commentator he concentrated on the game at hand, rarely dwelt on the past, and was always respectful of the players and their foibles and failures. A wild slog dismissal was clever bowling, a rank delivery urged a reflective comment, 'might have lost his length there'.

He played in an era of austerity. In his early years there were no celebrations at the fall of a wicket. It was a game. No one earnt any money from playing in the Australian team.

Richie was the first tactile captain, breaking the mould of restraint with enthusiastic enjoyment of the moment.

He was one of many heroes for a young lad at the SCG who was lucky enough to see so many great New South Wales and Australian players.

Between the stellar careers of Bill O'Reilly and Shane Warne, Richie was the match-winning wrist-spinner. Listening to his around-the-wicket performance at Manchester in 1961 on a crackling radio reverberates now as much as Warne's ball of the century at the same ground in 1993.

I first met and interviewed Richie in 1975 for a program on the 1961 tied Test series and looking back it was a disappointment that he was never asked to work on the ABC TV coverage in those years up to the start of World Series Cricket, which transformed the presentation of the game on television.

My respect and admiration for Richie deepened in the last decade when he was Twelfth Man, patron, of the Primary Club. Every appearance was greeted rapturously by audiences at our various functions, and he gave an ear to all comers who wanted a moment with him at the annual Marathon Cricket matches at the SCG.

Richie was unique. A great all-rounder and leader whose devotion to the game has been phenomenal.

Those were the words with which I memorialised Richie Benaud upon his death in 2015, words that I would like to expand upon.

I am both old enough and lucky enough to remember Richie Benaud before the beige jacket and the two for twenty-two.

He was *the* outstandingly popular figure in the game when I was a boy, the man who brought glamour to cricket. He was the first celebrity captain we ever had, emerging from a dour and repressed period of sport when people didn't dare celebrate wickets or centuries, when they didn't hug or high-five, when the game was undertaken in that very restrained, conservative British tradition.

Richie, however, was different. He took to the field with his shirt unbuttoned to the navel and he brought excitement to the game. He would embrace a bowler or a fieldsman when a wicket fell, he enjoyed the moment more emotionally and demonstratively than anyone had done in our cricket. Before Richie you were lucky to get a handshake when you got a century.

More importantly, he believed the game should be exciting.

I used to watch him in the Sheffield Shield playing for New South Wales and he was the main attraction. As I said earlier—but it bears repeating because it's unimaginable now—there were summers when there were no touring sides and the Sheffield Shield was all you had. Domestic cricket was wonderful because of it. Now the Test players rarely appear for their states, but we could go down to the SCG and see legends from the Australian team. It was so exciting to watch Neil Harvey, Norman O'Neill, Bob Simpson, Brian Booth, Grahame Thomas, Johnny Martin—and above all Richie—turn out for the state team. The Blues had a wonderful team—it was a Test team really—and there was a real atmosphere at a Shield match. You could expect crowds of 5000 on a weekday and 10,000 on a

Saturday (remember, there was no cricket on Sundays, it being a day of rest).

Of course, my strongest memories of Richie are of him playing Test cricket, particularly that 1963–64 series against South Africa when Simpson took over as captain.

I can still remember seeing his lovely smooth bowling action. Richie would have had fun in T20 because he would have just come out and played his shots. He batted at No. 8 and did so with freedom, seemingly scoring at will. It was the way Richie moved and carried himself that stood out. He had total composure on the field and that was echoed later on by his performances in front of a camera, where it seemed to me that he never made a mistake; there was never a word out of place, never a stumble. He didn't use autocue—he just looked down the barrel and delivered.

He trained for television in England and was a consummate professional by the time we saw him, learning the ropes before we even had coverage here. It would have been interesting to see his early work at the BBC, because with most of us it takes a while to be confident about where you are and how you are putting it across, whereas he had authority immediately. The ABC never used him, which was a huge mistake. He worked all those years for the BBC but never got a start at home.

I wonder now if he felt put out by that. I don't understand why it happened.

By the time World Series Cricket started he was eloquent and comfortable, well and truly established in his craft thanks to the work he'd done in England. And whatever he said was always *appropriate*, a highly underrated skill, especially when pushed by television to provide sensation and excitement. Fortunately, Mark Nicholas continues the tradition.

Richie was renowned for his silence, which sounds paradoxical for someone being paid to speak, but it actually demonstrated his profound understanding of television. It is a lot more constraining than radio, requiring constant discipline and awareness of what people are seeing on their screens. On television you add to the picture; on radio we make the picture. On radio you can go anywhere you like; it is a broad canvas—if the cricket is quiet I can go off on a tangent, but it's hard to do that on television, especially with advertisements at the end of each over.

Television, print and radio tend to share the same stand at the ground. We usually eat together, but move to different rhythms, shut up in our own little boxes. Sometimes I would find myself sitting outside the 'office' with Richie, who liked to find a quiet corner for himself, and we would talk. Melbourne was the best place for that, probably because there wasn't room in the Nine box to hang around. Richie had a little spot with a desk underneath one of the television monitors, where he faced the wall and would do research on his laptop. He never sought attention. If you spoke to him he was polite, but he didn't seek conversation. There weren't a lot of exchanges over the years. He kept to himself and he didn't drink with the boys in the evening. If he went out it was mainly with friends from around the world.

I got to know him in the last seven or eight years of his life because of the Primary Club, a cricket-based charity raising money for people with disabilities. I was president and he became our patron in 2002. We have a Marathon Cricket day at the SCG every year, our big fundraiser, and he was always there before the dinner, like a royal figure moving among the masses, shaking hands, having a chat, making connections with people.

At every one of those shows, when he came into the room people would stand and applaud. Here comes the king. I cannot remember any retired cricketer who had that much respect. He was the biggest cricket person in retirement since Bradman, in terms of presence and influence, even though he rarely said anything controversial. That wasn't his style.

Richie wasn't an establishment figure—he resigned his membership of NSW Cricket when his brother, John, was suspended for wearing ripple-soled cricket boots. And he was steadfast in his view that World Series Cricket was the right path. I think time has proved he was on the money there.

He was a proactive commentator with strong views on the game. He was forever on about the front-foot no-ball rule, but he never managed to force a change. He detested slow over rates, demanding that the cricketers entertain the crowd. When the Windies were getting away with 75 overs a day Richie was adamant something had to happen and something did happen, because people respected his opinions. People always listened because he was never one of those dial-a-quote types.

Richie did have an influence on what was happening in the management of the game and some of the laws and conditions of play. This influence, like everything else he did, was understated but wise.

There will never be another Richie. We miss you.

13

The Argus Report, homework and the Kat fight

I may have sat in the Windies and English dressing rooms as a young man back when cricket was a game and not an elite sport, not a multi-billion-dollar business, not part of the world of entertainment, but today the inner sanctum is fiercely protected. In fact the players guard their privacy and space jealously and few visitors are allowed to cross the threshold.

When I married my second wife, Jennifer, at the SCG in March 2014, we had the reception in the Members and I found a few guests had snuck into the Australian dressing room to get the results of the Swans' game on the television that's in the viewing room.

There's a lot of history in those rooms and that building. As you can imagine. A note by Bradman is framed above one of the doors and reads, 'If it's difficult,

I'll do it now. If it's impossible, I'll do it presently. D.G. Bradman 10.12.28.'

New South Wales had won the Sheffield Shield in the 2013–14 summer. The actual Shield is housed at the Adelaide Oval and is not going anywhere. It is, I think, one of the more ornate and beautiful trophies in sport. The victorious Blues decided they would make do and drew a replica on the wall to celebrate their win. Every player signed their name. There's a lot of graffiti in both change rooms and it can make for some interesting reading.

Perhaps the most infamous incident in the rooms in modern times happened between Michael Clarke and Simon Katich after the Test against South Africa in January 2009. Maybe the tension of the finish got to the boys that night, or maybe the tension had been there for a while before that.

For the second year in a row the Sydney Test had gone down to the wire. Clarke had knocked over Ishant Sharma with nine minutes left to play the previous season to win that controversial match and Mitchell Johnson got one to sear back from a crack and dismiss Graeme Smith with five minutes of play left in this game. Smith had showed extraordinary courage to come out with a broken left hand and a problem with his left elbow and had hung on for the best part of 30 minutes, but the Australians would not be denied.

There are a number of versions of what happened that night, but the basic story appeared to be that Michael Clarke, who was then vice-captain, wanted to go out on the town with his mates and got impatient because there is a team rule that nobody leaves until they sing the team song. The original version of the story was that he wanted to go and have dinner with his fiancée at the time, Lara Bingle.

Things got a bit heated, as they can after five long days in the sun and a long night drinking. One thing everyone agrees on is that Clarke said something to Simon Katich, who is a man with a bit of a temper, and 'the Kat' grabbed 'Pup' by the throat. Teammates had to separate the pair.

Katich now works for the ABC and opened up on his version of events in the summer of 2015–16.

'My understanding of it, and it always has been, is that it's up to the custodian of the song to determine [when the song is sung],' Kat said.

'It's his decision. Not anyone else's. There was a little bit of a rush that night to go on to the next venue. Michael Hussey was particularly keen to stay in the dressing rooms. Matty Hayden was sitting down there in what turned out to be his last Test match. He wanted to savour the moment in those SCG dressing rooms.

'As we all know there was a little bit of a disagreement in terms of when that timing should be; as a result of that I got a little bit . . . it bugged me.'

Katich explained that the song doesn't have to be sung in the rooms. When Justin Langer was custodian on a tour of Sri Lanka he took them to the Galle Fort for a rendition and another night they went up Cape Town's Table Mountain to do it (there is some story about Matthew Hayden riding down on top of the cable car with no clothes on after that night).

What happened was, I think, a sign that maybe not all was right with Michael Clarke and the rest of the team. Most people saw this scuffle as a clash between the old school and the new. Kat was a man who had begun his Test career under Steve Waugh. He was tough, hairy and not the sort to be on the social pages. There was a perception that Clarke was all about the bling and not about the thing called cricket. It may not have been fair—he was a marvellous and gritty batsman, let's not forget—but he certainly divided opinions and may have divided the dressing room.

Clarke had fallen out with Andrew Symonds over disciplinary issues and it became obvious from criticisms of him when he retired that he had fallen out with a few others. John Buchanan wasn't complimentary either.

I know for certain that there were concerns about him taking over from Ricky Ponting—at the time a senior Cricket Australia executive was concerned enough to seek out my opinion on the matter. Cricinfo journalist Daniel Brettig wrote in his book *Whitewash to Whitewash* that there had been a last-minute objection at board level to Clarke's appointment. Hayden, another member of the old school and a former teammate of Clarke's, was a director at the time and put it to those who had to approve the decision that he had been divisive. He also raised another unusual incident.

Clarke's relationship with Lara Bingle, a high-profile model, had been tabloid fodder and even if it hadn't been the source of the problem in the dressing room that night it certainly was when he left a tour of New Zealand in 2010 to deal with domestic dramas. He flew home, they announced their engagement was off and he flew back and scored 168 in the first Test, so the episode didn't have too big an impact on his performance.

Still, it was strange and another distraction caused by Michael's off-field life.

Things rolled on from there. Katich was controversially dropped from the Test team and eventually Clarke became captain. The Kat let it be known that he thought he would not get his place back because of his relationship with his former teammate. We will never know. It is true, however, that Katich did not go back into an Australian dressing room again until the night Mitchell Johnson retired in Perth, which was after his nemesis had also retired.

That fight in the dressing room is still one of the first things that gets mentioned wherever Katich goes. People are fascinated by it, possibly because it represented more than just a scuffle and a change in the way things were.

It might be possible to draw a link between that incident and what happened in India after Clarke got the captaincy. I doubt we will ever know exactly what was going on when coach Mickey Arthur, Clarke and the team manager made the decision to stand down four players for selection in Mohali for not handing in a written assignment. Obviously there were wider disciplinary issues involved, but for Mitchell Johnson, James Pattinson, Usman Khawaja and Shane Watson to be excluded from selection was extraordinary. It was no state secret that there was tension between Watson and Clarke and some think this was at the core of the incident. When Arthur sued Cricket Australia for wrongful dismissal he talked about that relationship being a 'cancer'. Again, Watson was from the old school.

It was probably no coincidence that 'Watto' stood down from the vice-captaincy some time after that, but it was just embarrassing that one Test after being suspended as punishment he was called back to India—he'd gone home for the birth of his child and said on the way that he was reconsidering his future—to step up and captain in the absence of the injured Clarke.

They were tumultuous times indeed and things didn't settle down until Arthur was unceremoniously sacked on the eve of the 2013 Ashes and replaced by the no-nonsense Darren Lehmann.

I wasn't there when Kat strangled Pup (the headline writers had so much fun with that), but I was there the day Kat gave a press conference after losing his Australian contract. I don't think I have ever heard a cricketer or anyone speak with such honesty and clarity. It was an extraordinary scene.

To that point the veteran of more than 50 Tests had not been known for his public utterances. Friendly, determined and a great batsman, but not a celebrity cricketer by any stretch, nor one that sought the spotlight.

After being treated a bit shabbily by selectors early in his career, he had forged a good opening partnership with Shane Watson and the statistics indicated it was one of Australia's best. Then he got injured in Adelaide during the 2010–11 Ashes when the wheels were falling off the team and he never got picked again. Selectors decided they would bunker down and do their best with Phillip Hughes, who it must be said was not in the best form at the time.

The Kat eventually decided he had held his tongue long enough.

We all suspected it would be an interesting morning when he summoned us to the mini lecture theatre behind the nets at the SCG that Friday in June 2011. There was a frisson of excitement in the air. He is a slight man, but has a deceptive strength, and when he speaks you listen. Kat gripped the lectern and gave cricket both barrels. It was as if he had been holding it in since they'd dropped him for Andrew Symonds in Sri Lanka all those years before (another injustice). He made it clear that the way the selection panel had been operating for some time had caused problems in the team.

'The facts are a week or two before the Ashes a squad of seventeen was named. Now, in my opinion, if you can't know what your best eleven is a week before our biggest series then that to me reeks of indecision. The fact that we've had ten or eleven spinners in the last three years, that to me is another indicator of the inconsistency in selection. There's been rules for some and rules for others.'

Katich said he thought the chopping and changing had caused disruptions in the side.

'There are so many guys looking over their shoulders about whether they were going to play or not. If you compare it to how England prepared—they were settled, they played the same team in all their warm-up games and it was no surprise that they had a very good campaign.'

Katich laid into Andrew Hilditch, the then chairman of selectors.

'As soon as he told me the reason, which was what was being trotted out in the press about wanting the opening partnership to be bedded down for the 2013 Ashes, that got me steaming,' Katich said. 'To hear that, when our opening partnership has been one of the strong points in the team and something that Watto and I enjoy doing. When I got picked for my first tour in 1999, you got picked because of your performance. Now it seems that's changed and it's not only about performance—it's about potential. This is not just about me, it is about a number of players who have felt aggrieved at the way they have been treated by the selectors in particular and not just the selectors, but by Cricket Australia, because there's people above the selectors who make decisions on their futures and also the players' futures because they ratify the decisions that are made.'

He made some good points. He said that having part-time selectors was farcical when the rest of the game was so professional. Hilditch was running a law firm, and often unavailable when teams were set to be announced; it was no way to run a professional team. I think even Hilditch conceded that.

There was so much going on at the time that nobody noticed Bob Simpson sitting front and centre as Katich made his attack in the lecture theatre. The former coach had often been credited by Kat for getting his game back in shape a few years earlier when he was having some technical problems, so it wasn't that strange he was there. It was, however, strange when you realise that Simpson is Hilditch's father-in-law. His daughter married the selector and you don't have to be Einstein to work out they may not be the best of mates.

Maybe Cricket Australia was listening to Katich that day, because a few months later they received the recommendations of the Argus Review into the structure of cricket in the country and appointed full-time selectors.

Some years later Cricket Australia chairman Wally Edwards admitted that dropping Katich was a mistake. When Ricky Ponting wrote his book at the end of his career he too was forthright on the subject.

'In my view, this was as dumb a non-selection as any during my time with the Australian team. Kato had averaged more than 50 in Test cricket during the previous three years. He had scored six fifties and two hundreds in his most recent ten Tests. More than any statistics, he was one of the grittiest and most sensible cricketers in my experience, a tough character in the Justin Langer mould, my sort of cricketer.

'I knew we couldn't afford to cast such a player aside so easily. If the selectors were now rating potential ahead of performance, this was the first we knew of it.

'Kat's poor treatment put us all on notice.'

14

Monkey business

Relationships are built on trust and when that trust has broken down the relationship can spiral out of control. When trust broke down during the India–Australia Test at the SCG in January 2008 things threatened to get completely out of hand. Catches claimed by fielders were disputed by the opposition and the game reached boiling point. A tense match was marred by umpiring mistakes. It reached fever pitch when Harbhajan Singh was reported to the match referee on a charge of racially abusing Andrew Symonds.

Things only got worse when more mistakes were made by officials.

The fact the game had one of the more exciting finishes of any Test match of the modern era has been completely forgotten.

When Harbhajan was suspended by Mike Procter it became the biggest cricket controversy since Bodyline.

The Indians ordered a plane and prepared to go home. Umpire Steve Bucknor *was* sent home. Peter Roebuck wrote it was surprising the Indians *hadn't* gone home—and called for Ricky Ponting, Adam Gilchrist and Matthew Hayden to be sacked. The whole place seemed to be in a state of hysteria.

India had lost face and a terrified Cricket Australia went out of its way to appease them, or so it seemed. In doing so, the trust between players and their employer suffered serious damage.

And then, right on the tail of the ugliest series of events witnessed in cricket in this country, the hammer fell at the IPL auction and the world changed. Everyone kissed, made up and moved on. The healing power of the rupee intervened!

The Australian players stuffed their pockets and stopped complaining about too much cricket (their hard-won holiday was now spent playing more). They also stopped their groaning about the difficulties of touring the subcontinent. More importantly, the barriers were broken down between the protagonists—men who had met only across the pitch now shared dressing rooms and common aims.

It's hard to think of a more ill-tempered and controversial Test match in the time I have been covering cricket than that one between Ricky Ponting's Australian side and Anil Kumble's Indians in Sydney.

No doubt Bodyline had its moments and if you are looking for ugly it's hard to go past the last day of the match between Australia and Pakistan at the WACA in 1979 when Alan Hurst mankaded tail-ender Sikander Bakht and Sarfraz Nawaz returned the favour by appealing when Andrew Hilditch picked up the ball and returned it to him. Maybe Greg Chappell's decision to get his brother Trevor to bowl underarm against the Kiwis that day at the MCG reverberated similarly at board level, but it never reached the courts. And then there was the time that Dennis Lillee and Javed Miandad danced the fandango . . .

The Monkeygate Test, as it became known, strained the relationship between the two sides, the two countries and eventually the Australian team and Cricket Australia. The players felt let down and that relationship never healed while Ponting was in charge. Trust was lost—and once lost, is rarely regained.

There seemed to be an angry edge to the cricket in that match and it wasn't helped by a number of controversial decisions, which inflamed a situation that was already bubbling away. We all knew that Andrew Symonds had been racially vilified by Indian crowds during the one-day series held in India, but at the time nobody was aware that there had been an incident with Harbhajan on the field in the game at Mumbai.

Symonds had apparently insisted that it be sorted out man-to-man and had fronted Harbhajan after the match. It was the way these things had traditionally been handled, but when it happened a second time a bureaucratic process was launched that was rigid and strict. Anil Kumble rang Ricky Ponting after the charges were laid asking for it to be dealt with man-to-man, but it was too late to stop what had been started.

Cultural differences were also at play. India was concerned about a loss of face when its player was put on trial. Australia, well versed in the politically correct approaches to the slightest whiff of racism, believed it to be a much more serious offence than their opponent's. It must have been galling for the Indians, who have had far more experience of the pointy end of racism than any Australian player, to find themselves being accused and lectured on the subject.

You could see how serious it was getting when Sunil Gavaskar launched an attack on match referee Mike Procter, saying: 'Millions of Indians want to know if it was a white man taking the white man's word against that of the brown man.'

There were a number of fiery characters playing that game. Symonds and Matthew Hayden both came from

Queensland and both played the game in that hard, uncompromising way. They homed in on any weakness in an opponent and did their best to drag them down. It was not pleasant—and those of us with access to the stump mikes were a little more aware of what was going on than the general public.

There was a long, long history with Harbhajan, going all the way back to 1998 in Sharjah when he and Ponting clashed. Both had their match fees docked and Harbhajan was suspended for a game. He had set a pattern for his career in what was just his first series. Then in 2001 he was all over Australia in the Test series: he got two ten-wicket hauls and that hat-trick in Kolkata. Ponting, who made 17 runs at 3.4 and was dismissed by him in every innings, was his bunny. The pair played fourteen Test matches against each other and Harbhajan got him ten times.

Harbhajan is feistier than most cricketers; I think even the Indians recognise that. He can't help himself, can't bite his tongue. I think the Australians were hoping they could find a way to unsettle him. When subcontinental spinners come to Australia it is the conditions that unsettle them as much as anything (as Murali found). True bouncing pitches mean you have to be a high-quality spin bowler to get anyone out. Harbhajan, understandably, struggled to have the same success here as he had in India. He averaged more than 70 per wicket in the four Tests he played in this country.

There was no doubt the Australian captain and most of his team had little love for the Indian spinner and I think Ponting was pretty happy to let his attack dogs—Symonds and Hayden—off the leash. But once the friction started—just as at the start of World War I—events spiralled out of everyone's control.

On day three Harbhajan was alleged to have called Symonds a monkey. The Australians became extremely angry over this. I remember Cricket Australia media manager Philip Pope coming into the commentary box and saying the Australians were upset with what had happened between Symonds, Harbhajan and Tendulkar. It was bubbling away.

You could tell watching the match how on edge Ponting's side was. There was a hostility to everything they did. A series of umpiring errors didn't help. There were enough moments in the game for you to think 'what is wrong with these blokes?'

Day four, after the Australians had levelled their allegations against Harbhajan, saw an extra tension to the game. When the spinner dismissed Ponting with his first ball, it triggered delirious celebrations, including a series of commando rolls from Harbhajan, which was par for the course he had set when they first met.

Then Michael Clarke was caught at slip for a golden duck but just stood there, almost as if he was in denial. It was right out of character and further upset the visitors.

On the final day the game was in the balance with India set 333 to win. Rahul Dravid and Sourav Ganguly were going well, but then Dravid was given out caught behind when the ball had obviously hit his pad and Ganguly was 'caught' in slip by Michael Clarke. The Indians disputed whether the catch was fair. It was impossible to tell from the replay, but Ganguly was on his way back to the pavilion. There was another 'catch' that Ponting claimed, which the visitors were unhappy about. The catch was disallowed.

These events were all the more galling for India as they had had Symonds out earlier in the game caught behind, only to have it denied by the umpire.

With two overs to go, India was seven down and a draw seemed the only result, but Clarke came on to bowl and took three wickets in the over to seal a remarkable victory.

In the box, Roebuck—like the Indian players—was growing increasingly angry with the way the Australians were playing—and he wasn't alone. Former captain Sunil Gavaskar was giving them both barrels on television for the viewers back at home. Things weren't helped when the Aussies got so caught up in their celebrations on the field they didn't shake hands with their opponents at the end of the game. It would have passed without comment any other time and I doubt it was intentional. It was all happening, as Bill Lawry would say. At the press conference Kumble invoked Bill Woodfull's old line about two teams being out there but only one playing cricket—which was greeted with applause from the Indian media.

In the past it would have been worked out on the field, but Ponting said later that they had been told by the match referee before the series that racial abuse and the like was serious and had to be reported. So that course was set.

Roebers was fixed on writing something fiercely critical of the Australians because of the way he saw Ponting behaving and even took aim at Gilchrist for appealing in the Dravid dismissal. It all piled up as we went.

This was what he wrote on the front page of the Fairfax papers:

> Ricky Ponting must be sacked as captain of the Australian cricket team. If Cricket Australia cares a fig for the tattered reputation of our national team in our national sport, it will not for a moment longer tolerate the sort of arrogant and abrasive conduct seen from the captain and his senior players

over the past few days. Beyond comparison it was the ugliest performance put up by an Australian side for 20 years. The only surprising part of it is that the Indians have not packed their bags and gone home. There is no justice for them in this country, nor any manners.

He got further worked up from there, taking aim at Hayden, Symonds, Gilchrist and Clarke. The Australians were getting attacked on all fronts—even from ex-players. Jeff Thomson didn't mince words: 'The Aussies act like morons and bullies and they can't cop criticism from someone like myself. I think it was appalling that none of the Aussies went over and shook Anil Kumble's hand at the end of the Test, they just played up and carried on like idiots like they normally do.'

And then things got really ugly. At the first hearing Harbhajan was found guilty and suspended for three matches. The Indians weren't pleased and threatened to go home. There was a stand-off at the team hotel: the players were told to get off the bus that was supposed to drive them to Canberra for a tour game. This was when Gavaskar chipped in with his brown man versus white man assessment.

There was an appeal against Harbhajan's conviction. The Australian players weren't pleased with what was happening behind the scenes, feeling that Cricket Australia was more worried about appeasing the Indians than defending their own employees. The appeal got ugly, with Justice John Hansen launching a broadside at Symonds over his sportsmanship. Harbhajan got off without a ban because the ICC made an error when asked about his prior convictions.

Ponting took no prisoners himself when writing about it all in his memoir, describing it as 'the most angry, acrimonious and difficult summer' he'd been involved in. He took aim at his former bosses saying a 'large chunk of goodwill was lost'.

> There was an incident on the field, an Indian player was charged and suspended by an independent arbiter and we were the bad guys. Indian officials threatened to call off the tour, their captain bad-mouthed us, sections of the media bad-mouthed us and Cricket Australia and its lawyers went looking for a compromise, as if they were the ones who had to save face.
>
> It was impossible for me not to conclude that they considered Australia's relationship with India more important than how they looked after us and communicated with us. They let me down and let the team down.
>
> I'm struggling to forget that.

The fracas derailed the Aussies and they got beaten in Perth in the following match. They just didn't seem to have their heads in the game—Ponting was spending a lot of time behind the scenes dealing with chief executive James Sutherland.

The best line came from fielding coach Mike Young, who was asked what was wrong with the Aussies in that match: 'They were too busy smoking the peace pipe with the Injuns,' he said.

The acrimony that we saw in Sydney 2008 has not been seen since, largely due to the retirement of the protagonists. Now the players have a healthy respect for each other and we don't have the stupidity, a lot of which went back to Harbhajan and certain characters on the Australian side. You can't condone the way Ponting ran the side in that regard; he had a couple of bovver boys there and he just let them go, I don't think he ever reined them in.

There was a good deal of stereotyping. The 'ugly Australian' tag had been around since Ian Chappell and his longhairs first put their feet on the boardroom table. Steve Waugh had a side that played with a snarl. 'Mental disintegration' was a phrase he popularised.

Much of the antagonism is ramped up by the media, it must be admitted. I see it when I am around the commentary box. You have a good day of Test cricket, but it doesn't provide a headline, then all of a sudden something happens and cricket is the main event. A stylish innings that would have kept Neville Cardus happy is never enough—there always has to be something else going on. It's like a Formula 1 race—the media are always looking for a crash. Personally I am happy to read Mike Atherton or Gideon Haigh, who focus on the cricket contest and not the peripherals.

That said, Monkeygate was as big a story as I have seen.

And it was but a few short years before Ponting, Harbhajan and Tendulkar ended up in the same dressing room at the Mumbai Indians. The IPL was about to change everything.

15

IPL, BBL, bloody hell!

Were I just a spectator and not a commentator, I could not go and watch the Big Bash. If this is what the new world of sport is all about, you can count me out. It's all based around that American concept of crowd involvement, like you get at the basketball or baseball.

Fans are continually cajoled by the public address system and the video screens to make noise. It seems to be all about making noise for the sake of it. Why can't we sit and enjoy watching elite athletes play? Why can't we focus on the contest, the experience, as most do at Test matches?

The world has gone crazy with noise—it's in your face and ringing in your ears. It seems to me to defeat the purpose of going to a sporting event, because it is *not* sport; it is entertainment. It's like a pop concert. A Test match is quiet by comparison, but not quiet enough. Before the game and at every break you are being berated by the public address system, or entertained by some silly event on the field or being informed of some trivial matter.

The constant message on the screen tells you to hydrate, to be careful of the folding seat, not to run on the field, not to offend anybody, not to do this, not to do that. The Mexican wave is banned, the beer snake is banned, umbrellas are banned, bottles are banned—the list of things banned is so long it might be easier to say what isn't.

The nanny state has gone mad. There is no sense of you being at an event you should enjoy as you see fit. You are being hammered all the time, being told what is happening, what to do, what to think, even when to kiss. The experience of being at the event has been diminished or tarnished by the twin obsessions of occupational health and safety and keeping people entertained. You have to tick all these boxes to be there and there is no chance to just be at the cricket and enjoy the game.

It is great that the BBL appears to be bringing people back to the game and that people have fun there, but the marketing men and women need to realise that central to the experience of going to the cricket is a game called cricket. It doesn't need dancing girls, fireworks, costumes or health and safety regulations.

The lunch and tea breaks traditionally were a chance to catch up on some reading or to discuss events with people around you. Now you have to leave your seat and go to the bar, because it is the only place you can get away from all the noise in the breaks, either blaring advertisements or exhortations to do one thing or another.

At the modern stadiums there is no escape, nowhere to go. If you are at the SCG the only place to escape is in the Members area, and that is a shortcoming of the ground. There is just no alternative for the rest of the crowd. The Gabba has no escape, the MCG is the same. I am sure the new stadium in Perth will be the same. Luckily Adelaide provides plenty of space, but again it's only for the Members. People need to have some space—that is what makes Lord's such a wonderful ground. You can go anywhere. Anyone can go to the Nursery End or behind the pavilion. You can buy a bottle of champagne and drink it—French champagne in glass bottles. You can even bring your own.

The catering system in Australian stadiums is ridiculous. Low-strength beer, wine in plastic cups, poor food at stadium 'restaurants'. I don't know why anyone would part with all the money that it costs to go to the game and then get treated like that. I remember sitting in front of the Noble Stand in 1965–66 with my scorebook and there were 55,000 people in the ground. You are never going to get that again. They were on the Hill and bunched in like sardines, but having a ball—you could take your own esky with your own food and booze. Sure it could get a bit out of hand, but relatively speaking it was a cheap day out.

Now everyone must have an undercover seat, but at what cost? I know officials are reducing the cost, but I think one of the reasons so many go to the BBL is because it is so affordable—$45 for a family ticket. You wouldn't get lunch for that at a Test or ODI.

And people have so much more choice now than we did. Some seasons back then you might have two Tests a summer if you were lucky, maybe four Shield games and a tour match, but that was all you got. There was no one-day cricket or T20. If you wanted to see cricket you could go to the suburban oval and hope somebody from the state side might turn up, or you would play yourself, which we did on Saturday and Sunday.

In the end it is all about getting more people playing the game. There is so much more choice now; people are not going to spend all their free time hanging around on the cricket field. They will do something that takes less time. Hopefully we can keep enough of them interested to see another generation play. One good thing about T20 is that it can induce more children to play. There is a belief they should be playing T20 in schools and I think they are right. I wouldn't say T20 is an antidote but it might lure back those who go off and play basketball instead, which is what I see happening in Sydney schools.

T20 is probably more attractive to children who are on the periphery of the game. I see plenty of them at my old school who would be very good first XI cricketers, but they don't want to play at a high level. They play basketball or muck around in Fourths. In terms of stimulating interest in cricket, if T20 keeps them in the game, that's better than them being out of it.

The other factor with the development of the game is the Women's Big Bash League. It will be a huge shot in the arm, encouraging more women to play. That is going to change things from the grass roots up. The WBBL is creating an event that people will aspire to be part of and they can only do that by getting a start in their school or their clubs.

I am feeling guilty as president of the Eastern Suburbs Cricket Club that we don't have any women's cricket at all, which is something we need to think about. We have a lot of female juniors but we really don't have a proper women's team. We have tried, but it hasn't worked out yet. We have 900 juniors at Easts and there are girls playing in those underage teams, but in terms of getting a proper set-up going with women's teams we are not there yet. It is on the To Do List.

T20 *might* encourage more kids to play the game, but it's certainly providing more employment—and exponentially more money—to cricketers. All the domestic T20 leagues crowding the cricket calendar around the world are luring players with their promise of quick cash. I am a fan of any reputable competition, but a lot of these leagues have a bit of whiff about them, with allegations—and findings—of spot-fixing and match-fixing. Even the IPL has been tainted, with teams and players suspended.

Yet anything that gives a player the opportunity to earn more from playing their chosen sport should be encouraged. I am not against it, although at times I get this feeling that T20 competitions like the BBL are becoming the *Days of Our Lives* of cricket. It's a serial that goes on throughout December and January providing all the appropriate melodrama, but what does it mean?

All formats have their value, but for an old hand who likes to watch Test match cricket, which is the ultimate challenge and examination of character, it sticks in the craw a bit to see the preponderance of T20 and how in our own backyard it is quite obviously going to become a bigger and bigger feature.

It is the natural course of events to a degree. Why wouldn't you monopolise television from mid-December to mid-January when nobody else is trying to take you on and you are getting such a wonderful response? It is bringing people to the game, and encouraging many youngsters to play.

If there hadn't been a Big Bash in the 2015–16 summer where would we have been? The West Indies series was a complete non-event, but the ratings and crowds for the BBL were going through the roof.

Cricket Australia is staring down the barrel of a fixturing problem—of just how to juggle Tests, one-day internationals, T20 internationals, the BBL and the domestic one-day and Sheffield Shield competitions. India managed to carve a hole in its international schedule so its players can participate in the IPL. Why can't we do the same here? I spoke to David Hussey after a BBL game at the time and he said Australian players should play every game in the tournament. I don't necessarily agree—I think they should maybe play the last couple of games going into the finals.

The question is, what comes first, the money or the greater good of the game? It's a bit of a chicken-and-egg argument with so much money coming in from television and players required to play to earn their living. Everything is dictated by commerce in big sport these days. Cricket Australia is winning the argument with the decisions they have taken to ensure the financial viability of the game, but how you prioritise scheduling is another matter. At the moment it is hard to argue against the paths they have taken, but I am not sure where they will lead.

The rise and rise of day–night pink-ball Tests, which potentially endanger the integrity of the game by producing very short contests, is another looming issue. We will be watching closely as momentum builds towards day–night Ashes Tests in 2018–19.

Looking at T20 the other way, as a broadcaster as opposed to my preferences as a spectator, it is undoubtedly a good thing. You sit in a box describing what you see and the noise creates atmosphere and the sense of an event taking place.

Before Big Bash, when T20 was an interstate series, there were some amusing nights at the Olympic Stadium. NSW Cricket tried to promote the matches with celebrities and Andrew Johns, a brilliant rugby league player, was drafted in as a player to market the game to a wider audience. On one occasion the marketing men decided to have speed dating and for an extra $10 fans got to sit in a section of the ground, where they were sorted into age groups. The idea was that every time a wicket fell or a six was hit you would change partners. Thinking that might not provide enough opportunities to switch partners, they added fours to the switcheroo. In one over

Luke Ronchi struck 4 4 6 4 6 and was out off the final ball, which meant you were back with your first 'date'.

In the box working with Kerry, Geoff Lawson and David Morrow, the ABC tech Wayne Davis got into the tempo of the action and punched out bursts of 'Love is in the Air' and 'Can't Get Enough of Your Love, Baby'. So the box was heaving with John Paul Young and Barry White while Craig Hamilton was keeping tabs on the speed daters and we were commentating. It was one of the most entertaining 'commentaries' I can recall—and speed dating needs to make a comeback. For all of the above, you have the example of the IPL to thank—or blame. Cricket Australia has spent a lot of time tippy-toeing around Indian cricket. They've been shirt-fronted, if I may borrow a phrase from former PM Tony Abbott, more than once by the fickle BCCI, which is fond of flexing its financial muscle.

Past chairman Wally Edwards learnt that on his first days in the job when he received a letter from the BCCI saying they were having second thoughts about the 2011 tour—which was a matter of weeks away. India generates the majority of income in world cricket, close to 80 per cent of all money in the game. For many cricketers, it provides the biggest pay cheques they get. When India tours your country you sell the rights back to the subcontinent and you are set up to host other nations in the down times. Only the Ashes come close as a money-maker. Edwards had to fly straight to India when he received that letter. As soon as they saw him everything was alright and the tour went ahead. They just wanted to let him know who was boss right from the start. Edwards eventually cut a deal with the BCCI and England board to carve up world cricket among themselves. It guaranteed the Big Three more money, but the move was universally criticised outside the Big Three. Edwards argued it was the only way to keep the Indians in the tent.

Then the wind changed again.

Shashank Manohar signalled early on in his reign at the BCCI that he might be a bit more flexible. I said this to former PM John Howard at a lunch soon after Manohar was appointed. Mr Howard wasn't so sure. He pointed out that Manohar was the man who blocked him from becoming president of the ICC—another example of India flexing its muscles and Cricket Australia backing down.

Interestingly enough, it was the near-death experience of having India threaten to go home after Monkeygate that caused Cricket Australia to realise it needed to find other income streams. The result was the T20 Big Bash League, modelled after India's IPL.

The economic power has not just changed the landscape for Cricket Australia. As I said earlier, when that first IPL auction happened, ironically at the end of the Monkeygate summer, the players' relationship with India changed too. Suddenly Indians and Australians were teammates—mates even, all getting along fine—and a lot of players were earning money they had never dreamt of. It also changed for coaches and physiotherapists and the like, who are also part of the IPL caravan.

Yes, IPL had changed everything.

16

Phillip Hughes

On a cloudless day on 8 December 2014 the international cricket summer got off to a belated start with a tribute to Phillip Hughes played on the Adelaide Oval video screens. A simple, touching voiceover by Richie Benaud finished with the words 'forever rest in peace, son'. A sadness hung over the morning as it had hung over cricket since the boy from Macksville had been struck at the SCG and fallen to the turf two weeks earlier.

It was a terrible time. The sadness extended over the entire summer.

It was, too, basically the last time we heard from Richie. He had been sick for a few years and at the end of the season we lost him too. He had not been well enough to make it to the commentary box for a few years and had pre-recorded the tribute to Hughes.

Phillip Hughes was the son of a Macksville farmer, brought up alongside the vast expanse of the Nambucca River. He had started his Sheffield Shield career at the SCG but moved to Adelaide to further his cause. Here was a kid who made a half-century on debut for the Blues and his first century in the Shield final. It was a shame to lose a player like that to another state, but it has been happening since Bradman's time and you can see why. NSW produces so many talented cricketers that some have to leave. I am not sure that was the full story with Hughes' exit, however; I know there were tensions between him and the administration there.

Hughes was a precocious talent by any measure. He hit 201 of NSW's 345 runs for the match on a green top at Bellerive that nobody could master—and in doing so broke Bradman's record for the highest contribution to a team's score. He loved making runs. Sam Robson, who played at Easts and for England, recalls a time before a state Under 17 trial game in Canberra where the group started talking about how many centuries they'd made. These were the best young batsmen in the country. Someone said two, a couple had three, one had made six. They looked at Phillip and he whispered that he'd made 50, maybe 60.

Then one day, it all came to a halt. It was a blessing not to be there that dreadful day at the SCG when he was felled. The scenes that unfolded were terrible: the way he fell, the resuscitation on the boundary, helicopters and ambulances . . .

The ABC had long since lost interest in covering the Sheffield Shield; the only thing we do these days is give score updates from the various grounds on the weekend. Anyway, I was on the golf course on that November day. There was a bit hanging on the Shield game because there was a lot going on behind the scenes. Australian captain Michael Clarke had got himself into a stand-off with the selectors and head honchos at Cricket Australia, who were insisting he play a certain game to prove his fitness, which he was refusing to do. It was really heating up and almost certain he wouldn't be available for the first Test in Brisbane, which meant Hughes was batting for a place in the side. He'd been out of the team since the second Ashes Test, at Lord's in 2013.

I wasn't far away at Royal Sydney. Andrew Sinclair, president of the South Australian Cricket Association, was playing the same course, but not with us. I'd seen him as I wandered around and at some stage I heard that Phillip had been felled. As we came off the eighteenth hole I saw Andrew again and asked how Phillip was and he said he was going to see him in hospital. It sounded pretty serious, but I don't think we had any idea of just how serious at the time. Only a few people did. Michael

Clarke would have been one, as he too had headed to the hospital.

Phillip was 63 not out when he got hit and in one of those 'nobody is getting me out' frames of mind that typified him. I had heard a whisper that he'd already earnt his way back into the Test team and said that to Andrew, who said he'd heard the same thing. It turned out later that this was a bit premature. Shaun Marsh was batting the same day, and was also in the frame.

Events moved quickly. I rang the press box at the SCG to see what was happening. There was hardly anyone I knew at the ground (which tells you just how far Sheffield Shield has slipped). Geoff Lawson was bowling coach for NSW, so I rang him and he told me how awful it was. How the players were just so shocked that they sat in the rooms for hours and wouldn't leave. It was becoming apparent that this was really serious.

We all wandered around in a daze for the next 48 hours.

And then Phillip was dead. I remember having to talk a lot on the television and radio as all the players had shut themselves away. Everybody was in shock.

During those days I spent a lot of time thinking about David Hookes, who had died some years earlier when he was king hit outside a pub in Melbourne. I liked 'Hookesy', who was always winding me up for being a

New South Welshman. He was a proud South Australian and they always have a chip on their shoulder about places in the Test team going to NSW players. He would carry on about the baggy green being handed out in the same bag as the baggy blue. I'd interviewed him in Newcastle when he was coaching Victoria and they had pulled off an extraordinary win. It was the week before he was killed. The Vics scored 7–455 in the last innings to win the match. Hookesy had been chipping me all day and I invited him to come on air and talk about it and it was some wonderful radio. He was very cheeky.

Phillip had played a Shield game at the same ground in Newcastle to earn his first Test selection. He and NSW teammate Phil Jaques, who had played eleven Tests, had been in the running to fill the space left vacant by Matthew Hayden. Hughes was nineteen years old and Jaques was almost 30, but his back was buggered and that was what had cost him his place in the side in the first place.

Hughes made 151 in the first innings of the game and that was that. He was on the plane to South Africa and Jaques never played for Australia again.

●

My first memory of Phillip was when he came down from the bush to live in Sydney and one of the charities had a match on Australia Day during the 2006–07 Ashes series at Reg Bartley Oval at Rushcutters Bay. He was an emerging star and he was kind enough to come down and help out. He was nervous, quiet and incredibly shy. I remember he was still the same when we did those first interviews in South Africa when he had made the Test team two years later. He was an innocent abroad.

The South Africans bowled badly in Durban when he got those two hundreds in his second Test, but that's how good batsmen make you bowl.

He was instinctive. His batting took me back to the days of Doug Walters. It was just sheer instinct and an adrenaline high and he was very hard to bowl to. A bowler thinks such a brazen batsman will make a mistake and get out. He'd done that in his first Test innings, taking a swipe at the fourth ball to make a duck on debut. He was swiping away in Durban but it was coming off and the bowlers kept thinking that it had to stop soon. It didn't stop until he had made a pair of centuries. I think that word got around cricket and by the time he got to England the bowlers had worked out they just had to tuck him up, bowl tight.

Still, he wasn't a one-trick wonder and he worked very hard. Every time they dropped him he demanded they reconsider their actions by the work he did and the runs he scored. I was never sure if he could ever get back and play the way he had initially, because he had that homespun method that was fallible, but we will never know. He was only 25 going on 26, so there was plenty of time. Or so we thought . . .

The day Phillip died—two days after being struck—was a horrendous day for everyone. I was sitting in the ABC offices when the news came through. I remember going on Richard Glover's program. I wasn't close to Phillip, but nevertheless it was like a death in the family; it just hit you. The nation, the whole cricketing world, had been waiting for news. Hoping that there would be something positive.

I was on live within five minutes of it becoming official and I broke down while I was talking to Richard Glover. It was so emotional. We had feared the worst but when it happened it was incomprehensible. It just hit everyone like a bomb had been dropped. I can't remember getting upset like that before. When Peter died I didn't do anything for a few days until the ABC said I should, so I did an interview with Ginny Stein and I lost it a little bit, but not like this.

Richard Glover and I spoke on air, but I was a mess and he let me go after a little while so I could compose myself.

One thing tipped into another, then I was on JJJ, the youth station, talking again. I must have done every radio network and then I did the television news live at the top and *The 7.30 Report* live. The BBC were on the line a lot. It was emotionally tumultuous. Working helped protect you in a little way from the awful emptiness we all felt.

The guy who came up with the idea of putting bats out in front of your house was a genius. What an imaginative, brilliant way of marking Phillip's passing. I would see bats out for a year after it happened. It was a sign that we were all part of a wider community. We were all going through something together.

Phillip's death reverberated internationally. Pakistan and New Zealand abandoned the second day of their Test match in Sharjah. In Germany, Elton John dedicated a song to Phillip at a concert.

The ABC decided to do a full coverage of the funeral using Channel Nine's feed on News 24. I was back doing what I had done when Bradman died, but this was so much sadder.

It was a strange, hot day in Macksville. We were set up in a little area opposite the hall where the funeral was held, at the bottom of the hill, next to the high school he attended. It was an enormous event, with so many people in town. The Australian cricket team, Ravi Shastri, Virat Kohli and other members of the Indian side, Brian Lara and many state cricketers were there. Prime Minister

Tony Abbott and a host of politicians descended. It was like the death of the king.

I did the broadcast with Joe O'Brien, who is a very good operator. The organisation was amazing given how little time there was to prepare. It was hard work, there was no script, you just had to be ready to wing it. If I say it was like covering a sporting event, it is with no disrespect. We had to keep the audience informed about what was going on.

The tributes to Phillip from his family were heartbreaking. His sister Megan spoke with great dignity, as did his cousin Nino. Nobody who heard Michael Clarke's speech that day will forget it. He got to the heart of things. Others weren't so successful. Alan Jones was in the audience; I was told he was keen to talk but there wasn't much appetite for that.

The chief executive of Cricket Australia, James Sutherland, spoke but his name was not on the order of service. There was some tension between the organisation and the cricketers, who felt they were being railroaded into playing again before they were ready. His speech about getting back to the game caused a few ripples.

I remember that it hit me sometime during the day—maybe it was during that slow, sad procession through town—that this was Australia's Diana moment.

17

A sporting life

Rudyard Kipling posed the question 'what should they know of England who only England know?', which the wonderful West Indian cricket writer C.L.R. James rephrased to ask 'what do they know of cricket who only cricket know?'

I am not sure if I am condemned here or not. Hopefully not.

At the ABC we did not only cricket know. In fact, I have had to specialise in many sports over the years and it is only in recent times that the summer game has occupied most of my year.

In the 1970s I cut my teeth on country rugby league matches and also dabbled in soccer. I still cringe about one memorable faux pas on a 1974 Saturday afternoon when I was subbing for Martin Royal, the resident newsreader cum soccer commentator, who had gone to Australia's first World Cup. Remember that on Saturday afternoons the radio *Sports Panel* tried to cover everything that moved. So listeners would hear horse racing from Geoff Mahoney in Sydney, Joe Brown in Melbourne and Larry Pratt in Brisbane wrapped around John O'Reilly's call of the rugby league match of the day, Ron Davies at the club rugby and me at the soccer.

In the Forbes Street dungeon studio the presenters were mainly newsreaders like Kevin Chapman, Geoff Howard, Rod McNeil and John West. On my first day at the soccer Kevin Chapman was in the chair. He loved the punt and was constantly ringing the bookie to get on anything a coat-tugger—that's a tipster—had mentioned.

I was at a place called Arlington Oval in Sydney for the South Sydney Croatia match against Western Suburbs. I sat in the crowd wearing the harness and microphone that was the rig of the day, and ne'er a word of English could be heard. The NSW soccer competition was a collection of ethnic and suburban-based teams, such as Hakoah, Marconi, Apia Leichhardt and the two clubs already mentioned. My task was to provide succinct updates, which I embellished with mind's eye replays of any goals scored.

So it was deep in the first half when the first cross came to me. 'It's Western Suburbs up one–nil out here.

(Sound effects of a crowd rising in a cacophonous swell of foreign tongues.) In the fifth minute Milanesevic swept from the right, passed to Ilich who centred to Woznavic and his searing left-footer beat the goalie Smith into the back of the goal.'

I was trying to call a match between two teams I had never seen before being played by players I had never seen before. Confident that my homework research was accurate I felt relieved to have spat out the story so competently. A few minutes later Kevin talked down the line, discouragingly, 'Hey, Jim, a few listeners have rung to say that those blokes you described play for South Sydney Croatia, not Western Suburbs.'

Oh well.

Calling rugby league was a challenge. At the country grounds I sat at a table on the sideline, with a fractured view of the action. Even in Sydney through the 1970s and 1980s we had that problem with our broadcast positions, which were all on the sideline unless you were at the SCG or the Sports Ground. We used to pray it wouldn't rain—if it did you got wet. An umbrella was worth a fortune. Sometimes you got very wet, but you had to keep going.

We were thrown into the deep end at those country assignments. I know one time I made it a bit harder for myself than it should have been. There was a good ABC man at Orange by the name of John Clarke. For the listeners there were two John Clarkes, one who did sport on the weekend and his alter ego who morphed into a humourist on Monday.

The sports John was a friendly guy who, like everybody at the time, enjoyed a drink. One of my earliest work memories is flying to Dubbo the night before the game and meeting John, who'd driven from Orange, at the rugby club. That took a while and when we broke up late in the evening he announced that we needed to reconvene at 10 a.m. the next morning before the game. Which we did. After lunch we wobbled down to the ground, Victoria Park, had a peek in the dressing room, set up on the sideline and began the broadcast.

I would have the program in front of me and he would point out who was who and I would try to put together a half-sensible call of what was going on. It wasn't very professional and I shudder at the memory of it now.

I remember visiting again in 1975 with Tony Cozier to cover a tour match with the West Indies back in the days when the visiting teams would have a few hit-outs in the country. That match was a massacre. The Western NSW Country XI did their best, but were humiliated by the clearly superior visitors. Viv Richards hit a century in 70-odd minutes as the team scored 6–312 from just 35 overs. We sat on the cycle track to cover that game and spent a bit of time ducking missiles—from the middle, not the crowd.

In 1978 the ABC decided we should have somebody at every rugby league match on the weekend, which meant we spread out around Sydney to file updates while Alan Marks and Reg Gasnier called the main game.

The early around-the-grounds coverage included some interesting would-be commentators. John Coates, now supremo at the Australian Olympic Committee, was a keen Wests supporter; Ian McNamara, the voice of *Australia All Over*, followed Parramatta; yachtsman Peter Shipway was involved; and the voice of rugby, Gordon Bray, was on board with tyros Peter Longman and Bob Vincent.

In the early 1980s, when Alan moved over to television, I did the Saturday game on radio. We would set up at places like Lidcombe Oval, Cumberland Oval, Redfern . . . all sorts of grounds where you were again sitting in the open, sometimes getting sunburnt, sometimes getting wet. Basically I did it on my own. I had a wingman called Graham Hartman, who was known as the track watcher because of his tipping expertise at the trots, but on these occasions he accompanied me as my statistician.

It was a great experience; rugby league still had a bit of that connection with suburban culture and tribalism that is slowly dying out. You talk to Australian

Rules fans from Melbourne or Adelaide and they often mourn the passing of that. Once upon a time you lived in Carlton or Port Adelaide or Redfern and that was where your team played; every other week you ventured into hostile territory for away games. These days they have rationalised it all so everyone trudges off to the modern stadiums, where the facilities are better but that connection is gone.

In 1985 I graduated to covering league for television. Mike Stephenson, Debbie Spillane and I did that every Saturday for two years until Kevin Berry dumped me in 1987.

It was the year I got married to my first wife, Madonna, so it was a bit of a relief not to have that weekend duty, and clearly the hierarchy, somewhere between Kevin, who was the TV sport boss, David Hill, head of the ABC, and John Quayle, CEO of the rugby league, thought I wasn't cutting it, but I continued covering the game right up until 1990 on the radio, when Peter Wilkins took over.

Looking back I recall the Monday morning discussions about which game ABC TV would get on Saturday. Given that Channel Seven was getting the pick game of the round on Sundays, we normally got the third or fourth best. I remember saying to John Quayle that it would be great to get some more quality matches on Saturdays, and he replied, 'Jim, every game is a good game.'

I did eight grand finals on radio, working with Les Johns, Ted Glossop, Reg Gasnier, Mark Levy. They were good years, really good years. In 1986 when the ABC covered the Commonwealth Games on TV and radio from Edinburgh we were one short on the commentary roster for rugby league. We needed a radio caller for two Saturdays. I had a brainwave and rang Frank Hyde, who had recently retired from his long-serving distinguished career with 2SM. His signature call was 'it's long, it's high and it's straight between the posts'. Frank said that he'd always wanted to work for the ABC. I caught up with him after his first call at the SCG and he was exhausted. He said that he didn't realise how tough it would be without any commercial breaks!

In 1992 I got my first chance to cover an Olympic Games, which meant a trip to Barcelona. I would be covering the hockey. I knew nothing really about the game so they sent me to Cairns to familiarise myself with the sport and the players. Hockey is one of the great amateur sports of Australia and has some outstanding people involved. It hasn't been polluted by all the professional nonsense like the more high-profile pursuits have. People play the game because they love it and they volunteer to keep it going because they love it. I remember around this time that highly talented but troubled rugby league star Julian O'Neill got in trouble again. Hockey coach Ric Charlesworth said he could keep the women's team afloat for a whole year for the same money O'Neill was getting on contract.

In 1992 the men made the Olympics final. Mark Hager, a member of that team, ended up helping me out as an expert commentator because we didn't have anyone accredited who could do the job. He was accredited as an athlete but was injured, so we drafted him.

The games were at the Estadi Olímpic de Terrassa venue, about an hour's drive by bus from Barcelona. I was covering both the men and women; the women didn't do so well, but the men were very good. They defeated the Netherlands in the semi-final but had to console themselves with a silver in the final, losing to Germany.

It was pretty isolated out there and a long way from the action, but during siesta time I would hook up with the guys from Channel Seven for lunch at the Pink Panther restaurant. It was a quirky little spot, serving schnitzels and salads, and I enjoyed the company of David Christensen and Richard Aggiss and then drifted into afternoon slumber, escaping the heat.

I called the 1996 Games in Atlanta on my own until the finals. The women were outstanding this time. Ric Charlesworth was their coach and they won the gold medal in a match against South Korea. Katrina Powell scored off the reverse stick from Alyson Annan, who was brilliant. Charlesworth, who had aspired to coaching the Australian cricket team in the 1980s, had a remarkable record as a coach. The Atlanta gold medal game was Australia's 38th match without a defeat.

Then in 2000 at Sydney the women won again and the men got a silver.

I also covered hockey at the Commonwealth Games in 1998 in Kuala Lumpur and 2002 in Manchester.

At Kuala Lumpur I also got to cover the cricket, which was a one-off experience featuring teams like Barbados and Antigua. Trivia question: who has taken the only hat-trick in Commonwealth Games cricket? Yes, Brad Young, the left-arm spinner from South Australia. Expecting gold, Australia had to settle for silver when Steve Waugh's team was beaten by South Africa in the final.

Then in 2004 the late Wally Foreman took over and that ended my Games career until 2016 when I was again pitched into the hockey, but not from Rio, fortunately.

Rugby union is my favourite pigskin sport. I was an ordinary player but kept the best and fairest competition going at Cranbrook for three years, keeping the stats and assessments in small blue notebooks, which now reside in the school archives. Martin Pitt was the ringmaster coach, who kept everyone motivated with various notices on the board like 'Rugby is a substitute for War'. Under his guidance the school produced some prominent players, including Andrew Stathopoulos, who became infamous for various company swindles later on. He was the half back in the first Australian Schoolboys team that went to South Africa in 1969.

In 1996 ABC television decided to restart their coverage of Saturday club rugby, pitching me alongside Brett Papworth and Toby Lawson.

I did that for thirteen years every Saturday except when I was on a cricket tour. Again, that was a lot of fun; as I said about the hockey, the grassroots sporting experience is always healthy. You develop a connection with the people and the sport more than when you are doing the major stuff.

The pleasure of calling club rugby was sometimes improved by refreshments. Ray Dearlove from Sydney University produced a good bottle of red at University Oval and the habit kicked in. At Woollahra, Yalumba wines was the major sponsor of Easts, and Greg Pullen, their go-between, planted a bottle on our desk, which was alongside all the Easts fans on the club balcony.

The Senate Committee missed this free plug on the ABC, which went 'and there's Easts prop Rob Bartrop yalumba-ing in for a try'.

On another occasion when club rugby had a weekend off we covered a match in the GPS competition between two of the great rival schools, St Ignatius and St Joseph's. A very young Kurtley Beale was the rising star at Joeys and a massive crowd created plenty of atmosphere at Riverview's spacious Lane Cove ground in the historic battle between the Jesuits and the Marist Brothers. Again a bottle appeared to keep us lubricated and one lingering memory is directing a well-hosted Cardinal George Pell in the dark towards his waiting transport.

The days of schools enjoying this type of publicity are long gone. As a group the GPS and other schools reason that boys shouldn't be put on a pedestal.

The ABC's coverage of club rugby on television sadly disappeared a few years ago when the bean-counters moved in. Alas the ABC rarely covers any sport on TV unless it's given to them, or is a rebadging of someone else's coverage. The decision not to compete for major sport was made decades ago and arguably contravenes the ABC charter. Yes, cost is a factor, and if commercial TV and subscription channels are paying big money, then why should taxpayers' money be spent chasing it? The BBC survives on the largesse of licence fees, abolished long ago in Australia. Triennial funding gives the ABC some certainty about what they can spend, but major sport is too expensive. The growing profile of women's sport is an opportunity for the ABC to get on board and grab a niche. Luckily radio, with its audience reach, sustains full coverage of major sport and with contractual commitments to AFL, NRL, Cricket Australia and a giveaway deal with the FFA on A League football, the immediate future is okay.

There were a few golf tournaments sprinkled over the 1980s and that was always fun. I was a roving reporter at a couple of big events which we used to do on television. In 1976 I was assigned to cover the West Lakes Classic at The Grange Golf Club in Adelaide and was on hand to witness a fair-haired young fellow by the name of Greg Norman win his first tournament as a pro. The following season he joined the European Tour, promptly won the Martini International at Blairgowrie in Scotland and he was off.

I was on hand at my home course, Royal Sydney, when the Australian Open was played there. I used all my rudimentary knowledge as an amateur golfer who knew every trap and every bit of rough on the course to tell everyone what I thought was going on. My friends still badger me about the bunker in front of the eighth tee, which I described as an Alister MacKenzie design, one of two holes created by the master golf course architect when he was Down Under in the 1920s. Apparently not, but the message has stuck and the current Royal Sydney Club captain, Tim Rankine, says as far as he's concerned it's now known as the Maxwell hole. Fortunately the coverage of golf at the Australian Open has continued on the radio since TV coverage moved to Channel Seven.

Unfortunately my radio voice doesn't quite get to the whisper that is necessary on a golf course. It's amazing how much sound carries out in the open when one of the golfers is over a chip or putt.

I remember I got a very dirty look from Andre Stolz when he was leading one year. I thought I was whispering, but apparently my voice is quite megaphonic. I don't come with a volume switch in real life.

I was lucky to get some all-round exposure as different fads came and went in the organisation.

There was a period up until the late 1980s when we used to have a sports program on television on Friday nights around the coverage of harness racing that I mentioned earlier. When Norman May wasn't doing it, I often got a chance.

I may have got a bit carried away one night in the late seventies when I was still young and foolish after making the mistake of going to a friend's bucks party before doing the broadcast. I had a couple of quick ones before going to Gore Hill studios for the 9.30 p.m. start. There was a pacer called Rip van Winkle and its driver was a chap called Michael Vanderkemp. It was the backmarker and just too good for any other pacer around at the time. I think it was 20/1 on and I may have picked up the yellow racing guide and started waving it towards the camera, saying 'If you don't know the favourite in the next you are a fool.'

I was to be reminded of that for many years after by my friends—and it was noted higher up. The following week I went out on Pittwater to do a fishing story before doing the show and I got badly sunburnt. I really struggled that night because I think I had a bit of heat stroke.

On Monday I got called into the office by the director of sports, Bernie Kerr. He had obviously been told about my performance the previous week. Bernie had started in the ABC as a cable runner during the synthetic tests and developed into an outstanding rugby league caller, also covering the 1953 Ashes tour and a number of Olympic and Commonwealth Games. And he did tick my box for the trainee's job in 1973.

He said to me, 'Now, Jim, I hear that you had been drinking before you went on last Friday night and weren't in the best of shape.'

'Last Friday night?' I asked.

'Yes, last Friday night,' he said.

Fortunately I could say in all honesty that I had not

had a drink last Friday night before going on air. I'd had many drinks the Friday before, but that wasn't what he asked.

I got a very stern warning about how much trouble I would be in and how my job would be in jeopardy if I was found to be intoxicated on air. Another warning to a brash youngster which I have taken on board. Mostly.

Every Saturday afternoon from 1976 there was a show called *Sportsview* on television. We used to split the city and the country, so that in the city you were watching the rugby union live and in the country the rugby league, and then at 6 p.m. they would replay the league to the city and the union to the country. This strategy came about because the league didn't want their games going out live against the gate in the city.

I was the presenter of the one that went out to the NSW regionals for a couple of years.

In that era until the early 1980s we had a 6.30 p.m. sporting program every night on radio. From Monday to Thursday it was called *Sporting Highlights* and on Friday it was *The Sportsman's Parade*. It involved the dash across William Street from our offices to the studio at Forbes Street. The show kicked off with the 'Thunder and Lightning Polka' by Johann Strauss and ended with the 'Pastorale', the theme that introduced Australia's longest running radio serial, *Blue Hills*.

All the interviews were pre-recorded on tape or in our tiny studio because you weren't allowed to record people on the telephone until the mid-1970s. You may recall they used to have beeps to indicate the person was being recorded. The very first one I did was with rugby league champion, and later coach and commentator, Bob Fulton—it sounded like we were swearing a lot.

One of my occasional gigs was appearing on the breakfast show at 6.45. It started with Clive Robertson in the 1970s, who was a sharp wit and took the mickey out of everyone. He'd back-announce a Neil Diamond disc with, 'I wish his name was sapphire, he'd wear out faster.' Later there was Philip Clark, who'd put up with my youngsters eating breakfast and complaining about the choice of cereals, and then Angela Catterns and Adam Spencer wound me up or vice-versa. Now Robbie Buck is pulling an audience. Robbie once took fright when I said 'have you heard the one about the frozen balls?' In fact, it was a story about Sepp Blatter claiming that the draw for UEFA competitions had been rigged by freezing the ping pong balls. I think the joke was on Sepp there.

So the sun rises and the show goes on. Yes, and I'm trying, as Richie suggested, not to take myself too seriously.

18

Looking forward— and back

Cricket is flourishing. Can you name another sport that has so much diversity? From cricket on the street, six-a-side frolics, 50-over competitions, Test matches and the burgeoning T20 bashes, the game is booming.

For me the most exciting recent developments are the growing profile and participation of women, and the gospelling force of T20.

The women's game has languished for a long time in the shadows, the backwaters of the men's juggernaut.

In the 1990s I enjoyed many chats with Belinda Clark, arguably the best bat produced until Meg Lanning arrived. The ABC occasionally covered some women's matches on TV and radio, and Belinda has worked as a commentator occasionally on some Test matches.

It was clear that women's cricket had a problem. They simply didn't play enough major matches. No cricket, no profile. Zoe Goss momentarily gave the game a spotlit star when she dismissed Brian Lara in a televised testimonial match in 1994, but this was fluff that had no longer-term substance. Gradually the interstate series took prominence and matches were scheduled more frequently between the major powers, Australia, New Zealand and England.

In one of those series, in 2011, ABC TV involved the Chaser comedians Julian Morrow and Chas Licciardello. Dressed up in Richie Benaud blazers, their humour fell flat, despite the best help from the players. Skits replaced the commercial breaks seen on Channel Nine, and it was a bizarre cross-promotion for the Chasers. It still got more laughs than the corny endorsements Nine's commentary team were forced to spruik about network programming.

The women's game deserved to be taken more seriously. Subsequently Cricket Australia moved to professionalise women's cricket with central contracts and the results have been stunning.

CA's strategy has paid off and any reluctance from their own marketers and commercial television to give wider exposure to women's cricket was blown away by the staggering WBBL numbers; televised matches averaging 250,000 viewers last summer indicate that there is an audience.

And cricket needs the women's game to prosper so that it can become a more universal game. The ICC seems to be moving from self-interest and narrow agendas to embrace participation in the Olympic Games. The AOC chief John Coates has long complained to me about cricket not having a crack at the Olympics.

The development of women's cricket, like field hockey and more recently rugby sevens, could create the opportunity to put cricket on a bigger stage than the Commonwealth Games.

•

For four decades and more I have been so lucky to have had the opportunity to watch the game's best players in action, to see every ball of fascinating contests and to share the whole experience of Test cricket. Cricket on the radio is a summer perennial for many Australians and the ABC has been a supportive, proselytising force since the synthetic commentaries in the 1930s.

The administration of cricket has changed dramatically since I started at the ABC in 1973. Alan Barnes was the board secretary who ran the game out of a shoebox office above the Cricketer's Club in George Street, Sydney.

Gradually, then dramatically after the explosion of World Series Cricket, the game became a serious business, and the players are now generously rewarded if they win a central contract.

The commercial growth and branding of cricket, the CA imprimatur, has been hugely successful, thanks mainly to television deals with Channel Nine. Now the revenues from India, England and most recently Channel Ten with the BBL entertainment are underpinning CA's finances.

Their duty of care, to 'put fans first', has been compromised by excessive entrance prices for international cricket, and it's good to see that they have reduced ticket prices for 2016–17 in line with the cost of going to a BBL contest.

Several former CA operatives have expressed surprise to me about the ABC's contractual relationship. Why is the ABC paying a fee to broadcast? Surely CA should be paying the ABC?

The ABC gets no commercial advantage from the deal. It certainly gets a lot of goodwill and appreciation for delivering the national game to a wide audience, wider than any other radio network could. For many years the ABC had an exclusive radio deal in place, but with its commercial agenda CA wanted new markets—essentially more income.

The decision of CA to stream the ABC commentary on the CA website—not the ABC website—hints at the possibility of it providing its own radio coverage in the future. By comparison, England's board allows, indeed welcomes, the BBC live-streaming its commentary on its own website, putting fans first.

Hopefully the relationship between the ABC and CA will mature so that both organisations get what they want. For CA it's about reaching a new audience but making sure they don't disengage with those who enjoy an authoritative and untainted commercial-free coverage of the national game.

For the ABC it's about 'broadcasting programs that contribute to a sense of national identity and inform and entertain'. And doing it on all media platforms.

I dream that one day we will see a T20 World Championship played in the US and Canada, and some form of the game at the Olympic Games. There is huge potential for cricket to grow beyond its Commonwealth limits. The adrenaline hit of athletic frolics, the sometimes manic, often extraordinary, virtuoso skills of the players, can pull plenty of new audiences.

Against the noise of this razzamatazz, Test cricket has a place. Ashes contests are eagerly anticipated and

India wants to play and compete strongly in the traditional form of the game. South Africa and the West Indies need rejuvenation and leadership to compete, but for their players the financial imperative is playing T20.

For me, cricket—and broadcasting—has provided a path in life to the young man who came from the sheltered world of white 1950s Australia, emerging from Cranbrook School in the 1960s with no sure idea of a way forward in the world. Cricket has taken me to the most extraordinary places—from the heaving megacities of India to the back streets of Birmingham, from rowdy Caribbean parties to pleasant lunches in the English countryside. Broadcasting more generally has taken me everywhere from the Harold Park trots and country rugby league in Dubbo to the Olympic Games in Barcelona, Atlanta and my home town of Sydney—the former no less entertaining and instructive than the latter. Being part of the travelling cricket caravan has brought me into contact with everyone from prime ministers (and would-be prime ministers) to eccentric West Indian fans and wholly unique Indian scorers—and this time, the latter are definitely more entertaining. A career at the ABC, an organisation central to the national conversation, has been a great privilege, at its best uplifting, often challenging and on occasions disappointing.

As a commentator I still look forward to any match that has a crowd and a sense of occasion. In cricket's secular world it doesn't matter whether it's a red, white or pink ball, as long as the game is a contest.

Cricket has given me a passport to many places and my life is richer for the many friendships that have radiated from this captivating game. For this, I am grateful. I don't know what the future holds but I do know I want to continue to be involved in the game that has played such a big part in my life.

Acknowledgements

This book has been inspired by many people. Patrick Gallagher and Tom Gilliatt from Allen & Unwin persevered and got me motivated with the help of Peter Lalor's skill. Thanks for pushing me along. Michael Epis has done brilliantly too with his editing and suggestions, aided by the diligent guidance of Angela Handley.

Thanks to Kerry O'Keeffe for making me laugh and for writing a foreword. And to Rob Padbury for casting a surgical eye over the manuscript.

The constant love and support of my wife, Jennifer Kirkby, has kept us strong and made me laugh. And laughter is contagiously stimulating.

To my two sons, Hamish and Oliver, thanks for keeping me from ageing, and for flourishing, in line with the Maxwell motto, *Reviresco*.

The Queen Street coffee club is a source of inspiration. Thanks to team leader Peter Bavin and his acolytes Mick Halliday, Michael Doyle, James Bush, John Tierney, Peter Shipway, David Newgrosh, Gordon Bray and occasional drop-ins who get top coffee from Harry and Arthur at Nostimo's.

Big Pete is one of a clan of old Cranbrookians through the OCCC who have been players, friends and tourists, including the Cohens, the Thiedemans, the Loves, the Newtons and the Morrows.

Special thanks to Dominique Novak d'Hennin for sourcing material in Cranbrook's archives.

Thanks to all my golfing mates, particularly the Tuesday Group at Royal Sydney captained by Jim Morrow and one of their stars, Paul Pemberton, for his skilful navigation of the Whitsundays.

Thanks to Ian and Greg Chappell for their friendship and candour, and to cricket's most charming couple, the late Arthur Morris and his widow, Judith.

Lifelong friends from the ABC like Peter Wilkins, Janie Lalor, Peter Longman, Caroline Davison and the best fast-moving caller of them all, David Morrow, have stimulated me as much as the late Billy McGowan when we were creating audio cricket documentaries on cassette in the 1980s. The roll call at the ABC is a long one, starting with Bernie Kerr and continuing through to Drew Morphett, Karen Tighe and Glenn Mitchell.

Acknowledgements

At the BBC, the friendship of Peter Baxter, Shilpa Patel, Adam Mountford, Henry Blofeld and Aggers on TMS has been stimulating, and seriously indulgent. No more cakes please.

At the Primary Club of Australia, the commitment from Geoff Verco, Rick Glover, Jim Winchester and the new breed of strategists has been outstanding. Marathon Cricket at the SCG, encouraged by former chairman Rodney Cavalier, should thrive around the recent Richie Benaud Trophy initiative.

I owe much to Max Abbott and now Peter Lovitt and Adrian Tham at the Eastern Suburbs Dolphins for their support in making Easts cricket strong again.

To many relations on the Maxwell, Bury, Kirkby and Kinnane teams, and to the Maxwells who are not related, Peter, Jennifer and James, thanks for the friendship and long lunches. A recipe for living.

There are many friends from different places who are like regulars in the pub of life and great company too. Alan and Jo Bridge from Brisbane, Bill and Pamela Slocum from Canberra, Wayne Bristow from Lake Macquarie, Mike Coward and Peter Boully from Annandale, Ted and Merrin Harnett from Hardy's Bay, John MacKinnon from East Melbourne, Bob Massie from Perth, Norman and Nancy Johnson from Cheltenham, and from the UK, James and Deborah Welsh from Salisbury.

The list gets longer, and optometrist cum fast bowler Geoff Lawson—Henry to everyone—has been a strong friend on tour with me to the West Indies, South Africa, the UK, Darwin, Cairns and few golf courses in between.

As a lifelong victim of the punt, thanks to Peter Falk and Peter Horwitz for encouraging me to buy a share in the ownership of thoroughbreds. Several trainers are happy too, looking after The Big Bomber, Mr Hurley, Kind Heart, Poldark and a colt that could win the Golden Slipper. Dream on.

Thanks for listening, and for reading this book.

CRICKET QUIZ

A prize of 20 cents will be awarded to the first correct solution to reach the EDITOR, 2 Bradley Av., Bellevue Hill by January 31st, 1968. All entries must be submitted on an official entry form, which can only be obtained by buying "CRICKET CHRONICLE."

1. S.F.Barnes was chosen to tour Australia in 1901 after playing only 4 county matches in 8 years. For which county(ies) did he play, and in which years?
....

2. How many centuries did W.R.Hammond score in first class cricket? ....

3. Who is the youngest bowler to take 100 test wickets and how old was he?
....

4. Name one of the two batsmen who have scored 6 centuries in successive innings?
....

5. Who was manager of the 1921 Australian team in England? ....

6. How many dismissals has H.Strudwick to his credit? ....

7. What was Ray Flocton's highest score in first class cricket? ....

8. Prior to World WAR II what was Australia's highest partnership for the fifth wicket against England, and who made it? ....
....

9. When still at school he was chosen to play for Victoria, he played for Australia in 1936-37, but was passed over for the 1938 tour of England, and was subsequently killed in action during World War II. Who was he?
....

10. Who wrote "Green Sprigs"? ....

ACROSS

1. Son of a policeman, or almost, was W.H.C.
3. 'Sketch in' turns out to be a former South Australian.
4. Invariably makes runs, this 'Sandgroper.'
6. A Hindu batsman with another skill.
8. Add 'ed' to 'draws' to get a West Australian wicket-keeper.
9. Ernest and J.T. were brothers.
12. Take 'al' away from it, for a synonym of 'state.'
13. ... out.
16. An umbrella field makes an ... of fieldsmen.
17. A New Zealand 'great' of the early 'thirties
19. 'Shale' in another form, is a post war South African.
21. Bob was a Yorkshireman, semi-fruit.
22. Scored 122 not out against England.
20. Jack was a pre war Australian, who often made a 'ton.'
25. Umpired with Kidson.
27. Slow scoring Bill was a New Zealander.

DOWN

1. West Indian all-rounder, or Roman Emperor.
2. Victoria's Jack plays with clay.
4. Jack toured in 1946-47.
5. It's better than none.
7. He made 191 for the fifth wicket with 'Maurice' at Manchester in 1934.
10. Preceded Waite.
11. Johnny followed Iverson.
14. Change 'Goblet' to get a former Australian fast bowler.
15. Add 'S' to a word meaning behind time to get a former West Australian.
16. 'Tape' is an Indian cricketer in another form.
18. Percy, was a man, by name.
20. Charlie puts it into batsmen's minds.
23. "Brightly Fades the ..." by J.Fingleton.
24. Holds ninth wicket record for India with Hazare.
26. P.A.Perrin scored a triple century for them in 1904.
28. ... Jordon.
29. Wes was large in ....
30. Don used to get his in quickly.
31. He scored two centuries against England in 1950.
32. There's usually eleven in one.
33. This former Middlesex player really blew in.
34. Hon. ... Bligh or Lord Darnley.

A prize of 20 cents will be awarded to the first correct entry
to reach the　　　　EDITOR,
　　　　　　　　　　2 Bradley Av.,
　　　　　　　　　　Bellevue Hill.　　　　by January 31st, 1968.